HOW TO WORK, TRAVEL, AND STUDY IN JAPAN

NATALIA DOAN

INTRODUCTION

How do you find a job in Japan? What are the best resources for improving your Japanese? Where should you go to find cool restaurants and fun activities? And what *exactly* is the best way to transport a samurai sword? *How to Work, Travel, and Study in Japan* answers all of these questions and provides practical advice on working, studying, and traveling in Japan, including how to write a resume in Japanese, how to choose a study abroad program, how to meet people, and more.

Before moving to Japan, I read every travel guide on Japan that I could find. These books discussed Japan's economy, but not how to read a Japanese paycheck or conduct a bank transfer on a machine with no English options. Some of the books outlined Japan's medical system, but never explained which American over-the-counter medicines cannot be brought into Japan. Some travel guides shared accounts of teaching in Japan, but said nothing about American USB drives not always working with Japanese printers, especially ten minutes before the start of class.

That's why I wrote *How to Work, Travel, and Study in Japan*. This guide contains the tips and tricks I've learned (sometimes the hard way) from living in Japan, so that you can get the most out of your international experience—whether for a few months on study abroad, or for a few years working with a company.

There are lots of links and suggestions included in this book to help you plan your trip, so I recommend reading this book *before* leaving your home country. For those already in Japan, I hope the tips in this book will help you discover new ways to navigate and enjoy your experience abroad.

It wasn't until college that I first started studying Japanese. Since then, I've studied at Ochanomizu University in Tokyo, as well as at Nanzan University in Nagoya. After graduating from Vassar College with a BA in

English and Japanese, I started teaching English to elementary and middle school students in Osaka, where I lived during the 2011 Tōhoku earthquake. At the end of the school year, I moved to Tokyo, where I began working at a Japanese company in an all-Japanese workplace environment. While in Japan, I also modeled multiple collections for a Kyoto fashion house and for one of Japan's premier women's magazines.

Although all the advice in this book comes from tested experience, my opinions, ideas, and research are not meant to replace the advice of trained financial, legal, or medical professionals. If you require serious financial, legal, or medical planning, please consult an accountant, lawyer, or doctor. Basically, stay safe and use common sense. Another disclaimer—I recommend several companies and services that have, in my personal experience, been helpful during my Japan travels. I have not received paid compensation for any of these recommendations.

May your travels in Japan be wonderful and story-filled.

Ganbatte! ("Good luck!")

TABLE OF CONTENTS

AUTHOR'S NOTE

This book is intended to help you prepare for an extended stay in Japan whether or not you can speak Japanese. That being said, perhaps nothing can as dramatically define your experience in Japan as your familiarity with the Japanese language.

If you would like to improve your Japanese during your stay in Japan, give yourself a head start by practicing basic greetings, numbers, and simple words related to your interests before you arrive. (See "Study—Essential Studying Resources" for helpful tools to begin your studies of Japanese or "Recommended Reading—Snapshot Guide to Japanese" for a breakdown of the three Japanese alphabets: *hiragana*, *katakana*, and *kanji*.)

Japanese words that have been integrated into the English language, such as "*sushi*" and "*kimono*," will from this point onward be italicized and accompanied with their Japanese pronunciations. (Japanese words adopted into the English language are often pronounced differently in Japanese.) Japanese cities will be spelled using their English pronunciation.

I hope this guide can help you enjoy the true adventure that is living in a foreign country and learning about a different culture. If you have any questions about learning Japanese, studying abroad, or working in Japan, feel free to send me a message through this book's website: http://www.worktravelstudyjapan.com.

Have a great time in Japan and good luck!

BEFORE YOU LEAVE

Before you leave, make a list of all the goals you have for your experience in Japan—places you want to go, foods you would like to try, and any language milestones you wish to reach. Post this list somewhere prominent in your apartment or dorm room so that in all the excitement of a new experience, you stay focused on what motivated you to move to Japan in the first place.

Itterasshai! 「いってらっしゃい!」—"Have a nice trip!"

THINGS TO BRING

Gifts

If, for any portion of your trip, you will be staying with a homestay family, bring a nice gift for them from your home country. A coffee table photo book of your hometown can make a great conversation piece. Other easy-to-pack gift options include calendars, magnets, locally-made goods, and boxes of candy. Distinctly American brands, even if they are available in Japan, will always be well received.

> **TIP**: **Starbucks** (http://starbucks.com) makes excellent travel-sized gifts, especially the bags of coffee beans and mugs with the names of American cities on them.

> **TIP**: Bigger is not always better in Japan. Avoid large, obtrusive gifts, such as vases or wall-mounted picture frames.

In Japan, the way a gift is wrapped is almost more important than the gift itself. I like to use gift bags, especially when giving fragile or hard to wrap items, like candy or t-shirts. Gift bags make it easier for the gift recipient to carry the gift home, which is especially important in business situations.

If you will be working in a Japanese office or school, bring a box of individually-wrapped American snacks or candies to share with your co-workers. For large groups, it is always better to bring a gift, such as food, that everyone can enjoy.

If you get to Japan and realize you forgot to pack a gift for your homestay family, pick up a souvenir box of sweets at a local tourist site. Obviously, buying a Japanese souvenir for your Japanese homestay family is not as good as bringing a gift from home, but it is better than showing up empty-handed.

> **TIP**: If you brought two gifts, give one to your homestay family upon your arrival and one the day you leave. Giving your homestay family

your gift right away will help start conversation and make a good impression.

If you will be studying or working abroad, leave room in your luggage for gifts! Japanese people tend to be generous, even to strangers, and host families will often give parting gifts just moments before you say goodbye. (I always keep a roll-up tote bag or some extra space in my luggage. It's much easier than trying to carry a bunch of individual cards and gift bags through a train station.)

Bring a set of non-Japanese Thank You notes with you before leaving for Japan. It is always exciting to receive a letter on foreign stationery, and your Japanese friends and colleagues will appreciate the extra effort. I always bring a few birthday cards, too, just in case.

Home

Before leaving for Japan, print address labels in both Japanese and English for your friends and family members. Japanese addresses can be long, so preprinted labels will make it easier for your family to write you letters.

> **TIP**: You can order inexpensive business cards, address labels, and other stationery goods from **Vista Print** (http://vistaprint.com). Don't forget to keep some return address labels for yourself!

If your family members are interested in helping furnish your apartment from overseas, set up a wish list on **Amazon Japan** (http://amazon.jp). Though nearly all of Amazon Japan is in Japanese, there is a translate option that will provide brief English descriptions of Amazon Japan's prices and shipping information. Walk your family through Amazon Japan's site before you leave and preload your Japanese address into their account to make checkout as easy as possible. Ordering items from Amazon Japan is much cheaper than shipping food items or appliances from home. (If you buy Japanese appliances, you also do not need to worry about power adaptors.) Amazon Japan can deliver within days, whereas getting a friend to ship something to you from your home country can take over a week.

You may be tired when you first arrive in Japan. Pack a pair of scissors and a towel in an easy-to-find section of your luggage if you will be directly moving into a new apartment or dorm.

Bring your skin care solutions from home in bulk. Your preferred toiletries might be unavailable or slightly different in Japan, even if the brand name and packaging is the same.

> **TIP**: When buying Japanese cosmetics or toiletries, look for the word
> 美白 *bihaku*, which means "skin whitening," to see if the product
> contains skin whitening agents. Whitening skin treatments are a
> thriving industry in Japan, and many American products have these
> chemicals added before reaching the Japanese market.

Download a metric converter app for your phone. You may be surprised
by how often you need to convert from Celsius to Fahrenheit or take
measurements.

Work & Study

Business cards, known as *meishi* 名刺, are crucial to your professional
success in Japan. Not all English teaching companies provide their
employees with business cards, but I highly recommend ordering your own.
These business cards can simply have your name and e-mail address on
them. I recommend including your contact information in both English and
Japanese.

If you are coming to Japan to study or work, set up your computer's
Japanese-language capabilities in advance. You can look up a tutorial online
for your computer's specific operating system.

Bring a LAN cable from home. Many Japanese hotels do not have in-
room WiFi.

Japanese teachers, especially those who teach elementary school, often
stamp their students' papers with a "Good Job" or "Well Done" stamp. If
you will be teaching in Japan, bring your own stamps and/or stickers from
home to wow your students.

> **TIP**: **Oriental Trading** (http://www.orientaltrading.com) is a great
> place to order inexpensive stickers, craft supplies, and American-themed
> novelty goods before you leave.

> **TIP**: Bring a few novelty office items from home. When students stop
> by your desk, an oversized pen or American flag notebook will be a fun
> conversation starter for shy students.

Entertainment

Avid readers should stockpile an e-reader (ideally one with wireless Internet access) with books before leaving for Japan. Most of the English-language print books available in Japanese bookstores are either classics (e.g. Charles Dickens) or so popular you've probably already read them (e.g. Harry Potter).

> **TIP**: **Project Gutenberg** (http://www.gutenberg.org) offers an enormous catalog of public domain books in multiple languages. These books are free because of their expired copyright, so you can find a plethora of free titles and genres.

Due to copyright laws, once in Japan, you will not be able to directly access American television through legal streaming sites like Hulu or through the network's website. Keep up-to-date on your favorite shows and songs through **iTunes** (http://itunes.com) instead.

The Long Flight

Take a picture of your luggage before your flight. In the event that your luggage gets lost, a photo will make it much easier for the airline staff to identify your bag.

Rotational wheel luggage is sturdy and easy to push across crowded train stations. This type of luggage is increasingly available outside of Japan and can make hauling luggage across crowded train stations much easier.

I suggest packing a lightweight, collapsible duffel bag with you in your suitcase. Many international airlines allow two checked bags per person, but charge an extra fee if the bags exceed a certain weight. In the event of overweight baggage, you can divide your items between the two bags to avoid the extra charge.

CLOTHING

Japanese clothes are Japanese-sized, which means that if you're of a different body build, finding well-fitting clothes in Japan may be challenging.

Record your height, chest, waist, and hip measurements in centimeters. Knowing your detailed measurements will make finding a perfect fit easier, both at home and abroad, especially if you ever need to order clothes online. Japanese shoes are also sized in centimeters.

Both women's and men's clothes in Japan use the S, M, L system of sizing.

When buying clothes in Japan, it's usually safe to assume one size or one half size larger than your normal size in the U.S.

If your size is not represented on the charts below, it may require extra effort for you to find well-fitting clothes while in Japan.

Men's Shirt Sizes in Japan		S	M	L	XL
Neck	Inches	14½-15¼	15½-16	16¼-16¾	17-17¼
	Centimeters	37-39	39-41	42-43	43-44
Chest	Inches	37-38	39-41	42-44	45-47
	Centimeters	86-91	96-102	107-112	117-122
Waist	Inches	29-31	32-33	34-36	37-40
	Centimeters	74-79	81-84	87-92	94-102
Sleeve	Inches	33	34	35	36
	Centimeters	84	86.5	89	91.5

Though many stores selling imported Western suits give sizes in American-style letters (S, M , L,), many Japanese suit stores use a different lettering system.

The following chart is a translation of the men's suit size guide used by popular suit company **Aoki Style** (http://www.eshop.aoki-style.com/guide/

sizemap.php). ("XL" is also written as "LL.")

Bring your measurements with you when you visit the store and ask a store assistant for help to get the perfect fit.

Men's Suit Sizes in Japan								
Japan	U.S.	5'1"~5'3"	5'3"~5'5"	5'5"~5'7"	5'7"~5'9"	5'9"~6'0"	6'0"~6'1"	6'1"~6'2"
Y	XS	27"~30" 69-75 cm Y3	28"~30" 71-77 cm Y4	29"~31" 73-79 cm Y5	29.5"~32" 75-81 cm Y6	30"~33" 77-83 cm Y7	31"~33" 79-85 cm Y8	32"~34" 81-87 cm Y9
A	S	29"~31" 73-79 cm A3	30"~32" 75-81 cm A4	30"~33" 77-83 cm A5	31"~33" 79-85 cm A6	32"~34" 81-87 cm A7	33"~35" 83-89 cm A8	33"~36" 85-91 cm A9
AB	M	31"~33" 79-85 cm AB3	32"~34" 81-87 cm AB4	33"~35" 83-89 cm AB5	33"~36" 85-91 cm AB6	34"~37" 87-93 cm AB7	35"~37" 89-95 cm AB8	36"~38" 91-97 cm AB9
BB	L	34"~37" 87-93 cm BB3	35"~37" 89-95 cm BB4	36"~38" 91-97 cm BB5	37"~39" 93-99 cm BB6	37"~40" 95-101 cm BB7	38"~40" 97-103 cm BB8	39"~41" 99-105 cm BB9
E	XL	37"~39" 93-99 cm E3	37"~40" 94-101 cm E4	38"~41" 97-103 cm E5	39"~41" 99-105 cm E6	40"~42" 101-107 cm E7	40"~43" 103-109 cm E8	41"~44" 105-111 cm E9
K	XXL	X	X	44"~46" 112-118 cm K5	46"~48" 117-123 cm K6	48"~50" 122-128 cm K7	X	X

Women's clothes in Japan use the letter system (S, M, L), which can change depending on the store, measurements in centimeters, or numbered sizes (as shown below).

Ladies, I recommend bringing your own bras from home. If you decide to buy bras while in Japan, increase your cup size by one letter.

Women's Clothing Sizes	
U.S.	Japan
0	3
1	5
2	7
3	9
4	11
5	13
6	15
8	17
10	19
12	21

Bra Sizes					
	U.S.	Japan		U.S.	Japan
A	30	65	D	30	65
	32	70		32	70
	34	75		34	75
	36	80		36	80
B	30	65	E	30	65
	32	70		32	70
	34	75		34	75
	36	80		36	80
C	30	65	F	30	65
	32	70		32	70
	34	75		34	75
	36	80		36	80

If you will be staying with a homestay family, try to bring pajamas that you don't mind wearing in front of the whole family while relaxing in the evening or eating dinner with the family. (Ladies, it also might be a good idea to wear a bra under loose tank tops.)

TIP: Bring nice underwear, but leave your sexiest lingerie at home if you will be staying with a homestay family. Most Japanese homes do not have heat-using dryers, so your homestay family will see your undergarments when they help hang your laundry up to dry.

If you will be teaching in Japan during the summer, which is monsoon season, don't bring expensive suits. Sweat and humidity can ruin your jackets in just a few weeks, and many Japanese school have a relaxed code of professional attire. Many public schools do not have air conditioned classrooms, and you might be asked to help with outdoor activities. Your elementary school students might invite you to play outside during recess, so after the first few days of work, stick to a business casual wardrobe. (See "Work—Teaching English" for details.)

Japanese washing machines have a spin-dry feature that essentially centrifuges the water out of your clothes, but this does not dry your clothes completely. If you will be participating in a short term study abroad program, bring a clothesline and some clips so you can hang your clothes up to dry. (Most Japanese apartments do not come with a heat-using clothes dryer.) You'll be able to wash your clothes right away instead of having to run to the nearest 100 Yen Store, the Japanese equivalent of the dollar store, for detergent and supplies.

Shoes

Bring or buy a few pairs of shoes that are easy to slip on and off. Many families and restaurants with tatami 畳 (rice straw)-floors will ask you to take off your shoes before entering, so don't forget to wear nice socks too!

> **TIP**: The Japanese store **Tabio** (http://www.tabio.com) sells a variety of women's knee-highs, socks, and stockings. They also sell socks for men. Tabio has a point card system and locations throughout Japan.

Men's Shoe Sizes		Women's Shoe Sizes	
U.S.	Japan	U.S.	Japan
6½	24.5	5	21
7	25	5½	21.5
7½	25.5	6	22
8	26	6½	22.5
8½	26.5	7	23
9	27	7½	23.5
9½	27.5	8	24
10	28	8½	24.5
10.5	28.5	9	25
11	29	9½	25.5
11.5	29.5		
12	30		
12.5	30.5		
13	31		

If you will be teaching in a Japanese school, you will need a pair of "school shoes." Street shoes aren't allowed indoors, even for teachers. Work shoes are left in the shoe cubbies, *geta-bako* 下駄箱 , at the entrance of the school, the *shōkōguchi* 昇降口 . Teachers and students usually use different shoe cubbies.

Natalia Doan

TIP: For school shoes, I recommend black flats or loafers made by **Crocs** (http://www.crocs.com). Crocs are comfortable, allowed on the floors of Japanese schools, and come in a variety of surprisingly professional styles. Though many Japanese teachers wear the original Croc clog, dress shoe-style Crocs will give you a more professional look. Professional-looking Crocs are a worthwhile investment since you will wear your "school shoes" every day of work.

TIP: Students wear uniform indoor-shoes, known as *uwabaki* 上履
き . In elementary school, *uwabaki* are made of white canvas. In upper grades, these indoor-shoes may be a type of plastic sandal. Students may also have a separate pair of *uwabaki* solely for the gym. To prevent confusion and looking unprofessional, avoid bringing white shoes or plastic sandals as your school shoes.

America has a much more casual dress code than Japan, but during your visit, dress to impress! You never know what will happen or who you'll run into.

HEALTH AND MEDICAL

If you have specific medical needs and/or concerns, before you leave for Japan, order a copy of *The Japan Health Handbook* by Louise Picon Shimizu, Meredith Enman Maruyama, and Nancy Smith Tsurumaki. Though published in 1998, this book still boasts an impressively comprehensive collection of information on Japan's medical care system. It is a definite must-have if you are currently on prescription medication and plan on an extended stay in Japan. Many of the sections in this book, such as "Having a Baby," are intended for permanent residents of Japan.

Many American prescription and over-the-counter drugs are illegal in Japan. The Japanese Embassy does not provide a comprehensive list of banned medications, but you are allowed up to a two-month supply of over-the-counter medication and up to a one month's supply of allowable prescription medicine, provided you have a doctor's note and an explanation of the drug and its effects.

TIP: The doctor's note does not have to be in Japanese, but photocopy the doctor's note just in case someone requests a copy. More information on bringing medicine into Japan is available on the U.S. Embassy's website (http://japan.usembassy.gov/e/acs/tacs-medimport.html).

TIP: Do not ship prescription medicine from your home country to your Japanese address. It will be confiscated by Japanese Customs and you will have to pay a fine.

Products that contain stimulants or codeine, inhalers, and most allergy and sinus medications are illegal in Japan. If you try to bring any of the following banned substances into Japan, they will be confiscated by Customs and you may be fined.

Natalia Doan

American Medicines	
OK	NG (No Go!)
Liquid Tylenol	Tylenol Cold
	Advil Cold & Sinus
Benadryl	Claritin
	Inhalers
Chloraseptic Throat Spray	NyQuil, DayQuil
	Sudafed
	Actifed
	Vicks Inhalers
Ritalin (not legal as an ADD medication; may only be used to treat Narcolepsy)	Adderall
Concerta (must be between the ages of 7-15)	
Midol, Midol PM	Muscle Relaxants
*This list is subject to the discretion of Japanese Customs.	

If you plan (or hope) to be sexually active in Japan, bring your own birth control and/or condoms. Birth control and Plan B are prescription only in Japan, but you can bring a one month supply into the country. Condoms, or "skins" *sukin* スキン , are available in convenience stores and pharmacies. You may have to experiment to find the right size and fit. If you anticipate being sexually active while in Japan, avoid the guesswork and bring your own supplies from home.

If you require more than one month of prescription medication, you must apply for a special import certificate, or *Yakkan-shōmei* 薬監証明 , and bring it with you to Japan.

The application form is available on the Kanto-Shinetsu Regional Bureau of Health and Welfare website (http://kouseikyoku.mhlw.go.jp/kantoshinetsu/gyomu/bu_ka/shido_kansa/documents/medicines.doc), in a document after the Q&A pages.

Epipens, pronounced the same (*epipen* エピペン) in Japanese, were introduced to Japan in 2012, and require a *Yakkan-shōmei* to pass Customs.

TIP: If you plan on bringing an epipen to Japan, I recommend printing this Japanese explanation (http://www.epipen.jp/download/siyoujyoho. pdf) of how to use an epipen. If you are staying with a homestay family or find yourself in an emergency situation, this handout will explain what an epipen actually is and how to use it.

Always carry hand sanitizer, especially since many Japanese bathrooms do not stock paper towels. Most people carry their own cloth handkerchiefs with them, but keep a pack of portable Wet Wipes with you too, just in case.

If you will be living in Japan for an extended period, research the nearest hospital and the nearest English-speaking doctor. Copy the hospital's address in both *rōmaji* (so you can pronounce it) and *kanji* (so you can ask for directions.)

As of this time, Japan only requires immunizations for those traveling to rural farm areas. It's always a good idea, though, to keep your shots up-to-date.

HOW TO CALL HOME

International Dialing Codes

To make an international phone call, first dial the country's exit code, then the code of the country you wish to dial, then the phone number you wish to reach.

If the phone number you wish to reach starts with a zero, omit that number when you place the call.

(Country Exit Code) + (Country Code) + (Phone Number)

Calling a Japanese Number from America:
011+81+Phone Number

Calling an American Number from Japan:
010+1+Phone Number

*For more country codes, visit Country Code (http://countrycode.org).

Country Codes	
America	1
Australia	61
Brazil	55
Canada	1
China	86
France	33
Germany	49
Hong Kong	852
India	91
New Zealand	64
Russia	7
U.K.	44

FINANCES

The Japanese currency is the yen, pronounced *en* 円 ^{えん} in Japanese. Yen prices are written as either 500 円 ^{えん} or ¥500.

Cash

Bring cash! Withdrawing cash from a Japanese ATM once you're in Japan might give you a better exchange rate, but don't wait until your arrival to get Japanese cash. Though many restaurants and department stores accept credit cards, many smaller stores, street vendors, and taxis will only accept cash. Always carry at least ¥5000 (about $50), in case of emergency. You will need cash for your bus or train ticket from Narita International Airport. (See "Upon Arrival" for more details.)

For the best possible exchange rate, visit your local American bank and place a currency order in advance. It may take up to a week for the yen to arrive, but banks usually offer better rates than airport kiosks.

If you need to present someone with money in Japan—whether you're paying in advance or returning money that you borrowed—it's customary and polite to slip the bills into an unsealed envelope. Providing an envelope makes accepting the money less awkward for the recipient.

Credit Cards

International ATM service is available 24/7 at all Japanese 7-11s and during the postal service's business hours. ATMs at other locations might not take your American credit card. (See "Bills, Bills, Bills—How to Withdraw Money from a Japanese ATM" for details.)

NOTE: You can withdraw up to ¥30,000 a day from a Japanese ATM.

Japan Post (http://www.post.japanpost.jp), Japan's postal service, offers ATM service, but not on Sundays. (See "Bills, Bills, Bills—How to Withdraw Money from a Japanese ATM" for more details.) Japan Posts are usually open from 9 am to 5 pm on weekdays and from 9 am to 12:30 pm on Saturdays, but the Japan Post ATM often has different hours than Japan Post. Check your local branch for exact hours.

As of April 2013, 7-11 ATMs no longer accept non-Japanese MasterCards, Maestro, or Cirrus cards. You can still use these credit cards to make purchases, just not to withdraw cash.

Prepaid cash cards will not work in Japanese ATMs, so if you plan on withdrawing money while in Japan, please bring a traditional credit or debit card.

Before you leave for Japan, write down the phone number of your credit card company, as well as your credit card's number and expiration date. This information will greatly expedite the recovery of your credit card, should it get lost or stolen.

See if your bank offers access to **ShopSafe Online** (http://www.shopsafe. com). ShopSafe generates auto-expiring credit card numbers based off the number of your original card. ShopSafe's service prevents unwanted recurring fees, as well as credit card theft. ShopSafe is a great service to use when shopping online, especially from unfamiliar retailers.

Keep a ledger of all your expenses. I recommend **Quicken Software** (http://quicken.intuit.com), since it's easy to use and compatible with all operating systems.

HOW TO COMPLETE JAPANESE IMMIGRATION FORMS

While on the plane, you will be presented with two forms to complete for Japanese Customs. The first, shown below, is the self-explanatory Immigration Card.

Japanese Immigration Card for Foreigners

The Japanese Immigration Card for Foreigners is self-explanatory, but pay careful attention to the "Purpose of Visit" section.

If you will be traveling and/or sight-seeing, write "Tourism."

> **TIP**: Only those entering Japan as a tourist can use the Japan Rail Pass. (See "Out and About—The Japan Rail Pass" for details.)

If you will be visiting family, write "Visiting Family."

If you will be studying abroad and have a student visa, write "Study."

> **TIP**: Do not write "Study" if you are engaging in a short-term (i.e. less than ninety day) study abroad program. Japanese summer camps and three-week study trips are considered "Tourism." Study abroad programs exceeding ninety days require a visa.

If you are moving to Japan for a new job, such as teaching English, write "Work." Japanese Customs will then check the category of your visa.

If you will be going to Japan on business, but will not be engaging in income-earning activities, write "Business."

It is important to distinguish between "Business" and "Work" on your Immigration Card. "Work" requires a visa. If you write "Work," but do not have a work visa, you will have trouble with Japanese Immigration. Teaching English, even privately as a tutor, is illegal without the proper visa, as is any other form of paid employment. If you are working in Japan illegally, you may not receive equal protection under the law should any incidents arise, not to mention you may also be deported.

The back of the form requires you to complete the following questions:

以下の質問について、該当するものに☑を記入してください。Please check the applicable items.
어떠한 질문에 대해서, 해당하는 질에 □을 기입해 주십시오.

1 あなたは、日本から退去強制されたこと、出国命令により出国したこと、又は、日本への上陸を拒否されたことがありますか？
Have you ever been deported from Japan, have you ever departed from Japan under a departure order, or have you ever been denied entry to Japan?
귀하는, 일본에서 강제 퇴거 당한 일, 출국 명령에 의하여 출국한 일, 또는, 일본에 상륙을 거부 당한 일이 있습니까？
□ はい Yes 예 □ いいえ No 아니오

2 あなたは、日本国又は日本国以外の国において、刑事事件で有罪判決を受けたことがありますか？
Have you ever been found guilty in a criminal case in Japan or in another country?
귀하는, 일본국 또는 일본국 이외의 나라에서 형사사건으로 유죄판결을 받은 일이 있습니까？
□ はい Yes 예 □ いいえ No 아니오

3 あなたは、現在、麻薬、大麻、あへん若しくは覚せい剤等の規制薬物又は銃砲、刀剣類若しくは火薬類を所持していますか？
Do you presently have in your possession narcotics, marijuana, opium, stimulants, or other drugs, swords, explosives or other such items?
귀하는 현재, 마약, 대마, 아편 혹은 각성제 등의 규제약물 또는 총포, 도검류 혹은 화약류를 소지하고 있습니까？
□ はい Yes 예 □ いいえ No 아니오

4 あなたは、現在、現金をいくら所持していますか？
How much money in cash do you presently have in your possession?
귀하는 현재, 현금을 얼마 소지하고 있습니까？
〔例、$、￥、W、€, その他 Others（ ）〕
〔예, 달러, 위, 엔(한화), 기타（ ）〕

以上の記載内容は事実と相違ありません。I hereby declare that the statement given above is true and accurate.
이상의 기재 내용은 사실과 틀림 없습니다.

署名
Signature
서명

Japanese Customs Declaration

The personal information you enter on the Japanese Customs form should match the information you entered on the Immigration Form.

UPON ARRIVAL

International Japanese Airports		
NRT	Narita International Airport	Narita, Chiba
HND	Tokyo International Airport	Haneda, Tokyo
NGO	Chūbu International Airport	Aichi, Nagoya
KIX	Kansai International Airport	Izumisano, Osaka
ITM	Osaka International Airport	Toyonaka, Osaka

Narita International Airport (http://www.narita-airport.jp/en) is often called "Tokyo Narita," but Narita and Tokyo are completely different cities. The best way to get from Narita to Tokyo is by bus or train.

> **TIP**: Allow two hours (one way) for transportation. It actually only takes about an hour and a half by bus from Narita Airport to Shibuya, but factor in some extra time to your travel plans to allow for traffic, heavy baggage, and jet lag.

The ticket counter just outside the international arrival area sells tickets to various cities and hotels in Tokyo.

Taking the Bus

The bus timetable displays are written in English, but you can visit Narita Airport's list of bus/rail routes and destinations (http://www.narita-airport.jp/en/access/bus/index.html) or the **Airport Limousine Bus** official English website (http://www.limousinebus.co.jp/en) for specific price information. Tickets must be paid for in Japanese yen. No credit cards are accepted. (There is an ATM machine nearby.)

When you board the bus, you will receive a luggage ticket. Unlike many baggage claims in America, the Japanese bus employee will actually check that the numbers match before giving you your luggage, so keep your ticket in a safe place.

A taxi from Narita Airport to central Tokyo can cost up to ¥20,000, but even disregarding the cost, you are better off taking a bus. Unless you're going to a well-known Tokyo hotel, your Narita-based driver may be unfamiliar with your destination. Thanks to GPS navigation, this is not an insurmountable problem, but it may be easier to communicate your destination's whereabouts to a Tokyo-based taxi driver. Take a bus to Tokyo, then take a taxi from there to your destination.

Taking the Train

The **Narita Express** (https://www.jreast.co.jp/e/nex/index.html), or "N'EX" train, takes only 53 minutes from Tokyo Station to Narita Airport, and costs about the same as a bus ticket. The N'EX train stops at Tokyo, Shinjuku, and Yokohama, among other major stops. All N'EX tickets are reserved seats. Trains start at 7:30 am and make their last stops before 11:15 pm.

There is a reason you don't see a lot of Japanese people hauling heavy luggage on the train to the airport, and that reason is *takkyūbin* 宅急便. A *takkyūbin* service delivers your luggage directly to the location of your choice within two days. *Takkyūbin* is relatively inexpensive (around $30 per piece of luggage, more or less depending on the size and destination of your luggage). Bring your luggage to the *takkyūbin* counter, and have your destination address (in Japanese) ready and easily accessible. One of the *takkyūbin* employees will weigh your luggage and help complete the form for you. This service also works in reverse, though you will need to schedule the pickup in advance. *Takkyūbin* is a well-established service, and both safe and reliable.

> **NOTE**: *Takkyūbin* counters are separate from the airline counters—you will have to pick up your bags from the takkyubin company before getting in line for your ticket. This process should take under ten minutes.

Kuro Neko (http://www.kuronekoyamato.co.jp/en/personal/airport) can pick up your luggage from your place of residence and deliver it to the airline counter before your flight. If you will be traveling out of an international airport, specify which terminal your airline is in on your *takkyūbin* delivery slip. Kuro Neko requires at least three days notice for home pick-up.

SETTLING IN

Whether you're staying in Japan for a week or a decade, the following tips will help you have the most comfortable at-home experience possible.

AT HOME

Moving In

If you want to save money when you first move to Japan, search online and in local ex-pat magazines for "Sayonara Sales." Relocating ex-pats are desperate to purge their possessions, and will often give away furniture and appliances for free. The only catch is that you will probably have to pick up the items yourself.

> **TIP**: Amazon Japan is an easy way to get large and/or heavy items delivered to your residence, saving you the effort of trying to peddle a *futon* 布団 (traditional Japanese bedding, sort of like a padded mattress) home on a bicycle.

If your apartment comes with a TV, you're automatically required to pay for **NHK** (http://www3.nhk.or.jp), the government-sponsored broadcasting service. This is for "safety reasons," so that in case there's a typhoon or other natural disaster, you'll be able to know what's going on. Within months (maybe even days) of moving into your new residence, an NHK representative will knock on your door and ask for money. (Unless a previous tenant or your apartment manager has already paid this fee for you.) There is currently no penalty for not paying the NHK TV bill, but as a guest in Japan, you should be courteous and obey the law.

The Alien Registration Card (ARC)—a.k.a. The *Gaijin* Card

If you have a visa¬¬ and will be staying for more than ninety days, you must register for a Resident Card, or *zairyū-kādo* 在留カード . (The Resident Card was previously known as the the Alien Registration Card, or *Gaijin-tōrokushō* 外人登録証 . This card, pictured above, was known and known by foreigners as "the Gaijin Card," until July 9, 2012. Gaijin means "foreigner.")

Visit the Immigration Bureau of Japan's website (http://www.immi-moj. go.jp/newimmiact_1/en/point_1-2.html) for more details.

A ward office (市役所 *shiyakusho*) is a local government office branch. If you will be living in Japan more than ninety days, you will need to go to your local ward office to register for your Resident Card.

> **TIP**: If you change addresses while living in Japan, stop by your new ward office as soon as possible to get your address officially changed. Some businesses, such as cell phone providers, will not change your billing address until you can present them with the officially-updated Resident Card. An employee at the ward office will write your new address in pen on the back of your Resident Card. Do not write on your own Resident Card before visiting the ward office.

> **TIP**: Registering your change of address at the ward office will not redirect your mail, so you will need to complete a change of address form at the post office as well.

How to Read a Japanese Address

Japanese addresses are numbered in the order in which they were built, not sequential order. (Except in Sapporo, a city designed by Americans.)

> "There are no names on the streets; where there are numbers, they
> have no sequence, and I met no Europeans on foot to help me in my
> difficulty."
>
> —*Victorian adventurer Isabella Bird Bishop, upon her arrival in Japan in 1880.*

TIP:「ハンディ版」*Handei-han* guidebooks list easy-to-spot landmarks,
such as Starbucks and 7-11. The indexes in the back organize cities in
alphabetical order, by nearest train station and by prefecture. *Handei-
han* guides are available online and in many bookstores for about
¥1200.

100-0001
Tokyo, Shibuya, Lalaland 1-2-3

The Zip Code is 100-0001. The city is Tokyo. The ward, which is like
a county or district, is Shibuya. Lalaland is the name of the city within
Shibuya. "1" is the section in Lalaland. Once you're in Lalaland 1, search for
District #2, House #3.

〒 100-0001
東京都渋谷区ラーラーランド1丁目2番3号
Tokyō-to, Shibuya-ku, Lālālando, Icchome, Ni-ban, San-gō

〒 indicates the zip code and is written above the address. 都 (*to*) means
"city," 区 (*ku*) means "ward." 丁目 (*chō-me*) is the district number. 番
(*ban*) is the numbered section within the district, and 号 (*gō*) is the number
of the house. If the address is for a room in a building, the address might
instead say 号室 *gō-shitsu.*

〒 100-0001
東京都渋谷区ラーラランド1丁目2番3号

あおやまちょう
青山町 2 — 5 — 35
Aoyama-chō 2 — 5 — 35

Within "District 2" of the above sample map of "*Aoyama-chō*", look for "Block 5". Within "Block 5," is "Building #35."

Navitime (http://www.navitime.co.jp) offers free maps and route planning information for cars, buses, trains, and bicycles in Japanese. **Hyperpedia** (http://www.hyperdia.com) lets you browse train timetables in English.

GETTING A CELL PHONE

A *keitai-denwa* ケイタイ電話 ("*keitai*" for short) is a Japanese cell phone.

A *sumaho* スマホ is a smartphone.

You will not be able to buy a cell phone until you have a Resident Card. Since it will take at least three weeks for the ward office to process your Resident Card, I advise renting a phone in the airport, which requires a passport and an initial cash or credit deposit. (Your American cell phone may work in Japan, but expect heavy roaming charges.) You may have to return the rental phone to the airport kiosk in person.

> **TIP**: You may wish to rent a cell phone before you leave for Japan, through a service such as **My Japan Phone** (http://myjapanphone.com). The company will ship the phone to you before your departure, but this option can be costly. Confirm the company's return shipping address in advance to avoid late fees.

To purchase a cell phone, you must bring your passport, your Resident Card, and a major credit card with you to the store. The salesperson will photocopy your passport before selling you a phone.

Japanese Cell Phone Providers

au/KDDI (http://www.au.kddi.com/english)

DoCoMo (http://www.nttdocomo.co.jp/english)

SoftBank (http://mbsoftbank.jp/en)

Check your desired cell phone provider's website for a list of English-speaking branches, which may offer promotional materials and assistance in English. If you're going to a non-English branch and you speak some Japanese, it might help to prepare a list of any questions you may have in advance.

American iPhones can get roaming service in Japan, but just as in America, cell phone providers bundle the plan with the phone. You can't just bring your American iPhone and purchase a Japanese plan. Also, when you return to America, your Japanese iPhone (by which I mean the iPhone's telephone and texting capabilities) will not work with an American plan. There are apparently ways to get around this (involving phone hacking and prepaid SIM cards), but these are time-consuming and illegal.

Your phone company will mail you a copy of your phone bill each month, but this is really just a receipt. Your monthly payments will automatically be charged to the credit card you used to purchase your phone.

> **NOTE**: As a temporary resident of Japan, you cannot directly pay your phone bill through a Japanese or American checking account. You must have a credit card to purchase a Japanese cell phone plan.

If your visa expires within a year, contracted plans, such as gym memberships and cell phone plans, may require you to pay a year's fees in advance. Only those with visas registered for more than two years are eligible for "New Customer Discounts" known as *Shinki-keiyaku* 新規契約 . (Unfortunately, this includes most study abroad students and English teachers.) Fear not—many companies have plans where the phone itself is free and the customer just pays for monthly service and texting.

Keitai Mail

Japanese *keitai* come with their own e-mail address. Many people use their *keitai* address as their primary e-mail.

A text and an e-mail are both called *mēru* メール in Japanese. When someone asks for your *addoressu* アドレス , your address, they mean your e-mail/*keitai* address. (Your home address is your *jūsho* 住所).

Mēru set-up procedures differ depending on the model of your phone, so ask your salesperson for assistance before leaving the store.

> **TIP**: If you change your *mēru* address, inform all of your contacts. Incoming messages will not be forwarded automatically from your old address to your new one.

If you do a lot of texting or Internet browsing on your *keitai*, consider an unlimited data plan, known as *Paketto-hōdai* パケット放題 . For SoftBank phones, this unlimited data plan will let you access the Internet and text as much as you want for a set fee (usually $45 a month). There is also a reduced, pay-as-you-go *Paketto-hōdai* plan that charges up to, but never surpassing, the full *Paketto-hōdai* plan. The more expensive *Paketto-hōdai* option is often partnered with deep discounts on new phone models.

You can use your cell phone as an alarm clock, but adjust the "Manner Mode," マナーモード *Mannā-mōdo*, settings to protect your sleep from incoming texts and calls. The default Manner Mode settings usually negate all sound, so test your updated settings before trying it on a work day.

LINE (http://line.naver.jp/en)

This popular communication app lets you text and call your friends for free. When you message someone on LINE, you can choose from a range of free and paid "stamps" to accentuate your message. LINE contact information can be exchanged with the click of a button or by shaking your phone next to the phone of your friend, so this is an easy and fun way to keep in touch.

If you lose your phone, report the loss to the police. Japanese phone companies require a police report within thirty days before providing a refund to customers who purchased a cell phone protection plan, also known as *Zenson-hoshō* 全損保証 . If your phone gets damaged or lost, a cell phone protection plan may return up to 80% of the phone's original cost.

Most Japanese cell phone numbers start with "080" or "090", but a landline's area code depends on its location. Japanese area codes start with "011" in Hokkaido, increase to "075" by Kyoto, and end with "09" in Okinawa. Due to this numbering system, not all phone numbers have the same number of digits. If you're curious, you can look up each region's area code here: http://zatugaku.jp/tel-j.htm.

Digital Money

Denshi-manē 電子マネー , or "digital money," allows your phone to link to a Japanese credit card. Digital money lets you purchase items simply by swiping the phone over the clearly-designated data receivers in convenience stores, department stores, and restaurants. Digital money may be convenient, but foreigners are ineligible for Japanese credit cards unless they have proven "roots" in Japan (i.e. proof of a Japanese spouse or permanent residence).

See those barcodes on Japanese advertisements? These barcodes are called QR codes—short for "Quick Response" code. Take a picture of a QR code with your *keitai* and all the information will be sent to your phone.

Here's the QR code for a fun restaurant in Shinjuku, Tokyo called 座魚 *Zauo*

(http://r.gnavi.co.jp/g775103/menu1.html).

Purikura Photo Booths

Purikura プリクラ (short for "Print Club") photo booths let you choose an assortment of backgrounds and your ideal skin color (it can make your skin lighter or darker) for some quick, fun snapshots.

Purikura photo booths automatically smooth out your complexion and make your eyes bigger, brighter, and darker. After posing for a few pictures, you can digitally embellish your photos on the adjacent tablet screen. Your pictures print as a group of self-adhesive stickers. *Purikura* is popular with high school girls, who often use *purikura* photos to decorate their phones and binders.

TIP: Make sure your *keitai* mail address is easy to type. Many *purikura* booths text a free digital copy of one of your photos to your phone, but you have less than a minute (sometimes only 30 seconds) to input your phone's address. The *purikura* text will also contain a link to purchase digital versions of the rest of your photos. *Purikura* booths only send messages to Japanese *keitai*; you cannot send the pictures to a non-*keitai* e-mail address, such as @yahoo.com or @gmail.com.

Japanese Emoticons

Most Japanese cell phones come with a variety of animated emoticons, but *kao-moji* 顔文字 , emoticons based on standard ASCII characters, are still popular in digital communication. *Kao-moji*, though not always professionally appropriate, are sometimes present in business e-mails among coworkers.

Kao-moji Emoticons	
＾ ＾	Happy
(≧▽≦)	Excited
(⌒▽⌒)	Laughing
w	LOL (The Japanese word for laugh is *warai*.)
(□ ;)	Surprised
(˚Λ˚)	Shocked
ヽ(´ー｀)┌	Mellow
(T▽T)	Crying
(ToT)	Crying
＿│ ｜○	Depressed (A man slumped over in shame)
OTL	Depressed (Same as above)
(* m)	Dissatisfied
e(^｡ ^)9	Good Luck
(o^-')b	You Can Do It

For more *kao-moji*, visit Japanese Emoticons (http://www.japaneseemoticons.net), which is in English, or the Japanese-language website Face Mark (http://www.facemark.jp/facemark.htm).

JAPAN POST, AND HOW TO SCHEDULE A PACKAGE DELIVERY

If someone sends you a package when you are not home, Japan Post will leave a double-sided notice in your mailbox with information about rescheduling a delivery time.

Japan Post has an English call center, but sometimes it can be faster to schedule a delivery time using Japan Post's automated Japanese system.

The sample notice and instructions below will help you schedule a delivery time with Japan Post.

速　達

1 5 1 - 8 7 9 9

通信事務郵便
（依頼信）

代々木支店 郵便課 行

（1）インターネット再配達受付
http://www.post.japanpost.jp/
携帯電話からのご登録は右のQRコードから…→

※携帯電話でのご登録はご自宅への再配達に限ります。
ご自宅以外への再配達をご希望の場合は、パソコンまたはお電話でご登録ください。

（2）24時間自動受付 （一部ご利用になれない電話機があります。）

0800-0800-888（無料）
※おかけ間違いの
ないよう
ご注意ください。

携帯電話からのご連絡は **0603-155-3917**（有料）

自動音声に従って、プッシュボタンを押してください。
①お客様の郵便番号・種類番号
　（裏面 記号 に記載の9ケタをご入力）
②お客様の電話番号（市外局番からご入力）
③初回配達日（裏面 記号 に記載の配達日を4ケタでご入力）
　　　　　　　　　　　　　例：3月5日→【0305】
④お知らせ番号（裏面 記号 に記載の6ケタ番号をご入力）
⑤ご希望の配達月日（例：3月5日→【0305】4ケタでご入力）
⑥ご希望の配達時間帯（下表から該当の番号1ケタをご入力）

※ご自宅以外への再配達をご希望の場合は、上記の（3）、（4）の方法でご登録ください。

番号	ご希望の配達時間帯		受付時間
1	午前中	9時～12時	～当日 8:00まで
2	午後①	12時～14時	～当日11:00まで
3	午後②	14時～17時	～当日13:00まで
4	夕方	17時～19時	～当日16:00まで
5	夜間	19時～21時	～当日18:00まで
0	時間帯希望なし		～当日18:00まで

（3）郵便又はファックスによる再配達受付
　裏面に必要事項をご記入の上、この通知書をポストに投函
又はファックスにより送信（03-5790-0527）してください。
（ただし、お届けもしくは窓口でのお渡しは、投函日又はファックス送信日の
翌日以降となります。）

（4）コールセンター電話受付 （8時～21時）

0120-549-223
※おかけ間違いのないようご注意ください。

携帯電話からのご連絡は
0570-064-223（有料）

ご希望の配達時間帯		受付時間
午前中	9時～12時	～前日21:00まで
午後①	12時～14時	～当日11:00まで
午後②	14時～17時	～当日13:00まで
夕方	17時～19時	～当日16:00まで
夜間	19時～21時	～当日19:00まで

（5）当支店のゆうゆう窓口でのお受取り
　配達担当者が持ち出している場合がありますので、窓口での
お受取りを希望される場合、事前に03-5790-0526
（受付時間は8時～21時まで）へご連絡ください。当日配達分の
受取は23時以降となります。
　　24時間受け取ることができます。
なお、お越しになる際は、アこの通知書、イ印鑑、ウご本人様と確認
できる証明資料（免許証、健康保険証など）をお持ちください。

Call us for redelivery (English) 0570-046-111　8.00am-10.00pm Monday to Friday,
9.00am-10.00pm Saturday and Sunday

番ア 1 5 ０ ０ ０ ０ １ ８ ２ （情報番号）

Your Zip Code

受取人様
(Addressee)   **Your Name**   様

差出人様
(Sender)   **Sender's Name**   様からの

郵便物等をお届けにお伺いしましたが、ご不在でしたのでお預かりしております。
　再度配達いたしますので、裏面のいずれかの方法により、ご連絡ください。

Japan Post attempted to deliver your package on this date.

配達担当者
The name of the person who tried to deliver your package

番イ → 配達日時 4月15日5時００分頃

Japan Post will hold onto your package until this date.

保管期限 5月14日まで

Your package's number

番ウ → お知らせ番号 1584-27

お預かりしている郵便物等の種類と種類番号

内国郵便物 | 57 定形外・ゆうメール・未納通常等
Domestic Mail Fees
（備考）   引換金額（   円）

国際郵便物 | 61 書留・保険付   81 国際小包・EMS
International Mail Fees
62 税付   82 税付国際小包
63 上記以外   83 上記以外の国際小包
（備考）   引換金額 3 200 円

This package incurred international tax.

FAX又は郵便により再配達の依頼をされる際は枠内にご記入ください。

受取人様の電話番号

TEL（   ）   −   （ご自宅・携帯）

1 再配達をご希望の方は、ご希望の日と時間帯をご記入ください。

月   日 配達希望
☐ 午前中（9時〜12時）   ☐ 夕 方（17時〜19時）
☐ 午後①（12時〜14時）   ☐ 夜 間（19時〜21時）
☐ 午後②（14時〜17時）   ☐ 時間帯の希望をしない

2 勤務先への配達などをご希望の方は、下の欄にご記入ください。
（受け取られる際に、ご本人様であることを確認させていただく場合があります。）

☐ 勤務先に配達

☐ ご近所の方に配達

ご住所 〒
ご氏名
ご連絡先 （   ）

You can also request a delivery time via fax

☐ 他の支店、郵便局の窓口でお受取り ⟶   支店・郵便局

1. Japan Post will leave a double-sided notice (example shown above) in your mailbox.

2. First, call the number 0503-155-3917. The number 0800-0800-888 is free, but can only be dialed from a landline.

3. The automated voice on the other line will greet you and say something in Japanese. Press the number 1.

4. She will then ask for your zip code and the mailing code listed under the 「ア」 section, located above the name of the package recipient.) (Ex: 150000182) Type this number, but don't press #.

5. She will then ask for your phone number. This can be a cell or a landline. Type your phone number. (Ex: 080-1234-5678)

6. She will then ask for the date the post office attempted to deliver the package. This is under the 「イ」 section. (Ex: April 15th = 0415).

7. She will then ask for the package indicated in the 「ウ」 section. (Ex: 1584-27)

8. She will repeat the number back to you in Japanese. If you typed the number correctly, press 1. If you did not, press 3 and return to Step 7.

9. She will then ask for the date you wish the package to be delivered. (Ex: April 17th = 0417).

10. She will then ask what time you would like the package delivered. The options are listed in Section #4 on the front of the delivery slip, the side with the five red boxes. The available options are translated below.

番号		Desired Time	Call must be received by~
1	A.M	9時~12時	~当日 8 :00まで
2	P.M. (#1)	12時~14時	~当日11 :00まで
3	P.M. (#2)	14時~17時	~当日13:00まで
4	Evening	17時~19時	~当日16:00まで
5	Late Evening	19時~21時	~当日18:00まで
0		Any Time	~当日18:00まで

11. Choose and type the number that corresponds with your desired time slot. You must call within the "Call must be received by" time before selecting your desired time, otherwise you will have to repeat the whole reservation process from the beginning.

    TIP: Japan Post is reliable and prompt. If you select to have your package delivered between 5 and 7 pm, you will have your package no later than 7:01 pm.

12. The operator will repeat your selection, but don't hang up the phone just yet! Wait until she's finished talking, then she'll ask you one more time for confirmation.

13. If you have more package deliveries to schedule, press 1. Otherwise, press 3. Once you press 1 or 3, your package request has been placed. Your package deliveries are not scheduled until you press 3.

TIP: If your relatives send you new clothing while you're in Japan, ask them to remove the price tags in advance. Otherwise, Japanese Customs will charge the recipient tax upon delivery.

Signing For Your Package

An *inkan* 印鑑 , the Japanese equivalent of a signet ring, is a name seal used to sign official and important documents.

Leave your *inkan* inside an auto-stamp case (available at any stationery store) on a hook by your apartment door. When packages arrive, all you need to do is stamp the delivery receipt. No fumbling for a pen or exposing your house to a stranger.

NOTE: You can order these online or in stores like **Loft** (http://www. loft.co.jp) and **Itoya** (http://www.ito-ya.co.jp). Some Japanese banks require you to have an *inkan* before opening an account, though it's recently become acceptable to simply sign one's name.

Your *inkan* doesn't have to be a literal katakana-zation of your name. One guy I know had the last name "Barber," so he used the Japanese *kanji* for "hair cutter." You can even use English letters on your *inkan*.

Visiting the Post Office

Large post offices are open on weekdays from 9:00 am to 7:00 pm (5 pm for smaller branches) and on Saturday mornings.

Post Office boxes are red—put your mail in the "International Mail" slot. (There will be an English label.)

As of publication, it costs ¥70 to send a postcard and ¥110 to send a letter from Japan to America. Japan Post will increase the cost of its domestic postage in April 2014. You can check the exact cost of your postage on Japan Post's website (http://www.post.japanpost.jp/lpo/tax2014) (Japanese only).

In Japan, it is more expensive to mail a package if it contains a letter. The exact price depends on the size and weight of your package, but an international package containing a letter can cost ¥1000 more than a package without a letter.

Inkan are always stamped in red ink.

The same-sized package sent by airmail from Japan to the U.S. cost ¥2310 by itself and ¥3410 with a letter inside. Mail the letter separately for cheaper shipping.

When sending packages home, keep in mind that Japan Post only accepts cash. Japan Post ATMs are available for cash withdrawals.

EMS (http://www.post.japanpost.jp/cgi-charge), short for "Express Mail Service," is part of Japan Post and delivers to over 120 countries. EMS can ship packages and documents weighing less than thirty kg. Like Priority Mail in the U.S., EMS packages require special envelopes and/or boxes. EMS provides information in English on their website (http://www.post. japanpost.jp/int/use/ems_en.html).

Many Japanese envelopes, especially those from fine stationery stores, do not have flaps lined with self-sealing adhesive. Use a glue stick or some small stickers to properly seal your envelope. If you're in a rush, the post office supplies liquid glue sticks for public use. Look for the glue sticks on the ledges stocked with shipping forms.

GARBAGE SORTING

In America, there are usually two categories of garbage: recyclables and non-recyclables. In Japan, there are eight.

If you fail to sort your garbage correctly, you risk alienating your neighbors, getting in trouble with your apartment manager, and incurring fines. Different parts of Japan have different rules regarding disposal and collection rules, but Japan's garbage sorting categories are nation-wide.

Burnable Garbage 燃やすゴミ *Moyasu-gomi*

Food scraps, paper, and any waste that can be safely burned.

> **TIP**: Used sanitary products classify as burnable garbage. Their plastic wrappers go in the unburnable bin. Wrap your used sanitary products in toilet paper before disposing of them.

Plastic Garbage プラスチック *Purasuchikku*

Plastic containers, cellophane wrap, and any type of plastic that is not a bottle.

PET Bottles ペットボトル *Petto-bottoru*

Plastic bottles, washed, squashed, and with the labels—which are classified as unburnable garbage—peeled off.

The caps of PET bottles, known as "Eco Caps," *Eko-kyappu* 「エコ・キャップ」, can be recycled either with PET bottles or separately. Eco Cap containers are often located near vending machines or in office buildings.

Glass ビン類 *Bin-rui*

Glass containers rinsed clean and with the labels removed.

Metal Cans 缶類 *Kan-rui*

Metal cans rinsed clean and with the labels removed.

Non-burnable Garbage 燃やさないゴミ *Moyasanai-gomi*

Metal items, glass products, fluorescent lights, and other non-recyclables that cannot be safely burned.

Complicated Garbage 複雑ゴミ *Fukuzatsu-gomi*

Broken appliances, sharp metal, and any other garbage that requires extra precaution when handling.

Oversized Garbage 粗大ゴミ *Sodai-gomi*

Televisions, couches, futons, and anything else large and/or unwieldy. You may have to pay in advance for the disposal of oversized garbage.

Garbage Collection

Each type of garbage has a designated collection time (i.e. Burnable on Monday, Plastic on Tuesday, etc.). Garbage collection information is provided at your local ward office. In large cities, garbage sorting information is often available in English.

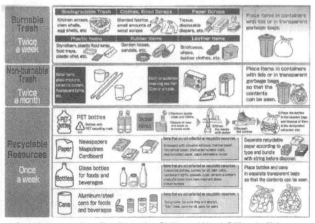

A garbage sorting flier from the Shibuya Ward Office in Tokyo.

Some regions of Japan may require you to use government-issued, color-coded garbage bags. In some cases, you may have to pick these bags up at your local ward office. These bags are free, but to avoid multiple trips to the ward office, gather your garbage into normal plastic bags first, then cram them into the government-issued one.

> **NOTE**: Since garbage bags often line the street on collection day, some businesses give away free bags with their company's information on the front as a form of advertising.

Perhaps because of garbage sorting rules, there are not many public trash cans in Japan. If you buy a drink or snack from a store, it is perfectly acceptable to dispose the resulting garbage in the garbage cans the store provides. It is not acceptable to do this with garbage you accumulated elsewhere.

> **NOTE**: It is acceptable, however, to bring your clean recyclables to the public recycling bins at your local grocery store. (Not all grocery stores open their recycling bins up to the public, so see what the locals are doing before hauling your cans and bottles across town.)

Wonder what those liter water bottles are doing tied around telephone poles and outdoor potted plants on the side of the road? They're not there to drink! These bottles act as a deterrent to stray cats, who may be repelled by the sparkle of water in sunlight.

HOW TO USE A JAPANESE
AIR CONDITIONER/HEATER

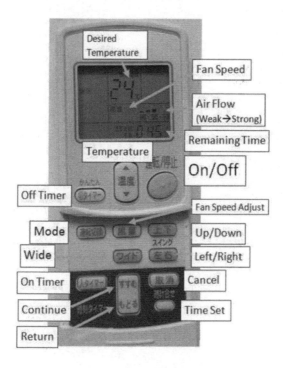

After turning on the remote, press 運転切換 ^{うんてんきりかえ} *Unten-kirikae*, "Mode."

Select either 冷房 ^{れいぼう} *Reibō*, "Cool," or 暖房 ^{だんぼう} *Danbō*, "Heat."

Adjust the temperature by using the arrow keys in the center of the device. Japan, like Europe, measures temperature in Celsius.

ドライ *Dorai*, "Dry Mode," is useful for when it is humid.

The fan setting, 送風 *Sōfū*, is self-explanatory.

The "Up/Down," 下上 *Jō-ge*, and 左右 *Sayū*, "Left/Right," buttons change the vent direction. If you hold down either of these buttons, the vent will circulate air back and forth. Release the button once the vent reaches the direction you prefer.

The On Timer 入タイマー *Iri-taimā* = Activation Timer

°C	°F	°C	°F
40	104	29	84.2
39	102	28	82.4
38	100	27	80.6
37	98.6	26	78.8
36	96.8	25	77
35	95	24	75.2
34	93.2	23	73.4
33	91.4	22	71.6
32	89.6	21	69.8
31	87.7	20	68
30	86	19	66.2

The Off Timer 切タイマー *Kiri-taimā* = Deactivation Timer

Energy Conservation

Many Japanese cooling and heating systems have a three hour energy save feature, meaning that unless you touch the remote, the unit will shut off after three hours. Some machines will let you designate a longer shut off time using 時計合わせ *Tokei-awase*, "Time Set." The number in the right-hand corner of the remote screen indicates how much time remains before the system shuts down.

> **TIP**: If your remote won't let you extend the shutdown time, buy a space heater that you can leave on during chilly winter evenings.

Japan has always encouraged its people to conserve resources, but ever since the Tōhoku earthquake, *setsuden* 節電 ("saving electricity") has become even more important. In response to the Tōhoku earthquake and tsunami, the Japanese government passed energy-restriction policies to conserve electricity and prevent unscheduled blackouts. Some *setsuden* restrictions have since been lifted, but many Japanese companies and households continue their conservation efforts.

COOKING AT HOME

Grocery Shopping

Certain Western food products, such as peanut butter or your favorite breakfast cereal, may be difficult to find in small, suburban supermarkets. The following sites can deliver your favorite foreign foods to your address.

The Meat Guys (http://www.themeatguy.jp/app/en) sells meat products that are hard to find in Japan, such as turkey, duck, venison, veal, and even kangaroo.

Tengu Natural Foods (http://store.alishan.jp) sells organic and vegetarian foods.

Foreign Buyers' Club (http://www.fbcusa.com/cs/index.php) sells turkeys, breakfast cereal, canned goods, and other imported Western food products. (They also sell teaching supplies.)

Are you a vegetarian or vegan? If you're in Tokyo, you might be able to live a 100% vegetarian/vegan life—it has been done—but if you're living in a rural area, you will spend a substantial amount of time and money acquiring food you can eat.

Surviving in Japan's guide to reading Japanese food labels (http://www.survivingnjapan.com/2012/04/ultimate-guide-to-reading-food-labels.html) can assist those with specific dietary restrictions.

You can also buy fresh produce as well as canned goods on the food section of **Amazon.jp** (http://www.amazon.co.jp). Look for the section labeled 食品 *shoku-hin*, or "foodstuffs."

Japanese grocery stores sell many premade or "ten minute" meals, such as instant noodles, prepackaged curry sauce, and reheatable precooked meals. If you're pressed for time, it might be faster to stop by the grocery store than cook at home.

Supermarkets in Japan often offer timesales タイムセール *taimusēru*—reduced prices for a short period of time. Arrive early to snag a good deal!

In the evenings, grocery stores will discount about-to-expire vegetables and meat products. Look for a a swarm of determined shoppers or a bright label with the word "half-price," *hangaku* 半額 , in bold. *Hangaku* sales are a great way to experiment with usually-pricey ingredients, but whatever you buy, you must finish that evening. Stocking up, even if you intend on freezing it—could just make you sick.

If you walk to the grocery store, use a basket to shop, not a cart. It's easy to lose track of how heavy your purchases are when shopping with a cart, which can make for a difficult walk home.

No need to lug bulky fruit home from the grocery store! Order it online from Amazon Japan and have it delivered to your home. Type フルーツ ("fruit") for a list of options.

Learning to Cook

If you've never lived on your own before, I recommend practicing a few recipes at home before moving to Japan. Knowing a week's worth of simple, go-to recipes will make your first weeks in a new country much easier.

> **TIP**: Learn how to make at least one "traditional" dessert and one main course from your home country. You never know when you will be invited to a party and asked to bring "traditional cuisine" from your country. These type of recipe-sharing potlucks are especially popular with study abroad students, who often come to Japan from a variety of different countries.

For cooks of all experience levels, I highly recommend Mark Bittman's classic cookbook *How to Cook Everything*. The book lives up to its title, and offers easy-to-make recipes for lots of ingredients, including ones you will be able to access easily in Japan, such as miso, squid, fish, and other types of seafood. The print version of this book would take up a sizable amount of space in your luggage. Fortunately, the **How to Cook Everything App** (https://itunes.apple.com/us/app/how-to-cook-everything-for/id367690249?mt=8) contains 2,000 recipes from the book. There is also a *How to Cook Everything* app for vegetarians.

Supercook (http://www.supercook.com) is a useful resource for making the most out of what you have in your fridge. Type in what ingredients you have in your pantry and this website will create a list of recipes you can make using what you already have on hand. You can save staples, such as "olive oil" and "sesame seeds," and keep your ingredient list current by registering a free account. Supercook is a fun and helpful website, but I recommend choosing a recipe *before* you actually need it. Late in the evening after a long day at work is not always the most fun time to try out new recipes.

There are lots of ways to improve your cooking while in Japan. **ABC Cooking Studio** (http://www.abc-cooking.co.jp) offers both one-day classes and year-long cooking and baking lessons. Taking a cooking class could be a fun way to improve your cooking and meet people at the same time. ABC Cooking Studio also offers classes in English at some locations.

If you don't want to sign up for an official cooking school, ask around your local community. Invite your friends or coworkers to your home and host a rotating cooking club, with a different person "teaching" a different recipe every week. Even if the people you invite are not necessarily interested in learning how to cook, many Japanese people are interested in learning about foods from other cultures. Just make sure to buy enough ingredients for everyone, and practice the recipe in advance!

Using a Japanese Rice Cooker

Even the most basic rice cooker, *suihanki* 炊飯器 , has a "warm" setting, which keeps your rice warm after it has cooked. Set the cooking timer before leaving for work in the morning and you can return in the evening to a pot of already-cooked rice! You can buy a rice cooker at any Japanese appliance store.

Understanding Your Japanese Rice Cooker		
炊飯スタート	*Suihan-sutāto*	Start
予約	*Yoyaku*	Reservation/Time Set
時	*Ji*	Hours
分	*Bun*	Minutes
切・とりけし	*Ki(ru)・Torikeshi*	Cancel
保温	*Ho-on*	Keep Warm

Making *Bentō*—Japanese Lunchboxes

A *bentō* 弁当 is a Japanese lunchbox that consists of two separate compartments—one for rice, and one for an assortment of vegetables and protein.

Just Bento (http://justbento.com) is an attractive and free resource of beautiful *bentō* recipes.

Kyara-ben キャラ弁 are *bentō* designed to look like cute characters. You can make your own *kyara-ben* using a variety of colorful toothpicks, cooking molds, and liners available at any Japanese grocery store.

These *kyara-ben* were made by the Japanese *bentō* blogger Kazumi Yusa, also known as "Monchi." You can visit her website **Nanka Iikoto Arukamo!** (http://blogs.yahoo.co.jp/yasukazutai777) for more amazing *kyara-ben*.

Takeout and Delivery

Most delivery chains in Japan, understandably, cater to Japanese speakers, so it may be difficult to find a restaurant with an English menu that also delivers. Many restaurants that serve non-Japanese food, such as Indian or Chinese restaurants, offer takeout if you call in advance, but might not have their menus online. Stop by the restaurant in person before placing an order, and take a picture of their menu with your phone for later reference.

A medium cheese pizza from **Domino's** (http://dominos.jp, in English: http://dominos.jp/eng) costs around ¥2000 (about $20). Many pizza companies offer seasonal promotions, though, so check the website of your local pizza chain for the best prices. Many takeout and delivery websites will let you pay with credit card.

> **TIP**: The Japanese Domino's menu has more options, such as the "Avocado Shrimp" *Abokado-Shurinpu* アボカドシュリンプ pizza, which has shrimp, mayonnaise, and avocado," or the "Quatro Super Delicious" *Kuwatoro Sūpā Derishasu* クワトロ・スーパーデリシャス , which is one quarter crab in white sauce, one quarter sliced short rib beef, one quarter tomato sauce and ham, and one quarter garlic chicken. If you're longing for a taste of home, the English menu has more traditional pizzas.

As of printing, **Pizza Hut** (https://pizzahut.jp/pc/top) is still developing their online English menu, so Domino's is your best bet for delivery pizza while in Japan.

Although there is no tipping in Japan, many restaurants will charge a small fee for delivery.

McDonald's (https://mcdelivery.mcdonalds.com/jp) also delivers in some locations, between the hours of 7:00 am and 11 pm., to some locations. When you click on the website's "English" menu, it will initially look exactly the same as the Japanese menu. Click on "Browse Menu" in the upper right-hand corner. You will have to register an account before being able to use this service. As of printing, your address must be inputted in Japanese. Delivery service is only available in some areas, and notice is required at least two hours before scheduled delivery time. Fortunately, you can place your order weeks in advance.

Japanese Tea

Tea cultivation in Japan first began in the ninth century, and tea has enjoyed popularity as Japan's beverage of choice since. (See "Culture and Language—Japanese Tea Ceremony.")

ぎょくろ
玉露 *Gyokuro*

Gyokuro, which translates as "jade dew," is a type of loose-leaf green tea enjoyed on special occasions. *Gyokuro* tea leaves are grown in the shade, and are high in Vitamin C, potassium, and caffeine.

まっちゃ
抹茶 *Matcha*

Matcha is made from powdered gyokuro leaves. *Matcha* is the type of tea served during Japanese tea ceremony, and is easily recognized by its vivid green color. Many Japanese desserts feature *matcha* as an ingredient or topping.

せんちゃ
煎茶 *Sencha*

Sencha is an everyday, loose-leaf green tea that can be served hot or cold. 80% of the tea produced in Japan is sencha. *Sencha* leaves are grown under full sun, and are high in Vitamin C and caffeine.

げんまいちゃ
玄米茶 *Genmaicha*

Genmaicha is sencha mixed with brown rice kernels, and is an everyday drink that can be enjoyed hot or cold. *Genmaicha* was originally meant as a "poor man's tea," since the rice kernels were used to stretch out the tea leaves. *Genmaicha* is now enjoyed by members of all classes.

りょくちゃ
緑茶 *Ryokucha*

When Japanese people say "tea" *o-cha* お茶 , they usually mean ryokucha. *Gyokuro*, *sencha*, and *genmaicha* are all types of *ryokucha*. *Ryokucha* is often called "Japanese green tea" in the West.

むぎちゃ
麦茶 *Mugicha*

Mugicha is a roasted barley tea made of loose barley grains. It is normally regarded as a summer drink, but can be served hot or cold. It contains no caffeine.

For detailed information on the production and preparation of Japanese tea, visit the **Ippodo Tea Company**'s website (http://www.ippodo-tea.co.jp/en/tea/index.html).

Scraping loose leaf tea leaves out the sink can be a hassle. Disposable sink filters, available at any grocery store, reduce unpleasant smells and keep used tea leaves from clogging the drain Check the tea section of the grocery store. Look for the sign that says *O-cha* お茶 , or "tea."

HOW TO USE A JAPANESE WASHING MACHINE

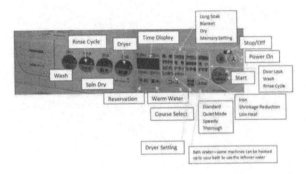

Turn on your washing machine by pressing the 入 *Iri*, "Power On," button. Input your desired setting using the corresponding buttons, then press スタート *Sutāto*, "Start."

The amount of time remaining for each stage of the washing cycle is indicated in the top black half of each circle. Many washing machines will lock shut during the wash cycle.

The ドライ *Dorai*, "Dry," setting dries your clothes without using water. This technology might not appear on older or less expensive washing machines. (The washing machine pictured is a Toshiba TW-741EX(WS), but most Japanese washing machines have similar control panels.)

If you live in a rural area, your wet clothes may attract bugs. If you hang your clothes outside in an urban area, you are potentially drying them in dirty air. Drying will take twice as long, but for hygienic reasons, I recommend hanging your clothes indoors.

Toiletries and cleaning product refills, such as laundry detergent, are often sold in loose plastic containers. Save money and help the environment by using these refills to replenish the bottles you have at home.

HOW TO USE A JAPANESE TOILET

There are two types of toilets in Japan: Japanese style and Western style.

Japanese style, or 和式 *wa-shiki*, is basically a flushable hole in the ground. You squat. Mission accomplished.

Japan is famous for its Western style, 洋式 or *yō-shiki*, toilets. "Western style" toilets in Japan often have functions and features unlike most toilets in the west. Many Japanese toilets are heated and can play music.

Though not all toilets are equally complicated, to avoid the discomfort of accidentally pressing "Bidet" instead of "Flush," here's a quick guide to using the control panel on a Western style Japanese toilet.

Not all Western style toilets in Japan are like the example below, but you may encounter similar models, known as "Washlets" ウォッシュレット , while in Japan.

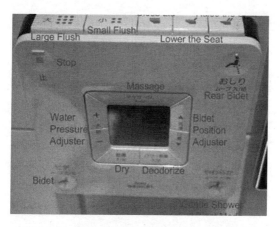

This model does not include musical background noise, but many toilets have an *oto-hime* 音姫 ("sound princess") button—usually identifiable by a music note—that plays music or the sound of rushing water to cover any bodily noises.

Toilets in public facilities often come with an "Emergency" button. If you press the "Emergency" button, someone will come rushing to assist you.

The Emergency Button will not usually be so obvious. Look for the word "call,"
呼出 *yobi-dashi*.

As mentioned earlier, many Japanese bathrooms do not stock paper towels, so it's a good idea to always carry some hand sanitizer, just in case.

THE DOCTOR'S OFFICE

You have two choices for medical treatment in Japan: a public hospital, *byōin* 病院 , or a private clinic, *kurinikku* クリニック .

> If your Japanese friends say you should "go to the hospital," they do not necessarily mean that you require emergency medical attention. Byōin means both "hospital" and "doctor's office."

Present the nurses at the front desk with your health insurance and Resident Card to receive treatment.

Hospitals and clinics usually have adjacent pharmacies. When you go to the pharmacy, the person at the front desk may give you a small book that looks like a mini-passport. This is called an *O-kusuri-techō* お薬手帳 , and is essentially a sticker book to help you keep track of your prescription medication.

Health Insurance in Japan

All foreigners residing in Japan for more than a year, permanent residents of Japan, and adult Japanese citizens are required to be enrolled in some sort of health insurance program. If you will be working in Japan, your company should sign you up for Japanese health insurance.

There are two types of health insurance in Japan: *Kenkō-hoken* 健康保険 Employees' Health Insurance" and *Kokumin-kenkō-hoken* 国民健康保険 "National Health Insurance."

Natalia Doan

Japanese Health Insurance		
Kenkō-hoken けんこうほけん **健康保険**	Employees' Health Insurance	An employment-based health insurance plan. Under this plan, the government will pay for 70% of your medical and drug expenses.
Kokumin-kenkō-hoken こくみんけんこうほけん **国民健康保険**	National Health Insurance	A health insurance plan for students, homemakers, non-citizens, and other residents of Japan who are ineligible for *Kenkō-hoken*. Copayment amounts vary based on income level.

There have been cases of companies discouraging their full-time employees from registering for Kenkō-hoken in an effort to avoid having to pay their share of the health insurance payment. If you are working full-time for a Japanese company, you are entitled to *Kenkō-hoken*.

TIP: Birth control pills are prescription-only in Japan, and are not covered by Japanese health insurance.

HOW TO REGISTER FOR A RE-ENTRY PERMIT

If you hold any sort of visa and wish to leave then re-enter Japan, even for just one day, you must have a *Sainyūkoku-kyokasho* 再入国許可書 , a "Re-entry Permit." If you do not have a Re-entry permit, you will not be able to re-enter Japan.

You can get a Re-entry permit at your local Regional Immigration Bureau, or *Nyūkoku-kanrikyoku* 入国管理局 .

1. Check the **Immigration Bureau of Japan**'s website (http://www.immi-moj.go.jp/english/info) for the Regional Immigration Office nearest you.

2. Plan ahead. The Regional Immigration Office has restricted hours: 9 am to noon and 1-4 pm, weekdays only. You may have to take a day off from school or work to process your paperwork.

3. Bring your Resident Card, your Passport, and your "Application for Re-entry Form." All the forms have English translations, and are available both onsite and online (http://www.immi-moj.go.jp/english/tetuduki/kanri/shyorui/06.html).

4. At the Regional Immigration Office, exchange your application form for a number. You will be directed to a nearby stamp machine offering two choices: Single or Multiple.

5. Bring ¥3000 for a Single Re-entry Ticket, which allows a one-time exit and re-entry into Japan, or ¥6000 for a Multiple Re-entry Ticket, which allows multiple exits and re-entries into Japan. Insert your money into the stamp machine, and press the button corresponding to your choice. Once you have a ticket, return to the lobby.

TIP: I recommend paying the extra money for the Multiple Permit, just in case you ever suddenly need to book a flight home.

6. When your number is called, present the ticket to the Immigration Official and he/she will insert the Re-entry Permit into your passport. Mission accomplished!

WORK

Maybe you're in college and thinking about working in Japan after graduating, or you're an English teacher already in-country and interested in changing careers. Maybe you just took a new job at a Japanese company and need some help understanding Japanese office culture. Whatever your situation, this section should help smooth the way to a happy, professional life in Japan.

BECOMING A *SENSEI*

If you meet a fellow foreigner working in Japan, chances are he/she is employed as an English teacher. Teaching English is a great opportunity for those interested in working in Japan.

The English teaching programs in Japan are as numerous as they are varied, but most fall into one of three categories: the JET Program, private dispatch companies, and *Eikaiwa* conversation schools.

1. The JET Program (The Japan Exchange and Teaching Program)

The only English teaching program sponsored by the Japanese government.

(http://www.us.emb-japan.go.jp/JET)

The JET Program offers two positions to the general public: Assistant Language Teacher (ALT) and, for those with a high level of Japanese language ability, Coordinator of International Relations (CIR). Less than 10% of incoming JETs are CIRs, but the CIR position offers an alternative to those not interested in teaching. In 2012, 4360 people from forty countries participated in the JET Program.

There is another JET Program position, Sports Exchange Advisor (SEA). SEAs assist in sports training and coaching, but this position requires recommendation by either the U.S. National Olympic Committee or another governmental organization. Visit the JET Program website for further details.

Benefits

Paid Airfare
> The JET program will pay for your flight both to and from Japan, a roundtrip fee that can sometimes cost $2000 or more. No other English teaching program will pay for any portion of your international travel costs.

High Salary

> JETs generally earn more than other entry level English teachers in Japan, perhaps because JETs usually live in rural areas, thus have reduced living expenses and shopping opportunities. Most JETs move into pre-furnished apartments, which also saves money. JETs are paid on a set day every month (as in America), instead of a month after the month they worked (as is usual in Japan).

Smooth Transition

> The JET Program will help set up your health insurance, find you an apartment, and assist you with all necessary paperwork.

Large Support Network

> The JET Program has a large community of JETs, both in Japan and abroad, who can provide advice and support. You might even be able to talk to the outgoing JET you are replacing for specific details on what to expect. Some JETs live in the same apartment complex as other JETs. **The JET Alumni Association International** (http://www.jetalumni.org), has chapters around the world, and this network may help you find Japan-related employment after the JET Program.

No Experience Required

> For better or for worse, you do not need any teacher's certification in order to teach English in Japan. Volunteer experience and/or TEFL certification will certainly enhance your application (and, for some non-JET positions, your salary), but the only qualification required in Japan to teach non-collegiate level English is a Bachelor's degree. Unless you are interested in ESL or EFL teaching as a long-term career, there is no need to get certified just to have something to put on your application.

Life After the B.O.E.
BY DAVID NAMISATO (AOMORI-KEN, CIR, 2002-04)

Why you wanted to go to Japan.

先生、5年間ありがとう

Why you stayed.

> Japanese language skills are not required for the ALT position. However, even a few weeks of Japanese class will dramatically improve your Japan experience.

School System

As a JET, you might teach any and all grades, ranging from kindergarten to high school. (If you teach elementary school, the school may provide you with a hot lunch—one less thing to worry about!)

Experienced Team Teachers

Schools with JETs have usually had JETs before, so they know what to expect from inexperienced English teachers. Your JTEs (Japanese Teachers of English) may also have an established pattern of how they would like the JET to be involved in the classroom. What this entails depends on your JTE, the competency of your JET predecessor, and your own personal motivation.

Fun and Games

As a JET, you may be expected to develop fun lesson plans, help introduce and/or explain grammar and vocabulary, assist with speech contests, administer oral interviews, and/or teach the students American songs, among other tasks. Your job is to get your students excited about learning English. It is the JTE's responsibility to ensure the students pass their exams.

Security

JET contracts start at one year, but if your Board of Education (BOE) is happy with your performance, you can stay on the JET Program for up to five years.

Inherited Apartment

JETs often live in the same apartment as their predecessor, meaning that the incoming JET is spared the significant start-up expenses of cooking utensils, tableware, and spices. The downside? Outgoing JETs caught up in the craziness of packing and moving often leave their clutter for the incoming JET.

Vacation Days

Non-JETs are lucky to have more than two non-national holiday vacation days a year. JETs have a minimum of ten days, plus national holidays, plus any additional days the school chooses to give. JETs will be expected to work (which is another way of saying that they will still be employed) during the summer, though what this entails is up to the school. JETs are highly encouraged to travel and experience Japanese culture.

Drawbacks

Location, Location, Location

JETs get a highly-authentic Japanese experience, meaning that they are often two to three hours away from the nearest major city. If you cannot survive without facials and fine dining, the *inaka* 田舎 , rural Japan, is not for you. That being said, the JET Program is a great way to experience parts of Japan many tourists may never see. I have met a few former JETs who worked in major cities such as Osaka and Kyoto, but this is the exception rather than the rule.

NOTE: As preparation for the upcoming 2020 Summer and Special Olympics in Tokyo, the Japanese government recently announced a plan to increase the number of English teachers in Tokyo. The plan is to bring 300 English teachers to Tokyo, then increase this number to 400 a year by 2028.

Time Management

A JET's duties may include afterschool participation in club events. Many JETs are thus not able to clock out at the end of the school day the same way other English teachers can. A teacher's schedule, like most aspects of an English teacher's experience in Japan, depends on the school.

2. English Dispatch

Private English-teaching companies that hire you to teach at different Japanese schools.

Examples:
Altia Central (http://recruiting.altmoot.com)
Heart English School (http://www.heart-school.jp/en/index.html)
Interac (https://www.interacnetwork.com/recruit)

Teachers who work for dispatch companies are called ALTs or NTEs (Native Teachers of English). Like the JET program, the main prerequisite of working for a dispatch company is being a native English speaker with a college degree.

Benefits

Visa Sponsorship and Health Insurance

Most dispatch companies will sponsor the visas of their overseas hires.

If you work full time, your employer is legally required to enroll you in *Kenkō-hoken*. (Part-time employees receive neither a visa nor health insurance.)

Provided Housing

Dispatch companies may provide their overseas hires with a company apartment. The company will contact the apartment manager and make all the necessary arrangements before you arrive. If your apartment is company-owned, you may be required to give your supervisor the extra key.

Location

Some dispatch companies advertise the locations of their open positions, so you have the option of applying only to areas in which you would like to work. Even if the company does not disclose details about the position's location, chances are you will not be more than an hour away from a major city. For those who fear isolation in the inaka, dispatch may be the best of both worlds: the excitement of a city and the fun of teaching at a Japanese school.

School System

Dispatch teachers, like JETs, teach in the Japanese school system. That means you get the fun of interacting with children and the safety net of team-teaching with a JTE. Some companies, such as Altia, provide their teachers with pre-made teaching materials. Premade lesson plans and teaching materials are a huge money and time saver, and, with a little creativity, can be tailored to the individual needs of your students.

Predetermined Hours

Though your company and fellow teachers may encourage you to get involved with clubs and after school activities, if there is nothing specified in your contract about after school involvement, you should be able to leave work at the time designated in contract. (For me, this was 4:35 pm.)

Special school events, such as the Sports Festival and Graduation, will require your participation, but helping out with these special occasions is fun, and a great way to support your students. Depending on the length and date of the event, you may receive a paid vacation day later in the week to make up for the weekend hours.

Fun and Games

Dispatch teachers, like JETs, are not their students' sole English teachers, and thus have more flexibility in their lessons than *Eikaiwa* teachers.

Drawbacks

No Paid Airfare

You must pay for your flight to and from Japan. Many English teachers in Japan choose to renew their contracts, so you do not need to buy a return ticket in advance.

Pay Schedule

You will be paid on a Japanese schedule, meaning that if you start work on September 1st, you will receive your September salary on October 20th. On November 20th, you will receive your October salary. There is no paid overtime.

Startup Costs

The upfront cost of airfare and rent may make dispatch a non-option, especially since your first two months of salary will be heavily taxed by the Japanese government. Most companies do not require proof that you have enough savings for the first few months, but most companies will also not provide any salary advances. Before you commit to working for a dispatch company, make sure the benefits of a unique cultural experience outweigh the initial financial expenses. (Or just apply to the JET program.)

Multiple Schools

You may be required to teach at more than one school. (I taught at one middle school and two elementary schools. One person I know taught at five.) Teaching at multiple schools can work in your favor if you enjoy variety, and it also lets you get more mileage from your lesson plans.

Unfortunately, if you are a transient presence at your schools (i.e. you work at the school only one day a week), you might not get your own desk in the Teachers' Office, the *shokuin-shitsu* 職員室 .

No Job Security

Most dispatch contracts run from August to March, the majority of the Japanese school year. Even if your company renews your contract, you may have to vacate your company-owned apartment in late March and find new employment until your renewed contract starts up again in August. Your company might move you to a different school, and might not provide you with another company-owned apartment.

You will not receive a paid summer vacation. Many dispatch teachers turn to English conversation schools, also known as *Eikaiwa*, for employment during the summer season.

Minimal Paid Leave
Your company determines the number of paid vacation days you will receive, but don't expect more than three, excluding Japanese national holidays.

Automatic Rent Deduction
Even if you choose to live somewhere else for the duration of your contract, your company will still deduct rent from your paycheck for the company apartment. This is usually not an issue for teachers who do not already have an apartment or family in Japan.

3. *Eikaiwa* 英会話

Eikaiwa means "English conversation." *Eikaiwa* schools are private English conversation schools, and range in size from small, ex-pat startups to national chains.

Examples:
Aeon (http://www.aeonet.com/aeon_index.php)
ECC (http://recruiting.ecc.co.jp)

Eikaiwa schools specialize in English lessons for adults and English-immersion, daycare-type programs for young children.

Benefits

Visa Sponsorship
Representatives from *Eikaiwa* franchises travel across the U.S. and other English-speaking countries to give informational sessions and to interview overseas candidates. *Eikaiwa* companies may provide visas to successful applicants, but due to the abundance of English teachers already in Japan, *Eikaiwa* franchises can afford to be picky. (And a part-time, in-country hire saves the company the expense of providing a visa or health insurance.)

Teaching Materials Provided

> *Eikaiwa* franchises will provide you with all the teaching materials you
> need. They may require you to teach a pre-prepared curriculum. This
> could be a drawback if you enjoy developing your own lesson plans, but
> pre-made lessons are a huge timesaver.

Convenient Locations

> *Eikaiwa* schools are usually located near train stations to be as
> convenient as possible for commuting students.

Drawbacks

Long Hours

> You may be expected to teach on weekends and/or in the evening, since
> these are the times most convenient for adult students. 11 am to 9 pm
> shifts are not unusual at an *Eikaiwa*.

> Your days off may occur in the middle of the week instead of on the
> weekend, which can make it difficult to meet up with friends who are
> not similarly employed.

> Just because you're teaching at an *Eikaiwa* instead of a traditional school
> does not exempt you from communal cleaning. All teachers are expected
> to help clean the school at the end of the day.

Minimal Paid Leave

> *Eikaiwa* companies do not offer as many vacation days as the
> JET Program.

Strict Dress Code

> Many *Eikaiwa* companies have strict dress codes, especially for women.
> Some, such as Aeon, require female employees to wear suit jackets at all
> times.

Mandatory Socializing

> You may be expected to exchange phone numbers with your students on
> your days off, since students who see you as a friend are more likely to
> sign up for more lessons. This "encouraged socialization" is great if you
> want some help meeting Japanese people (especially if you don't speak
> Japanese), but can infringe on your personal time if you're of a more
> independent disposition.

Sales Tactics

Some less scrupulous *Eikaiwa* companies may encourage and/or require you to sell textbooks or other company educational materials to your students. Your salary may be partly based on this type of commission.

No Paid Airfare

Like dispatch teachers, *Eikaiwa* teachers must pay for their flight to and from Japan.

Startup Costs

For the first two months of working in Japan, your salary will be heavily taxed by the Japanese government. Money should not be your main motivation for wanting to teach English in Japan. Living in Japan is expensive, and the job market for teachers in Japan is heavily saturated.

In 2007, the *Eikaiwa* company NOVA went bankrupt after multiple legal violations. Hundreds of English teachers became unemployed overnight, with no explanation or financial support. Obviously not all teachers will have this experience, but make sure you always have enough money in your bank account for a return ticket home.

Part-time tutoring may help you make a little extra money on the side, but giving private English lessons might violate your contract (as it would with most English teaching contracts, including the JET Program). Interacting with students outside the school in which you can teach can open your company up to liability and/or favoritism issues, not to mention it could cut into your company's business. Double-check your contract before committing to a part-time job.

High Turnover

Perhaps because of the grueling hours, or perhaps because most foreigners never intend on staying in Japan for more than a few years, *Eikaiwa* turnover is notoriously high. In 2005, the Japan Times reported that the "Justice Ministry estimates that some 90% of foreign residents in Japan stay for three years or less. For *Eikaiwa* teachers, however, that figure rises to between 96 and 97%."

Many foreigners are so eager to come to Japan that they will take any job they can get. Regardless of where you plan to work, make sure that your contract is a good choice for you—and not just the quickest way to get to Japan.

THE JOB SEARCH

You'd like to work in Japan or maybe change jobs, but where to start? The following resources, in my personal experience, are great ways to find employment in Japan. They are listed in order of helpfulness.

> Andy Fossett's *How to Get a Job in Japan: Get Hired and Get Here* walks you through the job application process and offers insight into working for a Japanese company, as well as honest advice on job-seeking and interview strategies. This book is a must-read for those serious about getting hired to work in Japan.

Kansai Flea Market (http://kfm.to)
A nice variety of job listings in the Kansai area (Osaka, Kyoto, and Kobe). Kansai is an awesome place to live, and this job board does not receive as much traffic as some of the better-known Japan job sites.

Gaijin Pot (https://jobs.gaijinpot.com/index/index/lang/en)
Gaijin Pot advertises both part-time and full-time positions across Japan, some of which offer visa sponsorship. This site is probably the most popular Japan job board, so competition is high. You can occasionally find non-teaching jobs on Gaijin Pot, especially if you have IT skills and/or hospitality experience.

Jobs in Japan (http://jobsinjapan.com)
This Craigslist-style job board mostly advertises part-time (i.e.: non-visa sponsoring) employment for in-country applicants. As some of the listed companies/schools do not have websites, e-mail communication is required.

Fukuoka Now (http://fukuoka-now.com/en/classifieds)
This website has a handful of job listings for those looking to work in the Fukuoka prefecture of Kyushu, Japan's third largest island.

MyShigoto (http://www.myshigoto.com)

MyShigoto mostly features part-time teaching jobs, but you might find a full-time position that will sponsor your visa.

Go Abroad (http://www.goabroad.com)
GoAbroad features various internships, jobs, study abroad programs, and volunteer opportunities, some of which may involve manual labor. (Volunteer programs usually require you to pay your own way, but this also means you can set your own time frame.)

Daijob (http://www.daijob.com/en)
Daijob is mainly geared towards fluent and native speakers of Japanese. This job site, like Gaijin Pot, allows employers to search your resume and contact you directly. Even if you have less-advanced Japanese skills, posting your resume online might help you catch the attention of a future employer.

American Chamber of Commerce in Japan
(https://japan.careerengine.org/accj)
The American Chamber of Commerce in Japan (ACCJ) advertises available positions on this job board site. These jobs almost exclusively require native-level Japanese fluency, but the ACCJ occasionally posts positions for those with IT skills.

Career Cross (http://www.careercross.com)
This website is geared towards native speakers of Japanese. Most of these jobs require technical skills and/or significant work experience.

WRITING A RESUME IN JAPANESE

If you are applying for a Japan-related job and speak some level of Japanese, a Japanese resume, or *rirekisho* 履歴書 , may enhance your application.

You do not need a Japanese resume to apply for a job as an English teacher, but evidence of Japanese language ability may help you ascend to a more senior position.

Traditionally, job seekers in Japan write their resume by hand. Not only does this reveal the quality of a prospective employee's handwriting and spelling, but having to write a resume by hand eliminates the not-so-serious applicants from the job pool. As a foreigner, you are neither expected nor encouraged to write your resume by hand. This works in your favor for obvious reasons, especially since you will most likely apply for jobs electronically.

The Japanese website **Resume Maker** (http://resume.meieki.com) has numerous blank resume templates available for free download.

> **TIP**: As in America, there is more than one way to write a resume. There are a variety of resume formats you can choose from, which can be altered according to your needs. For example, if you are not a minor, there is no reason to keep the section on guardian information.

The sample resume below is for a "Mr. George Smith," who is applying for a job as an English Teacher Manager at an English conversation school. (Normally, a resume should not contain *furigana*. The *furigana* provided in the examples is just to help you get your own resume started.)

履歴書

① 平成2△年1月11日現在

ふりがな	ジョージ・スミス		
氏 名	**George Smith**②		

③ 写真を貼る位置

1. 縦30〜40mm 横24〜30mm
2. 本人単身胸から上
3. 裏面にのりづけ
4. 裏面に氏名記入

生年月日	明治・大正・昭和・平成 ④ 6年1月1日生（満 △○ 歳）		卒⑤ 男・女
携帯電話番号	⑥(1○3) 4567− 89○△	E-MAIL	George.Smith△1 4@g.△.com⑦

ふりがな ⑧おおさか△ や○△し やす○まち		電話 (1△2) ⑫
現住所〒 581−0085 大阪府八○△市安○町4−8−18 プリンセスパラース320号室 ⑨		4△1−△212 (留守番電話あり)
		FAX ( ) ⑬ —
ふりがな ⑩		電話 ( ) ⑭ —
連絡先〒 ⑪	（現住所以外に連絡を希望する場合のみ記入）	FAX ( ) ⑮ —

年	月	学歴・職歴
		学歴 ⑯
平成25	5	○△○アカデミー卒業
平成25	9	△パー△ス大学英文科入学
平成26	6	東京△白△大学語学留学
平成29	5	△パー△ス大学英文科卒業
		卒業論文：「グローバリゼーションと和製英語」
		職歴 ⑰
平成25	10	Bookland 書店（ブックランド） アルバイト
		（書店、従業員：10名）
		販売スタッフとして○△店に配属。
平成26	5	一身上の都合により退職
平成29	8	株式会社ハッピーEnglish 入社
		○△府○△小学校で英語を教える。
		生徒のアメリカの文化に興味を力づける。
平成△	△	在職中
		ただし、会社都合により、△月末日退院決定
		以上

3：赤印のところは、該当するものを○で囲む。

年	月	免許・資格 ⑱
平成24	8	アメリカの普通自動車（第一種）運転免許
平成28	12	日本語能力試験2級取得
		※本年の7月の日本語能力試験1級を受験予定。

通勤時間　約　　時間 40 分 ⑲	扶養家族数 ㉑	配偶者 ㉒	配偶者の扶養義務 ㉓
最寄り駅　緑△　線　大○泉　駅 ⑳	（配偶者を除く）　　　0人	有 ・ 無	有 ・ 無

特技・趣味・得意科目等 ㉔
フランス語の日常会話レベル。
テニス（子供の頃、テニス部に参加する。）
大学時代、クッキングサークルに活動。

志望の動機 ㉕
英語教師のマネジャーを希望します。この仕事を目指し、英語とアメリカの文化を世界に紹介して、日本で新しい先生をサポートしたいです。以前、日本の英会話学校の教師をしたことがあるので、○△に関心があります。経験を生かして、新しい英語教師をサポートしたいです。○△の教師の多くは、日本で英語を教えるが初めてですから、いろいろな心配や問題の可能性が生じる。英語教師として、自分でレッスンプランを作った経験があるので、楽しい教科書の編集も手伝えると思います。このように教師をサポートすると、教師も生徒たちも楽しみながら、学習ができる思います。

本人希望記入欄（特に給料・職種・勤務時間・勤務地・その他についての希望などがあれば記入）
希望職種：英語教師のマネジャー
勤務地：もし希望配属制度あれば、道頓堀店か梅田店を希望します。㉖

保護者（本人が未成年者の場合のみ記入）		電話 （　　　） ㉙
ふりがな ㉗		―
氏 名 ㉘	住 所〒㉘	FAX （　　　） ㉛ ―

① The Date

① 平成２△年１月１１日現在

Write the date according to the Japanese era calendar. Unless Japan's emperor has changed since the publication of this book, the era should be
へいせい
平 成 *Heisei*. (See "Culture and Language—Culture Notes" for era calendar details.) The date should reflect the date the resume is submitted, so update this section each time you apply for a job.

Standardize your numbers. If you input half width numbers for the date, maintain half width numbers for the rest of your resume.

Full Width Numbers:　１０
Half Width Numbers:　10

Many Japanese applicants use full width numbers, but half width numbers may give you extra space.

② Your Name

ふりがな　ジョージ・スミス

氏　名

George Smith②

Write your name in English and provide the *katakana* spelling in the *furigana* section. You can also write your name in *katakana* in the main section and leave the *furigana* section blank.

If you have a Japanese name, write your name in *furigana*, surname first.

If you are not Japanese, write your first name first and your last name last.

Mr. George Washington would write his name as

ジョージ ワシントン
ジョージ・ワシントン or George Washington.

Only provide *furigana*, as a Japanese applicant would, if you have either a

Japanese first or last name.

Ms. Eliza Ishida would write her name as 石田エライザ.

Mr. Hiroyuki Smith would write his name as スミス博之.

③ Picture

③
写真を貼る位置
1. 縦 36〜40mm
横 24〜30mm
2. 本人単身像から上
3. 裏面このり付け
4. 裏面に氏名記入

Affix a professional, full-front headshot to your resume. This picture should be 4.5 cm x 3.6 cm, a little smaller than passport size. Japanese job-seekers usually do not have teeth-showing smiles in their photos. Scan the photo into your computer and crop accordingly. Take a USB drive to a convenience store and use the public printer/scanner if you don't have the ability to scan at home.

Photo booths for professional portrait purposes are often located in subway stations or outside of Japanese convenience stores. Many photo booths lightly retouch your photos, brightening and smoothing out your complexion. Look for the word *Kirei* キレイ ("beautiful") written on the outside in English and/or *rōmaji*.

> **TIP**: It's a good idea to have a few extra photos laying around, that way if you suddenly need to apply for something (or register for the Japanese Language Proficiency Test), you don't have to scramble to find a photo booth.

Professional Picture Attire

Ladies: For the "Japanese professional" look, wear a black or navy suit jacket and a modest blouse or button-down shirt.

Avoid blouses with lace or frills. Your makeup should look natural. It is fine to wear no makeup, as long as you look polished and professional.

Wear your hair either pulled back or behind your shoulders. Do not bring all your hair in front of your shoulders.

Do not wear jewelry. If you wear glasses, remove them for the picture to prevent glare.

<u>Gentlemen</u>: Wear a black or navy suit jacket, a button-down shirt, and a tie.

Your facial hair should be well-kept.

Do not wear jewelry. If you wear glasses, remove them for the picture in order to prevent glare.

④ **Birthday**

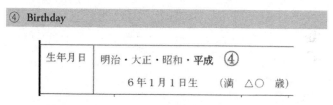

Circle or bold the era in which you were born, then write your birth year according to that era. Your current age goes between the parentheses.

Japanese Era Years		
めいじ 明治	*Meiji*	1868-1912
たいしょう 大 正	*Taishō*	1912-1926
しょうわ 昭和	*Shōwa*	1926-1989
へいせい 平成	*Heisei*	1989-present

(See "Culture and Language—Culture Notes" for details regarding Japanese era years.)

⑤ Gender

Circle or bold 「男」 for male or 「女」 for female.

⑥ Cell Phone Number

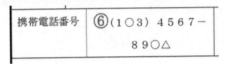

Your cell phone number. Include an international dialing code before a non-Japanese phone number.

⑦ E-mail

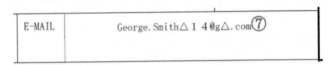

Your e-mail address should be professional, and ideally with a major e-mail provider, such as Google or Yahoo. (If you are living in Japan, this should be different from your *keitai* mail address.) As in America, this e-mail address should not be your current work e-mail address.

⑧ Address *Furigana*

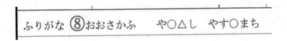

If you are currently living in Japan, write the *furigana* for your address in this box. If you are currently living overseas, leave this box blank.

⑨ **Current Mailing Address**

> 現住所〒 ５８１－００８５
>
> 　　大阪府八○△市安○町４－８－１８
>
> 　　プリンセスパラース３２０号室
>
> ⑨

Your current mailing address.

If you are currently living in Japan, provide *furigana* for your address. Write your zip code next to the 〒 symbol, then follow the normal procedure for writing an address. (See "Settling In—At Home" for details on how to read a Japanese address.)

If you live outside of Japan, write your address according to your country's postal standards. Do not provide *furigana* for a non-Japanese address.

⑩ **Alternate Address** *Furigana*

> ふりがな ⑩

The *furigana* for your alternate address. See ⑧ .

⑪ **Alternate Address**

> 連絡先〒　　　　　　　　　　（現住所以外に連絡を希望する場合のみ記入）
>
> ⑪

If you would like work-related communication forwarded to an address other than your current mailing address, write your desired alternate address here.

⑫ **Home Phone Number**

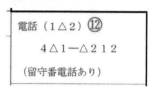

> 電話（１△２）⑫
>
> 　　４△１－△２１２
>
> （留守番電話あり）

The home phone number for your current address. An employer should be able to leave a voicemail at this number.

⑬ Fax Number

The fax number for your current address. If you do not have a fax machine, leave this blank.

As of March 2012, 59% of Japanese homes own a fax machine. Fax machines are a popular form of communication in the world of Japanese business.

⑭ Alternate Address Home Phone Number

The home phone number for your alternate address.

⑮ Alternate Address Fax Number

The fax number for your alternate address. If you do not have a fax machine, leave this blank.

⑯ Educational Experience

年	月	学歴・職歴
		学歴 ⑯
平成２５	５	○△○アカデミー卒業
平成２５	９	△バー△ス大学英文科入学
平成２６	６	東京△白△大学語学留学
平成２９	５	△バー△ス大学英文科卒業
		卒業論文：「グローバリゼーションと和製英語」

A Japanese applicant would list his/her educational experience in chronological order starting from elementary school. As a foreign applicant, this is unnecessary. Begin your educational history with your graduation from high school or college.

EXCEPTION: If you attended an all-girls school, an all-boys school, a private boarding school, and/or a prestigious, internationally-recognized school, it is worth mentioning in your educational history.

EXCEPTION: If you attended a Japanese elementary, middle, or high school for a significant period of time—not including study abroad—include your entire educational history in chronological order, starting with elementary school.

List the full name of your college and the department you entered. Students in Japan, like those in Europe, enter a university through a specific department.

Follow the school listing for the year you enrolled with 入学.

平成２５	9	△バー△ス大学英文科入学

Follow the school listing for the year you graduated with 卒業.

平成２９	5	△バー△ス大学英文科卒業

Double Majoring

Double majoring is almost unheard of at Japanese universities. As such, there is no traditional format for listing a double major on your resume. If you double majored during college, follow the example below.

平成２９	5	△バー△ス大学英文科卒業
		Major#1 と Major#2 の２科目を専攻しました

Major #1 と Major #2 の２科目を専攻しました。

This is not a perfect solution, but it works. If you have a major or minor, use the format below.

平成２５	9	△バー△ス大学英文科入学
平成２９	5	△バー△ス大学英文科卒業
		主専攻：Major、副専攻：Minor

主専攻（しゅせんこう）：Major, 副専攻（ふくせんこう）：Minor

Senior Thesis

平成２９	5	△バー△ス大学英文科卒業
		卒業論文：「グローバリゼーションと和製英語」

Feel free to give the topic of your senior thesis if you have space and your thesis somehow relates to the position for which you are applying.

卒業論文（そつぎょうろんぶん）：「Name of Your Thesis」

Study Abroad

平成２６	6	東京△白△大学語学

If you studied at a foreign university as part of a study abroad program, write the school's name, followed by 留学（りゅうがく）or 語学留学（ごがくりゅうがく）.

		職歴 ⑱
平成２５	10	Bookland 書店（ブックランド）　アルバイト
		（書店、従業員：１０名）
		販売スタッフとして○△店に配属。
平成２６	5	一身上の都合により退職
平成２９	8	株式会社ハッピーEnglish　入社
		○△府○△小学校で英語を教える。
		生徒のアメリカの文化に興味を力づける。
平成△	△	在職中
		ただし、会社都合により、△月末日退院決定
		以上

List the companies you have worked for in chronological order, starting with the least recent. Use the complete, formal name of the company. For example, if you worked for Coca-Cola Japan, you would write 日本（にほん）コカ・

コーラ株式会社 , not コカ・コーラ .

On my resume, I list my work experience in order of most recent, as you would in the United States. I want my most interesting work experience to be the first impression I give potential employers, even if it means they also notice the resume's peculiar format. (Just because you're in Japan does not mean you always have to do everything as if you're Japanese. I would rather get the interview than create the perfect Japanese resume that gets pushed to the side.)

If the companies you've worked for are not Japanese and/or have unusual names that a non-English speaking interviewer might struggle to read, spell the name of the company in English and, in parentheses, *katakana*. If the company is well-known or has branches in Japan, check online for the appropriate *katakana* spelling.

17. Work History

		職歴 ⑰
平成２５	１０	Bookland 書店（ブックランド）　アルバイト
		（書店、従業員：１０名）
		販売スタッフとして○△店に配属。

Include a short description of each job beneath each company listing. Normally, Japanese applications would list this type of information only on a *shokumu-keirekisho* 職務経歴書 , a detailed resume with a slightly different format. You can get away with merging the two because you are a foreigner.

Any time you enter a company, write 入社 after the company's name. When you leave, write 退社 .

平成２９	８	株式会社ハッピーEnglish　入社

TIP: If you have worked at a company part-time or as an intern, do not write 入社 after the company name. 入社 implies joining the company as a full-time employee.

If you are currently working at the company, write 在職中 underneath the company information, as in the example. Include the current month and era year.

平成２９	8	株式会社ハッピーEnglish　入社
		○△府○△小学校で英語を教える。
		生徒のアメリカの文化に興味を力づける。
平成△	△	在職中
		ただし、会社都合により、△月末日退院決定

A Japanese applicant would provide a reason for leaving one company for another. This is unnecessary for a foreign applicant, especially if you are a student or recent college grad. Here are some reasons, though, just in case you would like to provide an explanation.

平成２６	5	一身上の都合により退職

一身の都合により退職。 "Left for personal reasons."

契約期限満了につき退職。

"You came to the end of your contract and left of your own volition and on good terms."

会社都合により退職。 "Laid off for non-personal reasons."

平成△	△	在職中	
		ただし、会社都合により、△月末日退院決定	
			以上

Follow your work history with 以上 written in the right hand corner to indicate that you have provided a complete history.

⑱ Licenses and Certificates

年	月	免許・資格　⑱
平成２４	8	アメリカの普通自動車（第一種）運転免許
平成２８	１２	日本語能力試験２級取得
		※本年の７月の日本語能力試験１級を受験予定。

List any and all licenses and certificates you have in chronological order, starting with the least recent. Only mention skills for which you have official certification. Uncertified Microsoft Office proficiency and conversational French skills belong in Section ㉔ , "Interests, Hobbies, and Skills."

平成２４	8	アメリカの普通自動車（第一種）運転免許

Mention your driver's license, if you have one. Many Japanese people do not have driver's licenses due to the expense of the driving exam and the ease of public transportation. Your driver's license is a great way to fill this box. As in America, avoid leaving any section of a resume blank.

アメリカの普通自動車（第一種）運転免許

平成２８	１２	日本語能力試験２級取得
		＊本年の７月の日本語能力試験１級を受験予定。

If your Japanese abilities exceed your current JLPT Certification level, mention the next level JLPT you plan to take, as in the example above.

日本語能力試験（Level Number）級取得

＊（Year）の（Month）月の日本語能力試験（Level Number）級を受験予定。

⑲ Commute Time

通勤時間	約	時間 ４０ 分	⑲

List the approximate amount of time it would take you to commute to this company, not counting transfers. This section only applies if you are currently living in Japan. For example, if you would have to ride thirty-five minutes on the Blue Line to Station X, where you would then take a bus for five minutes to your office, your commute time would be considered to be forty minutes. Realistically, it would take more than forty minutes for you to get from your home to your office, but this section only counts time actually on the train/bus, not time spent walking, transferring, or waiting.

The company must reimburse you for commuting costs. It is in your best interest to find the shortest possible commute time, as this information could influence hiring decisions. If the position requires frequent overtime, a commute longer than an hour and a half (not counting transfers) may affect hiring decisions.

⑳ **Closest Train Station**

List the closest train station and train line to your place of residence. This information is factored into your commuting costs reimbursement.

㉑ **Number of Dependents**

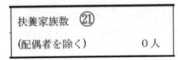

List the number of people you currently support, not including your spouse or yourself. If none, write "0."

㉒ **Presence of Spouse**

Do you have a spouse? Circle or bold 有 for "Yes" and 無 for "No."

㉓ **Spouse Support**

Do you financially support your spouse? Circle or bold 有 for "Yes" and 無 for "No." This information may influence your salary.

If your spouse is employed full-time, select "No."

If your spouse works part-time and does not receive health insurance, select "Yes."

If you are divorced and must pay alimony, select "Yes."

㉔　Interests, Hobbies, and Skills

特技・趣味・得意科目等　㉔

フランス語の日常会話レベル。

テニス（子供の頃、テニス部に参加する。）

大学時代、クッキングサークルに活動。

List any interests, hobbies, and/or skills that you have, especially those that could be useful in the office, such as language and computer skills.

If you have not taken the JLPT, estimate your level of Japanese ability.

You can mention belonging to a "Japanese Culture Club," but any mention of *anime* (アニメ、 Japanese animation) or video games on your resume may hinder your application. This is especially true for teaching positions. Only mention *anime* or video games if you have related certification and/or are applying for a job in one of those fields.

You might want to avoid mentioning hobbies that require extended time off from work, such as mountain climbing, playing in a band, or foreign travel.

㉕　Desired Job

志望の動機　㉕

英語教師のマネジャーを希望します。この仕事を目指し、英語とアメリカの文化を世界に紹介して、日本で新しい先生をサポートしたいです。以前、日本の英会話学校の教師をしたことがあるので、○△に関心があります。経験を生かして、新しい英語教師をサポートしたいです。○△の教師の多くは、日本で英語を教えるが初めてですから、いろいろな心配や問題の可能性が生じる。英語教師として、自分でレッスンプランを作った経験があるので、楽しい教科書の編集も手伝えると思います。このように教師をサポートすると、教師も生徒たちも楽しみながら、学習ができる思います。

In four to six sentences, explain why you want this job and what experiences and skills make you qualified.

Your reasons for wanting to join the company (at least the ones you write on your resume) should not be any of the following:

"I'm interested in this company."

"It's my dream job."

"I think I can learn many things while working at this company."

"I think this company would suit me."

   Why should the company care if this is your dream job? What's in it for
them if they hire you? Those are the questions you should answer in this
section. Tailor this statement of purpose to each job application and get your
sentences checked by a native speaker, if possible.

㉖ Desired Salary, Hours, Office Location

本人希望記入欄（特に給料・職種・勤務時間・勤務地・その他についての希望などがあれば記入）
希望職種：英語教師のマネジャー
勤務地：もし希望配属制度あれば、道頓堀店か梅田店を希望します。

   List any relevant work preferences, such as salary, hours, and office
location. You can fill out this section in complete sentences or just use bullet
points. Also mention any legitimate, recurring scheduling conflicts, such as
having to pick up a child from school in the afternoon.

希望職種：(Name of Desired Position)

勤務地：もし希望属制度、(Desired Location) を希望します。

   Avoid sounding difficult or making too many demands, such as "I want
to work at the company headquarters in Mr. Yamada's department and never
on weekends and no evening shifts."

   Do not outright request a specific salary unless it is the same amount as
the salary listed in the job advertisement. Salary negotiations will occur after
the interview.

   If you do not have specific desires, you can write ご相談させて頂きたい
と思っております ("I would like to discuss this with you").

㉗ *Furigana* of Legal Guardian's Name

保護者（本人が未成年者の場合のみ記入）

ふりがな ㉗

If you are under the age of twenty, provide the *furigana* spelling of the name of your legal guardian. (Twenty is the legal age of adulthood in Japan.) If you are above the age of twenty, leave this section blank.

㉘ Name of Legal Guardian

氏 名 ㉘

The full name of your legal guardian. Leave blank if not applicable.

㉙ Address of Legal Guardian

住 所〒㉙

The home address of your legal guardian. Leave blank if not applicable.

㉚ Phone Number of Legal Guardian

電話 （   ） ㉚

——

The phone number of your legal guardian. Leave blank if not applicable.

㉛ Fax Number of Legal Guardian

FAX （   ） ㉛

——

The fax number of your legal guardian. Leave blank if not applicable.

Job Hunting

Great jobs can pop up at a moment's notice. Keep your resume up-to-date at all times. It is much easier to steadily update a resume than to scramble something together with short notice.

There are many resume writing guides available in Japanese bookstores, especially around job-hunting season.

I recommend 「採用_{さいよう}される履歴書_{りれきしょ}・職務経歴書_{しょくむけいれきしょ}はこう書_かく」 *Saiyō-Sareru Rirekisho Shokumu-keirekisho Wa Kō Kaku* by Mitsuko Kojima. It offers examples of different types of model resumes, varying depending on the experience and desired job of the applicant. Kojima's handy guide also offers resume-writing advice according to specific situations, like applying for an entry-level position when having no previous work experience, as well as how to write a mission statement that makes a good impression. This book is a must have for those applying to a Japanese company.
When on an interview, expect to be seated in a small waiting or conference room, known as a *hikaeshitsu* 控_{ひか}え室_{しつ} , before meeting anyone.
When being interviewed, do not sit until the interviewer asks you to do so.

> **NOTE**: Some Japanese companies conduct simultaneous interviews with three or more people at a time. The interview candidates sit next to each other and take turns answering questions. There is almost no chance of this happening during your job search—group interviewing is meant solely to cope with the numbers of Japanese applicants during job-hunting season.

From October to March, college seniors engage in job hunting—*shūshoku-katsudō* 就職活動_{しゅうしょくかつどう} . During these six months, students search for jobs and participate in mass company presentations and interviews. Until recent years, the company you worked for after graduating from college would be your company for life. This tradition has become, for today's young Japanese people, the exception rather than the norm.

A "salaryman," *sarariman* サラリーマン, is a Japanese businessman. .
The stereotypical salaryman leaves for work early in the morning, spends at least an hour commuting on public transportation, and arrives home at 9 or 10 pm. Some salarymen are transferred across the country or overseas, sometimes separated from their families. Many wives and children of salarymen stay behind for the children to continue their education at their current school undisrupted.

TEACHING ENGLISH

Teaching English in Japan can be a rewarding way to learn about Japanese culture, while simultaneously gaining work experience.

The Japanese School System		
High School こうこう **高校** *Kōkō*	12th Grade	ねんせい 3年生 *san-nensei*
	11th Grade	ねんせい 2年生 *ni-nensei*
	10th Grade	ねんせい 1年生 *ichi-nensei*
Middle School ちゅうがっこう **中学校** *Chūgakkō*	9th Grade	ねんせい 3年生 *san-nensei*
	8th Grade	ねんせい 2年生 *ni-nensei*
	7th Grade	ねんせい 1年生 *ichi-nensei*
Elementary School しょうがっこう **小学校** *Shōgakkō*	6th Grade	ねんせい 6年生 *roku-nensei*
	5th Grade	ねんせい 5年生 *go-nensei*
	4th Grade	ねんせい 4年生 *yon-nensei*
	3rd Grade	ねんせい 3年生 *san-nensei*
	2nd Grade	ねんせい 2年生 *ni-nensei*
	1st Grade	ねんせい 1年生 *ichi-nensei*
Kindergarten ようちえん **幼稚園** *Yōchien*		

The Japanese school year runs on a trimester system, with the first term running from April to mid-July. Summer Break is between July and August, and the last trimester goes from September to March.

Many students continue to participate in club activities over the summer, though rising ninth and twelfth graders often forgo club activities to focus on studying for the year's upcoming entrance exams (high school and college, respectively).

A student's identity is strongly tied to his/her class year and homeroom. Students address upperclassmen with the suffix *-senpai* 先輩 and refer to underclassmen as *kōhai* 後輩.

Students never share classes with their *senpai* or *kōhai*. Classes are strictly organized by grade, regardless of individual ability. In many school sports clubs, *kōhai* perform the equipment cleaning and set-up for their *senpai*.

Your Japanese teachers will probably address their students with *-chan* ちゃん and *-kun* くん. You should not. (See "Culture and Language—Honorific Suffixes" for details.)

In Japanese schools, the students stay in the same classroom and the teachers rotate. There is usually a ten minute break between classes.

> In Japan, arriving five minutes early is showing up on time. Your students might slip into class late, but as a teacher, you should always be in the classroom before the bell rings.

All teachers should be addressed by their last name and the suffix *-sensei* 先生, which means "teacher." Never use another's teacher's first name unless invited to do so.

NOTE: Even if you are a teacher, *sensei* is a term of respect and should thus not be used to describe yourself. If you are a teacher and someone asks what your job is, say that you are a *kyōshi* 教師, which is another word for "teacher."

Principals, known as *Kōchō-sensei* 校長先生, and Vice Principals, known as *Kyōtō-sensei* 教頭先生, are always referred to by their rank. If you teach at a school and your fellow teacher is Mr. Ichiro Tanaka, you should call him Tanaka-*sensei*. If he suddenly gets promoted to principal, you must now call him *Kōchō-sensei*.

Dress Code

Students are not allowed to wear accessories, dye their hair, or use makeup. (These rules are often flouted in creative and amusing ways.) Nevertheless, teachers are expected to reflect the school's rules and set a good example for the students.

Dress Code for Teachers (Ladies)	
Do	**Don't**
Modest Blouses Button-Down Shirts Sweaters Cardigans	Visible Tank Tops
	Halter Tops
	Spaghetti Straps
	Exposed Bra Straps
	Strapless Anything
	T-Shirts/Athletic Apparel
	Sweatshirts
Skirt with Pantyhose Skirt with Black Tights Dress Pants	Skirt with Bare Legs
	Skirt with Knee Socks
	Skirt with Fashion Tights
	Above-the-Knee Skirts
	Jeans (Except in some schools)
School Shoes	High Heels
	Fur Boots
	Sneakers
	Open-Toe Sandals
	Flip-Flops
	No Socks
Natural Makeup Minimal Jewelry	Heavy Makeup
	Exposed Tattoos of Any Kind
	Perfume/Scented Body Lotion
	Non-Ear Piercings

Even more so than in the United States, it is unlikely that any of your coworkers will ever outright tell you when you are violating the school's dress code. As a teacher, it is your responsibility to project a professional appearance. (Ladies, Japanese coworkers who repeatedly ask "Aren't you cold?" probably want you to cover up a little more.)

Dress Code for Teachers (Gentlemen)	
Do	**Don't**
Long-Sleeved Dress Shirts Suit Jacket	Dress Shirts without Undershirts
	T-Shirts
	Anything Sleeveless
Suit Pants Khakis	Jeans (Except in some schools)
	Cargo Pants
	Shorts
	Anything Ripped/"Distressed"
	Skirts with Leggings (Yes, this has happened.)
School Shoes	Boots
	Flip-Flops
	Sandals of Any Kind
	No Socks
Tie (not required by all schools)	Cologne
	Heavy Jewelry
	Makeup of Any Kind
	Piercings
	Unkempt Facial Hair

Wear your full suit for the first few days at the school, even if the heat has you roasting underneath. After a few days of formal business attire, you can determine what level of business casual is appropriate.

When your local Board of Education (BOE) comes to observe one of your lessons, dress in formal business attire. Even Japanese elementary school teachers often wear full suit and tie when it is their turn to be observed.

Keep a suit jacket near your desk in case of cold weather and meetings/surprise visits from your boss.

> I always dressed professionally, but since most of my co-workers taught in athletic apparel, wearing a suit jacket to class seemed excessively formal. Nonetheless, I brought the suit jacket every day, which came in handy the day my supervisor stopped by the school for a surprise inspection.

Many Japanese teachers wear track jackets and athletic gear on a daily basis. Even in a button-down shirt and slacks, you may be one of the most formally-attired people at school. This is a good thing. As an outsider and a foreigner, you will be under constant scrutiny from your students, their parents, and your fellow teachers. Resist the temptation of casual wear, and never go to school in athletic gear unless you are participating in club activities or your school's Sports Festival.

If your students compliment you on your makeup, that means you are wearing too much.

A few tasteful pieces of jewelry can enhance an outfit, but avoid distracting and/or expensive-looking jewelry. The less jewelry you wear to school, the better.

> **TIP**: Brooches are a great way to accessorize without violating the unspoken "minimal jewelry" rule. Just don't wear brooches around young children because they might try to grab them. (I went through three shirts this way.)

Although you will wear rubber-soled school shoes inside the school, you should still commute to school in professional shoes. This means no knee-high boots or sneakers.

> **TIP**: Ladies—if you bike to work in a skirt, one day your pantyhose will inevitably snag on the bicycle pedals. Keep an extra pair in your desk drawer at work.

In the Classroom

Show your students some photos of your family and hometown during your first "Meet the Teacher" lesson. Bring props, also known as "realia" in the English-teaching world.

> **TIP**: You can also enlarge a few pictures on A3 paper so that even the students in the back of the class can see. Pictures can introduce your students to American culture, and will be much more engaging than a textbook.

Don't use your iPod, iPad, or laptop as a digital display for images. No matter how interesting your hometown may be, the excitement of a new gadget may make it difficult for the students to focus on your lesson.

If you decide to make your iPod a part of the classroom experience, bring speakers so the whole class can hear.

> **TIP**: Double-check any CDs you plan on using before the lesson. Some school CD players can't play computer-burned CD-Rs or CD-RWs.

Many Japanese schools do not have WiFi, so don't make YouTube videos or Internet clips a focal point of your lesson.

Jumpstart your students' energy by introducing a classroom game or activity that lets them get out of their seats and move around the classroom.

Japanese middle and high school students are often uncomfortable volunteering answers or raising their hands in front of their peers. Find a way to engage your students without singling them out.

If you decide to cold-call students by name, ask each homeroom teacher for a class roster list and check each name's pronunciation with the homeroom teacher in advance.

Buy at least ten magnets, and always bring them with you to your lessons. You can get cheap magnets at any 100 Yen Store, but it is worth the extra few yen to get the magnets that look like pushpins and are easy to remove. The flat, smooth magnets can be hard to pull off the board.

> **TIP**: Adhesive magnets, which are inexpensive and available at any stationery store, can be adhered to the backs of large flashcards.

> **TIP**: Don't get the cutesy magnets in the shapes of animals as these tend to distract the students.

> **TIP**: Magnets have a habit of disappearing, so keep yours together in a little bag that you can carry with you. Do not rely on the homeroom teacher's magnets.

Many of your elementary and middle school students may have a sheet of plastic that they slip between their papers when filling out assignments. This is not a cheat sheet! It's a *shitajiki* 下敷き, a paper protector used to keep the papers underneath from getting scratched or smudged with pencil marks.

> **CAUTION**: A *shitajiki* is a paper protector. *Shita-gi* 下着 is underwear. Be careful with your pronunciation in front of students.

Never make the thumbs-down sign in class. This means something along the lines of "Die and go to hell."

While trying to demonstrate an in-class activity, I wanted to confirm that my students understood the game's rules. I said "Yes?" and made

the thumbs-up sign, then said "No?" and turned my thumb down.
The whole class burst into laughter. Turns out I was the one who didn't
understand.

No one likes being embarrassed. If your JTE makes mistakes, don't point
them out in front of the class, *especially* if it's an issue of pronunciation. If the
JTE's mistake is truly heinous, let it slide (unless the teacher looks to you for
confirmation or correction during a lesson). Afterwards, make a fun handout
or game "for the students" with the correct grammatical structure. Hopefully
your JTE will recognize his/her mistake without losing face. If you don't
think you can pull this off with subtlety, just let it go.

Your job is not to ensure your students pass their English tests. Your job is
to provide your students with a fun, authentic insight into English-speaking
culture, and to increase your students' confidence and comfort with the
English language. You can't control what English your team-teachers use,
but you can make sure that
whenever your students are
around you, they only hear
perfect English in a positive
environment.

A culture board is a great way to
connect with your students and
encourage their interest in your
home country and the English
language. Use some wrapping
paper as a background and

A Halloween-themed culture board.

regularly update the board with interesting cultural information. (Ask a
fellow teacher's permission before hanging it up.) Leave a blank journal and
a pencil nearby for students to write questions.

From "What did your middle school look like?" to "What's your favorite
boy band?", my students asked all sorts of questions in the "Let's Learn
English" journal that they might not have had the confidence to ask during
class.

Bring a watch! A wristwatch is an essential component of the teacher's
toolbox. Take off your watch before class begins and set it somewhere
visible, but discreet, like the top of your desk. Nothing says "I'm bored"
like constantly checking your watch or your iPhone during your lesson. A
wristwatch will help you discreetly keep your lessons on schedule.

Natalia Doan

Lesson Preparation

The more effort you put into creating fun, interactive lessons, the happier both you and your students will be. Meet with your JTE ahead of time to discuss plans and activities for class. This meeting is called an *uchiawase* 打ち合わせ .

> **TIP**: If you're going to suggest a new in-class activity to your JTE, prepare samples of all the necessary materials beforehand. Use these samples in your explanation of the activity and the JTE is much more likely to say yes. Most teachers want their lessons to be fun and engaging, but it's a lot easier for them to rely on you if they know exactly what you have planned.

Print your handouts on size A4, B5, or A3 paper. A4 is slightly larger than standard letter size paper in America. B5 is smaller than A4, and A3 is the width of two A4 pages side-by-side.

Always hole-punch handouts and homework since your students will keep their papers together in their *fairu*, ファイル —or fastener folders. Students have one *fairu* per subject.

> **TIP**: Don't bother bringing binders from America. Japanese binders use a two-hole punch instead of three.

Before demonstrating games and worksheets in front of your students, enlarge copies of your worksheets and games on A3 paper. Demonstrating on the board with large visuals will help the students, especially those who sit in the back of the classroom, understand what to do in a game or activity.

You can create fun language-learning games using a set of dice and a homemade board game board (i.e. printed out on A3 paper). Elementary schoolers love dice games—just hand out the dice after you've explained the rules.

Always have a backup lesson prepared.

Keep a list of American idioms in your lesson binder. If one of your classes ever ends ten minutes earlier than expected, you can use the remaining time for a "cultural note."

If your lesson somehow runs twenty or thirty minutes shorter than planned, tell your students to create their own practice dialogues incorporating the lesson's target grammar. Afterwards, have the students perform their skits for you to check (but not in front of the whole class, unless you have some very confident students). The students will enjoy expressing themselves creatively, and skit-writing keeps them busy and engaged. This activity will go smoother if your JTE helps check dialogues too, that way you don't end class with a long line of students who have yet to present.

> **TIP**: Choose-your-own-partner activities work best in classes that get along well with each other. No matter what country you're from, no one likes being the kid left out of the group.

Always carry a glue-stick and correction tape for cutting and pasting minor changes to your handouts. Japanese tape is hard to remove and does not photocopy well.

If you plan on doing a lot of coloring for boards or visual aids, bring a set of crayons from the U.S. Crayons are great for filling out worksheets and demonstrating games on the board since they don't require tops, like markers, or sharpening, like colored pencils.

Never print or copy in color on school printers without first securing the permission of your supervising teacher. Color ink is expensive, so prepare a really good reason for wanting color handouts.

Life After the B.O.E.

Always be prepared.

TIP: For about ¥100, you can print and copy your own large, color handouts at a convenience store. I recommend printing at a convenience store for whenever you need big pictures for your class.

Japanese convenience stores, called *konbini* コンビニ , are very convenient. Besides offering all sorts of save-the-day fixes (office supplies, cosmetics, even button-down shirts), 7-11s have an all-in-one fax machine/copier/photo printer that lets you print double-sided, and in all sizes and colors. You can print from an SD card or USB drive, but 7-11 machines cannot read .doc, .docx, or .TIFF files, so convert your documents to PDFs first.

TIP: Buy a Japanese USB drive. Some American USBs have built-in software that Japanese copiers can't read.

TIP: Many schools are afraid of computer viruses and will not let you use your personal USB on one of the school's computers. If you will be teaching in Japan for more than six months, a decent printer/scanner is a worthwhile investment. For around $80, you can save yourself hours of stress and time spent at convenience store printers before work.

If your school lets you print directly off your USB, save your documents as .doc or .pdf files. Public computers that run older versions of Windows will not be able to read .docx files.

Lunchtime

Many schools will provide you with a free or subsidized school lunch, known as *kyūshoku* 給食 . Let your school know ahead of time if you need to bring your own lunch due to dietary restrictions.

As a teacher in the Japanese school system, you will eat with your students and, like everyone else in the school, be expected to finish what's on your plate. The "waste not, want not" mentality is very important in Japanese culture, and your fellow teachers may get upset if you waste food in front of your students.

One day I was eating lunch with the second graders when one kid snuck his half-eaten bowl of rice onto the dirty dishes cart. The teacher told the children to sit with their heads on their desks until someone confessed to wasting food. Lunch ended, and still no one came forward. I had to leave for my next class, and politely excused myself. The teacher came up to me and apologized for her students' terrible behavior, and said that she would cancel their lessons for the rest of the day until the culprit confessed. This is obviously an extreme example, but one I have never forgotten.

Soda and candy are not allowed in Japanese schools, but the school may make exceptions for packaged American treats if you bring enough for everyone—especially if this includes the teachers! Always check with your co-teachers and principal before giving anything to your students.

TIP: If you have permission to give out holiday treats, I recommend bringing candy corn for Halloween instead of candy canes for Christmas. Neither are available in Japan, but candy canes break more easily. Whatever treats you give should be individually-wrapped.

The Teachers' Office

When you enter the Teachers' Office, or *Shokuin-shitsu* 職員室, in the morning, say *O-hayō-gozaimasu* 「おはようございます」, "Good morning."

If you show up at work right before the bell rings, you might hear the phrase *Girigiri-sēfu* 「ぎりぎりセーフ」, which means "Oh, you just made it" as in "You're one minute away from being late and you arrived just in time." This is not a phrase you want people to use when talking about you. Get to work early, and in Japan, five minutes early is on time.

If you teach at an elementary school, join the students and teachers for the morning assembly. Some schools require this of their teachers, but might not actually tell you that you need to be there. Even if you just stand in the back of the auditorium with the other adults, your school will appreciate your participation.

You will be expected to help clean the school. You may or may not see your fellow teachers cleaning, many Japanese teacher supervise the students during cleaning time or use the time to deal with any situations that have occurred during class. Don't wait for someone to tell you how and where to help out. Just start cleaning.

Entering and Leaving the Office

When you leave work at the end of the day, say *O-saki-ni-shitsureishimasu* 「お先に失礼します」 to the people still in the room. This translates to "Excuse me for leaving before you," and is often shortened to a casual

O-saki-ni 「お先^{さき}に」.

Your co-workers will respond with 「お疲^{つか}れ様^{さま}でした」, which is basically "Good work." This phrase is often shortened to a casual *O-tsukare* 「お疲^{つか}れ」.

Always knock before entering the Principal's Office. Say *Shitsureishimasu* 「失礼^{しつれい}します」, literally "I'm being rude."

> **TIP**: In Japan, people usually knock on a door twice, not three times.

Your Students

Know your students! After a few weeks spent teaching and learning your students' names, you will start to understand the different personalities of the classes you teach. Knowing your students' energy level, language ability, and interests will help you structure your lessons.

Your students and fellow teachers will probably comment on your physical appearance. Even if their observations sound strange ("You're so pale! And your face is small!"), your students are probably just trying to compliment you.

> **TIP**: Normally when people compliment you, it is polite to reply in the negative with a smile and *Iie* 「いいえ」, "No." If someone compliments you on your Japanese, smile and say *Madamada-desu* 「まだまだです」, "Not yet."

A common question your students may ask you is "Who's your favorite character?" By "character" (*kyara* キャラ), they mean "cartoon character," like Mickey Mouse, Totoro, or Snoopy. Many Japanese girls have character school supplies and cell phone straps. Even "bad boys" may have character goods, like Cookie Monster pencil pouches. Come prepared with a few favorite characters, in case your students ask.

Even the most seemingly insignificant things you do can leave a big impression on the people around you.

Exam Season

Admission to high school, even public high school, is not guaranteed in Japan. Entrance exam season differs depending on a student's age and grade, but generally occurs in late winter and early spring. Entrance exam test-takers are called *jukensei* 受験生 .

> **TIP**: During exam season, increase the fun-level of your classes and incorporate active games that involve a lot of movement. Avoid complicated grammatical structures and/or anything that involves extended periods of sitting.

Tokyo University, nicknamed *Tōdai* 東大 , is the Harvard of Japan. Japanese society's general impression is that if you get into Tōdai, your life is made. *Doragon-zakura* 「ドラゴン桜」 , a TV show about a group of students at a third-rate school trying to pass the Tōdai entrance exams, can be an inspiring watch if you have exams coming up.

Around exam season, many *jukensei* adhere to test-taking superstitions. For example, avoid using the verb "to fall," or any other words connected to "falling," since "to fall" and "to fail" are the same word, *ochiru* 落ちる .

> **SNACK TIP**: Stressed out students munch on "Koala's March" (*Koara-no-Māchi* 「コアラのマーチ」 , small cookies shaped like koalas—since a koala never falls, even when it sleeps.

> **SNACK TIP**: Many students eat foods starting with the prefix "*katsu-*" かつ , since it sounds the same as the verb "to win," 勝つ *katsu*. *Katsu-don* かつ丼 , fried pork cutlet over rice, is especially popular.

> **SNACK TIP**: The Japanese word for Kit-Kat candy bars, *Kitto-katto* 「キットカット」 ,

Japan Post Kit-Kats

sounds similar to the phrase for "definitely win," *Kitto-katsu*「きっと
勝つ」. Around exam season, Japan Post provides mail-approved Kit-
Kats that you can send to your friends. Write a personalized message
on the back to wish your *jukensei* friends luck!

Caution

The *kanchō* 浣 腸 , literally translated as "enema," is the bane of (male)
English teachers everywhere. A *kanchō* is when some students—almost
always boys—put their fingers together and…poke them in your behind.
No, that was not a typo, and no, this behavior is not frequently punished.
I have never heard of a female teacher getting *kanchō*-ed, but if this does
happen, inform your fellow teachers and your supervisor.

Your more mischievous students may try to get you to say the word *chinko*
ちんこ, which means "penis." They may also try to teach you other
inappropriate words, especially in front of other students. Double check a
dictionary before relying on your students for language advice.

> One well-meaning English teacher arranged a class activity and told
> the kids they could choose their team names. The entire class (and the
> Japanese homeroom teacher) literally fell out of their chairs laughing
> when she wrote "Team Chinko" on the board. She didn't figure out
> what they were laughing about until months later. Many English
> teachers have a story like this.

Unfortunately, it is not uncommon for English teachers to get sexually
harassed by their students, even in elementary school. You may also be on
the receiving end of such wince-inducing questions as "What is your cup
size?" and "When did you lose your virginity?" Though some students do
not understand that these questions are inappropriate, inform your company
supervisor and JTE immediately after the inappropriate behavior occurs.
(This is worth breaking the "no cell phone calls during the school day" rule.)
When confronting the Japanese teachers about the problem, if possible,
mention the student's name and homeroom.

> **EXCEPTION**: Gentlemen—if you teach children, at some point
> in your teaching career in Japan, one or more of your male students
> will ask you "How big?" Prepare a deflecting response, because this
> is considered more of a "getting to know you" question than sexual
> harassment. (Stating a ridiculously large or small size, even as a joke, is
> not a deflecting response.) Perhaps in the history of U.S./Japan relations,
> there has been a foreign male English teacher who has not encountered

this question, but I have never heard of such a man. (E-mail me if you are the exception!)

Bullying, or *ijime* いじめ , occurs in every country and age group, but Japan's cultural emphasis on conformity makes *ijime* an especially serious social problem for Japanese children. Cases range from the mild (populars vs. unpopulars) to the severe: public humiliation, destruction of personal property, aggressive threats, and even assault. A number of Japanese students commit suicide every year due to intense cases of *ijime*. Inform your fellow teachers, especially the bullied student's homeroom teacher, as soon as you see a student getting bullied. As an English teacher, disciplining students is not and should not be part of your job, but alert as many teachers as possible about any incidents of bullying in your classroom. The other teachers may or may not take action, but at least you can try to protect your students.

Many schools have a "No Camera" policy, which may or may not be written into your teaching contract. (This is not true for Japanese homeroom teachers, who are often responsible for assembling their homeroom's yearbook and/or graduation album.) As an English teacher and a foreigner in the school system, it would be a major violation of your students' privacy for you to take their pictures without their parents' permission. No matter how much you want to show off your students to your family and friends back home, and even if the students themselves say it's okay, do not take pictures while on school grounds, especially if you are male. Your students and the other teachers are allowed to take pictures of and with you, so don't worry about finding material for your scrapbook. Your school and students will probably present you with some group pictures at the end of the school year.

I personally advise against Facebook friending your students. It's easier to maintain a professional level of distance through e-mail, and your students may enjoy having a penpal with whom they can practice their English. If you decide to Facebook friend your students, set up a Limited Profile so they cannot view your pictures or personal information. Never post pictures of your students on Facebook.

AT THE OFFICE

Once you start working for a Japanese company, the company will provide you with a set of business cards. When exchanging business cards, receive a business card with two hands and read the card carefully. If you're sitting at a table, place the card in front of you. Don't disrespect the card in front of its owner by bending it or slipping it into the back pocket of your jeans.

Buy a business card holder, called a *meishi-ire* 名刺入れ, and keep it in an easy-access section of your purse or briefcase in the event of sudden business introductions. When you get home, empty your new contacts' business cards into a business card holder binder, *meishi-horudā* 名刺ホルダー, for safe-keeping. *Meishi-ire* and *meishi-horudā* can be purchased at any stationery store.

> **TIP**: Japanese business cards are a few millimeters larger than American business cards (3.6" by 2.2" and 3.5" by 2", respectively), so wait until you're in Japan to buy a business card binder. (Or just snip a little off the top of the cards you receive.)

High-ranking employees in an office are often called by their rank instead of their name, though some companies have done away with this tradition.

Office Positions		
Temporary Hire	*Haken-shain*	派遣社員
New Hire	*Shinnyu-shain*	新入社員
Contract Hire	*Keiyaku-shain*	契約社員
Regular Employee	*Sei-shain*	正社員
Chief Clerk	*Kakari-cho*	係長
Section Manager	*Ka-cho*	課長
Department Manager	*Bu-cho*	部長
General Manager	*Honbu-cho*	本部長
Company Chairman	*Kai-cho*	会長
Company President	*Sha-cho*	社長

People holding the shaded ranks should be addressed simply by their rank, or by their last name plus their rank. For example, Mr. Sawada, the head of the Marketing Department, would be *Bu-chō* or Sawada-*bu-chō*, not Sawada-*san*. If you decide to talk to Mrs. Sawada and discuss Mr. Sawada in the conversation, he should still be referred to as Sawada-*bu-chō*, not Sawada-*san*.

If you hold one of the shaded ranks and are introducing yourself, do not refer to yourself as "Smith-*bu-chō*." The ranked titles are a show of respect, so directly using them to introduce yourself sounds arrogant. The same goes for when talking about a ranked superior to a customer. The customer is the higher rank, so you would then refer to yourself as "*Bu-chō-no*-Smith."

Using the example above, if you are talking about a ranked person to a customer, you would call that person "*Bu-chō-no*-Smith."

Never refer to anyone using one of the unshaded ranks. These are simply terms for different types of employees. You can use the unshaded ranks to talk about yourself, but, just as in America, you would not go up to a coworker and say "Hello, Temporary Hire!"

If you will be communicating with Japanese clients and coworkers on a daily basis for work, you may need to study honorific language, known as *keigo* 敬語 . There are different words you use when speaking about yourself and when speaking both about and to your superiors (i.e. customers and/or higher-ups). *Keigo* is a fundamental component of Japanese business culture, but also a double-edged sword; if you don't use it, you're not comfortable with it, but if you're not comfortable with it, you shouldn't use it. Even Japanese people struggle with *keigo*. The best way to learn *keigo* is through materials meant for native Japanese speakers.

TIP: Japan's **Agency for Cultural Affairs** has a series of free keigo explanatory video clips available on their website (http://www.bunka. go.jp/kokugo_nihongo/keigo).

TIP: The book *Keigo Surasura Benrichō* 「敬語すらすら便利帳」 by Tomoko Imai is a great guide to *keigo*. This book is intended for native Japanese speakers, but the chapters are organized into easy-to-understand sections, such as "Asking a Question," and "Exchanging Business Cards" that make this book ideal for advanced students of Japanese.

Business e-mails use *keigo*, as well as set phrases that might be unfamiliar if you've never worked in a Japanese business environment. Avoid professional

stress and confusion and buy a book about how to write business e-mails
before you start working for a Japanese company,

I recommend 「ビジネスメールものの言い方辞書」 (*Bijinesu Mēru
Mono No Iikata Jisho*) by シーズ者 (Cybernote Information System).

This book provides explanations and examples of how to make
common business phrases, like 「申し訳ありませんでした」 *Mōshiwake-
arimasendeshita* (a formal "I'm sorry"), more or less formal, as well as
how to tailor phrases to your specific e-mail. It also offers various sample
e-mails (congratulations, asking someone to do something, apologizing,
etc.), but what sets this book apart from many similar-style business
e-mail books is that this book breaks down complicated language
into understandable, easy-to-lookup chunks. This is a great book for
advanced learners of Japanese.

It is considered rude to leave the subject "Re:" in reply to business e-mails.
(Not to mention that your e-mail might not get past the server's spam
filters.) Take the time to complete the subject title.

E-mails to coworkers (but never customers) should start with the phrase
O-tsukare-sama-desu 「お疲れ様です」, which is a set office greeting that
roughly means "Good work."

Just like in a Teacher's Office at a Japanese school, when someone leaves the
office, that person should say *O-saki-ni-shitsurei-shimasu* 「お先に失礼しま
す」, essentially "Sorry for leaving before you." In reply, everyone else says
"*O-tsukare-sama-deshita*" 「お疲れ様でした」.

Many company employees are given PHS (Personal Handy-phone
System) phones for work purposes. PHS phones are basically low-range,
low-cost cell phones.

If you call someone on the phone to ask for something, it's polite to wait
for the other person to hang up first.

Don't board an elevator in the middle of a phone call; PHS phones often
cut out in moving vehicles and/or elevators.

Summer in Japan brings with it the relaxed dress code of "Cool Biz" クールビズ *kūru-bīzu*. Though women's professional attire stays pretty much the same, during the summer months, you'll see many men in short-sleeved, light-weight business shirts. Suit jackets and ties are also optional during Cool Biz.

In 2005, the Japanese Ministry of the Environment started the Cool Biz initiative to reduce electricity consumption by limiting the use of office air conditioners and relaxing the business dress code. Cool Biz has successfully reduced an estimated 1.14 million tons of CO_2 emission. During Cool Biz, air conditioners are set at 28° Celsius (82° Fahrenheit) until September, so don't ask your coworkers to up the AC.

Don't wear perfume or scented body lotion to work. A pleasing smell to you could be pungent to a coworker. On a similar note, don't take your shoes off underneath your desk.

In your office, you may see large snack bins with the brand-name **Glico** (http://www.glico.co.jp) written on the front. These are not free! Glico is a snack-company that does office-delivery based on the honor system. There should be a list of prices nearby, as well as a slot to deposit your coins. When in doubt, ask a coworker.

Nomikai 飲み会 or *enkai* 宴会 , drinking parties, are an integral part of Japanese office culture. Consider them mandatory. *Nomikai* are a chance for everyone to kick back and relax, but what happens at the party stays at the party. Don't bring up stories about Mr. Tanaka's table dance during the next tea break. Even though it's a work party, the emphasis is still on the work.

If you don't want to drink at a *nomikai*, order ginger ale. Order water and the party will stop so that everyone can try to explain that you can drink as much as you want.

People may want to go out for *karaoke* カラオケ after the *nomikai*. Even though they will probably want you to sing a song in English (for which I recommend a song they're likely to have heard before, such as anything by the Beatles, so your coworkers can sing along), it's not a bad idea to learn at least one Japanese song before your first

Life After the B.O.E.
BY DAVID SAMESATO (AOMORI-KEN) CIR. 2002-04)

Your supervisor vomiting in a urinal during an enkai is 'forgotten' the next day.

You vomiting in a urinal during an enkai will be talked about FOREVER.

company *karaoke*. Major *karaoke* parlors, such as **Big Echo** (http://big-echo.jp) are constantly refreshing their songs, so anything on the Japanese Top 10 chart is sure to be there.

> <u>TIP</u>: **All Charts** (http://allcharts.org/music/japan/singles.htm) updates its Japan Top 10 list regularly, but if you can read Japanese, visit **Oricon** (http://www.oricon.co.jp/rank) for the most up-to-date and detailed rankings.

Once everyone has gathered, wait for the group *kanpai* 乾杯 ("Cheers!") before taking your first sip. Never refill your own glass. If you'd like more, refill someone else's glass and that person will quickly return the favor. Once you've finished drinking for the night, leave some liquid in your glass or people may keep trying to refill it.

If possible, get your vacation days approved in advance, and remember that December 25th is a work day in Japan!

Sexual Harassment in the Japanese Workplace

Sexual harassment (known as *sekuhara*, セクハラ) is defined differently in Japan than in the West. Though some actions are universally acknowledged to constitute sexual harassment, some behaviors, such as asking the only female employee in the office to make photocopies, are considered normal, if not encouraged, in the Japanese workplace. Many men do not understand what does and does not constitute sexual harassment, so context is important when deciding how to respond to perceived or actual sexual harassment.

Examples of Sexual Harassment
A boss insisting a female employee sing a duet with him during karaoke.
Calling a female employee by the informal suffix ~*chan* 「~ちゃん」, without the employee's prior invitation.
Nude posters and/or swimsuit calendars in the office.
Asking female employees to "dress sexy."
Pressuring female employees to drink during business trips.

At a company Sexual Harassment Prevention lecture, the HR

representative told us that, although it may be confusing and not seem like sexual harassment, asking a coworker to sing a duet with you during karaoke does indeed constitute *sekuhara*.

Certain actions that constitute sexual harassment in the West may not be seen as clear sexual harassment in Japan. If your situation becomes too uncomfortable, tell your company's HR department.

Not Sexual Harassment (in Japan)	
Being asked about your "type" (See "Fun, Fun, Fun—Making Friends and Meeting People" for more details.)	This happens all the time. Consider it water cooler conversation.
Repeated comments on your physical appearance	Your co-workers and/or students will invariably comment on your appearance. They may just be trying to start conversation or compliment you. This is not sexual harassment—as long as the comments don't verge into the inappropriate.
Asking female employees about their plans for marriage and/or when they will have children	This question happens often. Some people are just generally curious and don't recognize this as a highly personal question. Judge context before writing up a complaint.
Pressuring female employees to quit work after getting married	This is considered normal, much to the chagrin of working women everywhere.
Asking the only female employee to serve tea and/or make photocopies	If you are an OL, or "Office Lady,"- this may actually be one of your job requirements.

BILLS, BILLS, BILLS

Understanding your paycheck and the intricacies of tax law can be just as confusing in Japan as it is in the U.S. Not all paychecks and bills are formatted the same way, but the following chapters should help you pay your bills and check your account balance in no time.

MONEY

Cost of Living

Japan is home to three of the "Top 10 Most Expensive Cities in the World," as reported in Mercer's 2012 Cost of Living Survey. (Tokyo is 1st, Osaka is 3rd, and Nagoya is 10th. New York City is 33rd.) Come to Japan with enough funds to keep you financially secure until you get settled and/or receive your second paycheck.

As mentioned earlier, Japanese companies pay you on the 20th after a full month of work, meaning that you get paid for working September 1-20th on October 20th. You will receive your October salary on November 20th. This delay in payment is why it is so important to have enough savings to support yourself during the first few lean months in Japan.

Japanese Bank Account

If you will be working for a Japanese company, you will have to register for a Japanese bank account.

Most Japanese banks are open only Monday through Friday, from 9 am to 3 or 4 pm, immensely inconvenient hours for the single, working professional! **Citibank** (http://citibank.co.jp/en), however, has locations all throughout Japan. Citibank also offers 24 hour ATMs, native-level English support, and English-language contracts and instructional information.

A Citibank account that you create in the U.S. is considered an American bank account. You will only be able to access it, like all American bank accounts, through an international ATM.

Electronic Money

Ever wonder why Japanese lines move so quickly? Many people in Japan use **Edy** (http://www.edy.jp), a type of electronic pre-paid money.

First, you'll need an Edy (pronounced "Eddie") card. You can get one from any place that accepts Edy electronic money. (I recommend getting your Edy card from your favorite grocery or department store, as you can often use your Edy card to earn double reward points.)

After you get a card, load it at an Edy charge booth, available in most grocery stores, or go to a convenience store, give your card to the person at the counter, and say "Edy charge." You can put as much money as you want on the card. Most Japanese stores are Edy-capable, look for the symbol pictured here.

Swipe your Edy card in front of the Edy reader by the register. You will hear a tweeting sound once the transaction is complete. The cashier will then give you a receipt, no signature necessary.

Point Cards

Many department stores have free point cards rewarding you with gift certificates or discounts after a substantial amount of purchases. Register for these free point cards. Sometimes stores will have double/triple point days that help those little purchases add up to big rewards.

> **TIP**: Many department stores offer their own credit cards, which give double points to their customers. For this reason, many department stores will not give you points on your point card if you pay with a non-department store credit card. If you wish to accumulate points, you will have to pay in cash.

Tax and Tip

Japan factors the 5% Consumption Tax into an item's price, meaning that the price of something in a store or restaurant is exactly how much you will pay.

If you're living in Japan and earning income, you must pay taxes. Even though you're a foreigner, you have to pay Municipal City Tax, Japanese Pension, and for Japanese Health Insurance. These fees will be a sizable chunk off your first paycheck. Since there are so many variables in regards to tax law (such as one's income level, dependents, and region), consult your employer if you have any questions.

<u>NOTE</u>: You will also need to file annual tax in your home country, so keep track of your paychecks. Holepunch your paychecks and store them in a binder.

There's no tipping in Japan. Ever. Hooray!

UNDERSTANDING YOUR PAYCHECK

If you're employed by a Japanese company, your payslip, or *kyūyo-meisai*
きゅうよめいさい
給与明細 , will be written entirely in Japanese.

Some English teachers may receive an explanation of the Japanese tax
system during their company's orientation, but those working in a non-
teaching position might not get an official line-by-line translation.

Paycheck formats differ depending on the company, but here's a sample
paycheck, in case you'd like to learn a little more about where your salary
goes.

給与 明細書 Year年 Month月分
Your Name 様

	所定就労日	出勤日数	出勤	欠勤日数	振替休日	慶弔日数	特別出勤日数	有休消化日数
68 勤怠	1	2	3	4	5	6	7	8
	残業時間 9	所定残業 10	残業60H超 11	法定休日時間 12	残業時間 13	有休休 14	遅刻早退時間 15	

	基本給 16	役職手当 17	管理職手当 18	超過手当 19	組合補助金 20	キャベツ金 21	その他支給 22	前月修正給与 23	慶弔見舞金 24	勤怠控除 25
69 支給	特定通勤費 26	通勤費 27	駐車場代補助 28							
								深夜手当 29	深夜残業手当 30	残業60H超手当 31

		固定休日手当 32		非課税通勤 33	課税通勤 34	運賃率連絡分 35	大数 36	課税 合計 37	非課税合計 38	総支給額合計 39

	健康保険 40	介護保険 41	厚生年金 42	厚生年金基金 43	雇用保険 44	職安出向金中金 45	雇用保 46	社会保険合計 47	課税 年金額 48	所得税 49
70 控除	住民税 50	年調過不足 51	組合費(控) 52	貸付金返済 53	弁当代 54	立替金 55	経費控除 56	その他 57	年調還付 58	
									控除 計 59	控除 合計 60

	差引総支給合計 61	前月 調整 残 給額 62	合 計 63	当月年末調整 64	振込1 65	振込2 66	銀行 支給日 67
71 集計							

きんたい
68. 勤怠 *Kintai*
   The combined total of working and vacation days.

しょていしゅうろうひ
1. 所定就労日 *Shotei-shūrōbi*
   The number of days you were expected to work.

2. 出勤日数　*Shukkin-nissū*

   The number of days you went to work.

3. 出勤時間　*Shukkin-jikan*

   The number of hours you worked.

4. 欠勤日数　*Kekkin-nissū*

   The number of work days you missed.

5. 振替休日　*Furikae-kyūjitsu*

   The number of holidays you worked (that can be made up). Some companies will give you a weekday off if you had to work on a weekend. Some companies will also do this if a public holiday falls on a Saturday or Sunday.

6. 慶弔日数　*Keichō-nissū*

   Congratulations and Condolences—days you missed work due to family-related events, such as marriages or funerals.

7. 休日出勤日数　*Kyūjitsu-shukkin-nissū*

   The number of holidays you worked.

8. 有給消化日数　*Yūkyū-shōka-nissū*

   Number of days of paid leave.

9. 残業時間　*Zangyō-jikan*

   Overtime hours.

10. 深夜勤務　*Shinya-kinmu*

    Late night hours. The specific hours are determined by the individual company, but this usually means between 11 pm and 5 am.

11. 残業60超時間　*Zangyō-rokujū-chō-jikan*

    Additional overtime hours after the first sixty hours of overtime.

12. 法定休日時間　*Hōtei-kyūjitsu-jikan*

    Mandatory vacation days. The legally defined number of vacation days you must take after a certain number of uninterrupted work days.

13. <ruby>残業時間<rt>ざんぎょうじかん</rt></ruby> 2 *Zangyō-jikan-ni*

    A different classification of overtime hours, usually absent from 9-to-5 jobs. This applies more to early-morning employment, as in a newscaster working overtime from midnight to six am.

14. <ruby>有給残日数<rt>ゆうきゅうざんにっすう</rt></ruby> *Yūkyū-zan-nissū*

    Remaining number of paid leave days.

15. <ruby>遅刻早退時間<rt>ちこくそうたいじかん</rt></ruby> *Chikoku-sōtai-jikan*

    Total number of minutes/hours you were late to work.

69. <ruby>支給<rt>しきゅう</rt></ruby> *Shikyū*
Salary

16. <ruby>基本給<rt>きほんきゅう</rt></ruby> *Kihonkyū*

    Base salary.

17. <ruby>役員報酬<rt>やくいんほうしゅう</rt></ruby> *Yakuin-hōshū*

    This is a special salary addition for bosses and upper-level managers.

18. <ruby>管理職手当<rt>かんりしょくてあて</rt></ruby> *Kanrishoku-teate*

    A manager's commission for the sales efforts of his subordinates. This is a pre-determined amount.

19. <ruby>超過手当<rt>ちょうかてあて</rt></ruby> *Chōka-teate*

    The sum of your overtime hours, equal to #9 + #11.

20. <ruby>歩合達成金<rt>ぶあいたっせいきん</rt></ruby> *Buai-tassei-kin*

    Sales commission earnings.

21. <ruby>キャンペーン金<rt>きん</rt></ruby> *Kyanpēn-kin*

    Campaign earnings, if your company was running a special type of promotion or event.

22. <ruby>その他支給<rt>たしきゅう</rt></ruby> *Sonota-shikyū*

    Additional salary/other earnings.

23. <ruby>前月修正給与<rt>ぜんげつしゅうせいきゅうよ</rt></ruby> *Zengetsu-shūsei-kyūyo*

    If there was a salary mistake from the month before, the proper amount will be added or deducted here.

24. 慶弔見舞金　*Keichō-mimai-kin*
    けいちょうみまいきん

    Congratulations and Condolences money.

    You will receive a small bonus in the event of a death in your
    immediate family, as well as for happier occasions, such as getting
    married or the birth of a child.

25. 勤怠控除　*Kintai-kōjō*
    きんたいこうじょ

    Salary reductions due to tardiness and/or missed days of work.

26. 修正通勤費　*Shūsei-tsūkinhi*
    しゅうせいつうきんひ

    Transportation Reimbursement Fee.

    If a calculation error was made before, or there has been a route
    revision and thus a need for additional/less transportation money,
    the correct amount will be added or deducted here.

27. 通信費　*Tsūshinhi*
    つうしんひ

    Phone/communication fees, if your company has given you a phone
    for work use.

28. 駐車場代補助　*Chūshajōdai-hojo*
    ちゅうしゃじょうだいほじょ

    Parking fee reimbursement for company cars.

29. 残業手当　*Zangyō-teate*
    ざんぎょうてあて

    Normal overtime salary, without surpassing the allowable number of
    overtime hours. Some companies do not allow excessive overtime.

30. 深夜勤務手当　*Shinya-kinmu-teate*
    しんやきんむてあて

    Late-night overtime salary.

31. 残業60超手当　*Zangyō-rokujū-chō-teate*
    ざんぎょう　ちょうてあて

    Salary for overtime totaling over sixty hours.

32. 法定休日手当　*Hōtei-kyūjitsu-teate*
    ほうていきゅうじつてあて

    Salary for working during holidays.

33. 非課税通勤　*Hikazei-tsūkin*
    ひかぜいつうきん

    Tax-free transportation reimbursement.

    Amount depends on region, method of transportation, and distance

from work. Reimbursement for travel by subway and/or bus is tax
free; transportation by car is not.

34. 課税通勤 *Kazei-tsūkin*

Taxed transportation reimbursement.

Amount depends on region, method of transportation, and distance
from work.

35. 遅刻早退控除 *Chikoku-sōtai-kōjo*
Amount of money deducted from one's salary due to tardiness.

36. 欠勤控除 *Kekkin-kōjo*
Salary reduction based on missed work days.

37. 課税合計 *Kazei-gōkei*
Sum of taxes owed.

38. 非課税合計 *Hikazei-gōkei*
Sum of tax exemptions.

39. 総支給額合計 *Sō-shikyū-gaku-gōkei*
Total sum of all additions and deductions.

70. 控除 *Kōjo*
Salary deductions.

Most of your salary deductions will be due to taxes and mandatory
insurance payments. The following terms will be used throughout the rest of
this section.

Japanese Social Insurance		
Nursing Care Insurance	介護保険	*Kaigo-hoken*
Pension Insurance	年金保険	*Nenkin-hoken*
Unemployment Insurance	雇用保険	*Koyō-hoken*
Medical Care Insurance	医療保険	*Iryō-hoken*
Worker's Accident Insurance	労災保険	*Rōsai-hoken*

40. 健康保険 *Kenkō-hoken*
けんこうほけん

Health insurance payments, calculated based on your monthly salary.

Your company divides the health insurance payment equally and deducts your half of the payment from your paycheck.

(MONTHLY SALARY) × (COMPANY'S *Kenkō-hoken* RATE) = PAYMENT

¥200,000 × 4.74% = ¥9,480

41. 介護保険 *Kaigo-hoken*
かいごほけん

Nursing Care Insurance.

Those above the age of 40 are taxed to help fund nursing care in old age. The *Kaigo-hoken* rate depends on the region of Japan.

(MONTHLY SALARY) × (*Kaigo-hoken* RATE) = PAYMENT

¥200,000 × 0.755% = ¥1,510

42. 厚生年金 *Kōsei-nenkin*
こうせいねんきん

Retirement pension.

This is only valid if you stay with the company until you retire. In the past, most employees in Japan began working for a company upon graduation and remained with that company their whole life. This has changed in recent years. Like the other pensions, this payment is matched by your company.

Paying Japanese retirement pension is not optional, even if you do not plan on retiring in Japan. (See "*Sayōnara*—Leaving Japan" for details on how to get some of this money back.)

You can receive *Kōsei-nenkin* payments after turning 65, like *Kokumin-nenkin* 国民年金.
こくみんねんきん

Unlike *Kokumin-nenkin*, *Kōsei-nenkin* is not available to those who are self-employed. Though a source of much controversy, a dependent spouse may also be registered under her husband's company's *Kōsei-nenkin*.

(BASE MONTHLY SALARY) × (*Kōsei-nenkin* RATE) = DEDUCTION

¥200,000 × 8.029% = ¥16,058

43. こうせいねんきんききん
    厚生年金基金   *Kōsei-nenkin-kikin*

    The portion of the Kōsei-nenkin payment paid by the company.

44. かくていきょしゅつねんきん
    確定拠出年金   *Kakutei-kyoshutsu-nenkin*

    A defined-contribution pension plan, like a Japanese 401k.

45. こようほけん
    雇用保険   *Koyō-hoken*

    Unemployment insurance.

    You are eligible for unemployment insurance seven days after getting
    fired. You will receive unemployment payments one month after
    the seven day waiting period. Benefits depend on your initial salary.
    If you work less than four hours a day at a part-time job, you can
    receive unemployment insurance. If you work more than four hours
    a day, you can still receive benefits, just at a reduced rate.

    If you resigned from your place of employment, the waiting period
    is three months and you must have worked for at least six months to
    qualify for unemployment insurance. In response to those suddenly
    unemployed by the NOVA *Eikaiwa* shutdown, **Let's Japan** ([http://
    www.letsjapan.org/collecting-unemployment-insurance.html](http://www.letsjapan.org/collecting-unemployment-insurance.html))
    created a detailed explanation of how to file for unemployment
    benefits.

46. しゃかいほけんちょうせい
    社会保険調整   *Shakai-hoken-chōsei*

    Additions or deductions due to changes in the percentage used to
    calculate social insurance.

    This one-time fee is only applied if you change companies. The fee is
    deducted on the 20th, so if you join a company on the 21st, you don't
    have to pay the fee to the new company. (The fee will have already
    been deducted from your paycheck from the old company.)

47. しゃかいほけんごうけい
    社会保険合計   *Shakai-hoken-kaikei*

    The amount deducted from your salary to pay for social insurance.

    This amount changes depending on your number of dependents and
    which types of insurance you don't have to pay for. (For example,
    those under forty years old don't have to pay *Kaigo-hoken*.)

48. かぜいたいしょうがく
    課税対象額   *Kazei-taishōgaku*

    The total sum of owed taxes. Equal to #39 - #33 - #47.

49. 所得税 *Shotokuzei*
   Income tax.

   This is deducted from your monthly salary, but calculated based on your annual salary.

50. 住民税 *Jūminzei*
   Municipal City Tax.

   Those who have never worked before or, in some cases, those who had previously worked in a different region of Japan do not have to pay Municipal City Tax in the new city of their employment until after two years of living in the new city. Until then, Municipal City Tax is paid to the city of former residence. The Muncipal City Tax rate varies from city to city.

51. 年調過不足 *Nenchō-kafusoku*
   Changes to one's yearly salary, which can be either additions or deductions.

   December salaries usually include end-of-the-year bonuses.

52. 社宅・寮費 *Shataku・Ryōhi*
   Rent. Only applies to those living in company housing.

53. 貸付金返済 *Kashitsukekin-hensai*
   Repayments for a loan/advance from the company.

54. 仮払金 *Karibaraikin*
   Advance repayment deducted from one's salary in the case of a temporary advance.

55. 立替金 *Tatekaekin*
   A temporary advance.

56. 経費精算 *Keihi-seisan*
   Reimbursements for business trip expenses.

57. その他 *Sonota*
   Other.

58. 年調過不足2　*Nenchō-kafusoku-ni*
    Year-end tax adjustment.

    Companies pay the majority of their insurance premiums in
    December, but deduct a small amount from your monthly salary
    each month instead of all at once. (Thus the monthly social
    insurance payments.) If the tax rates change, the appropriate amount
    will be added or deducted here in December.

59. 控除計　*Kōjokei*
    Deductions carried over from the Salary section (#69).

60. 控除合計　*Kōjo-gōkei*
    Total subtractions.

71. 記事　**Kiji**
    Final tally.

61. 累積課税合計　*Ruiseki-kazei-gōkei*
    Your accumulated total of paid social insurance taxes, starting from
    January.

    This monthly tax varies depending on the month, though tax
    payments often increase as the year progresses towards December.
    The Japanese business year begins in April and continues
    in four-month increments (January→April, May→August,
    September→December).

62. 前月調整残　*Zengetsu-chōseizan*
    Adjustments left over from the previous month.

63. 端数合計　*Hasū-gōkei*
    This is your salary for the month, after deductions, and rounded
    down in case of a small decimal point.
    (EXAMPLE: 150,000.1 円 →150,000 円)

64. 当月端数調整　*Tōgetsu-hasū-chōsei*
    This is the total sum of money rounded down, in case of a very small
    decimal point. (EXAMPLE: 0.1 円 → 0 円)

65. 振込 1 *Furikomi-ichi*

    Furikomi means transfer. The two main transfer points of a paycheck are one's Japanese bank account or Japan Post, which has its own bank (Japan Post Bank). This section could refer to the amount going to either one of those locations, depending on the account listed with the Human Resources (HR) Department.

    The HR Department is called *Jinji* 人事 in Japanese.

66. 振込 2 *Furikomi-ni*

    Same as #65, but sent to a different account.

67. 差引支給額 *Sashihiki-shikyūgaku*

    The total of additions minus the total of deductions. The amount you will receive in your bank account.

HOW TO WITHDRAW MONEY FROM A JAPANESE ATM

The following pictures will show you how to withdraw money from an ATM at Japan Post. (The ATM screen has a reflective coating so that your neighbor can't glance over and easily see what you're typing. This is great for privacy, but not for photography!)

STEP ONE

To withdraw money from the ATM, first hit "ENGLISH GUIDE."

STEP TWO

Select "WITHDRAWAL" from the upper right-hand corner. You can tap the buttons on screen or the plastic buttons on the left and right of the screen.

STEP THREE

You will be asked to insert your passbook or card. Insert your credit card in the slot above the machine.

STEP FOUR

The machine will recognize that you are using an international credit card. Tap "Cards Issued Overseas."

STEP FIVE

Confirm that you are willing to receive a foreign transaction fee.

STEP SIX

Type your PIN using the keypad.

STEP SEVEN

Enter the amount of money you would like to withdraw.

STEP EIGHT

Confirm the amount by hitting "ENTER."

STEP NINE

Collect your cash and
your receipt.

HOW TO PAY BILLS AND TRANSFER MONEY

Most Japanese bills must be paid using a post office ATM during business hours. Allow yourself time to figure out the machine (or ask someone who works at the post office for help.)

Paying a Bill at the Post Office

Here is an example of a bill that you would pay at a Japan Post ATM.

The left side of the bill is perforated, but don't separate the perforated sheets of the bill.

Insert the complete bill as one set into the part of the machine labeled "PASSBOOK."

Insert your money. Confirm the amount you wish to pay, and wait to receive your receipt.

Paying a Bill at a Convenience Store

If your bill has convenience store logos on it, you can pay the bill at the counter of any of the convenience stores listed on the bill.

If you're paying a bill at a convenience store, all you need to do is hand the bill and the money to the clerk at the counter. Save the stamped receipt, just in case.

Bank Transfers

Japanese ATMs do not provide English directions for conducting bank transfers. I recommend that you visit the local branch of your Japanese bank during business hours and let the bank staff help you with the electronic transfer. In case you're unable to visit the bank during business hours, here's a basic guide to completing a bank transfer using Citibank.

STEP ONE

Tap the button that says "Local Funds Transfer," お振込み *O-furikomi.*

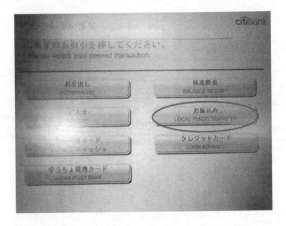

STEP TWO

From this point onward, there won't be any English support.

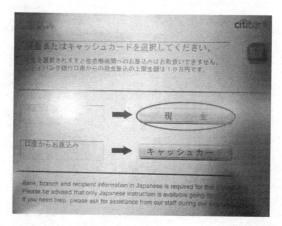

The bottom button says "Cash Card," キャッシューカード *Kyasshū-kādo*.

Paying by "Cash Card" means that you will pay directly out of your Citibank bank checking account.

The top button 現金 *Genkin*, says "Cash."

Press 現金 "Cash," and you will be greeted with the following list of payment methods.

STEP THREE

The screen will show a list of different Japanese banks.

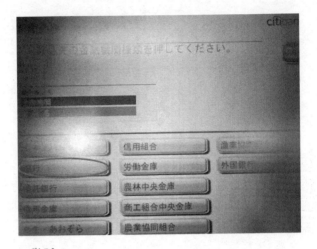

Tap 銀行 *Ginkō*, which means "Bank," to send money to a non-Citibank Japanese bank account. Send money to a foreign bank account by pressing 外国銀行 *Gaikoku-ginkō*. The other options are translated below.

シティバンク	信用組合	漁業共同組合
Citibank	Credit Association	Fishing Cooperative
Shiteibanku	*Shinyō-kumiai*	*Gyogyō-kyōdō-kumiai*
銀行	労金金庫	外国銀行
Bank	Workers' Credit Union	Foreign Bank
Ginkō	*Rōkin-kinko*	*Gaikoku-ginkō*
信託銀行	農林中央金庫	
Trust Bank	Norinchukin Bank	
Shintaku-ginkō	*Nōrinchūō-kinko*	
信金金庫	商工組合中央金庫	
Shinkin Bank	Shoko Chukin Bank	
Shinyō-kinko	*Shōkō-kumiai-chūō-kinko*	
新生・青空	農業共同組合	
Shinsei-Aozora Bank	Agricultural Cooperative	
Shinsei・Aozora	*Nōgyō-kyōdō-kumiai*	

STEP FOUR

Type in the account number.

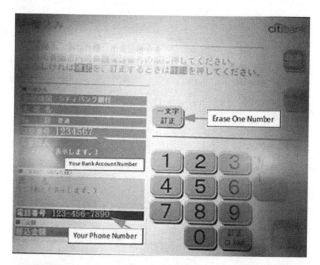

STEP FIVE

A screen should pop up with information about the receiving party. Type in how much yen you wish to transfer.

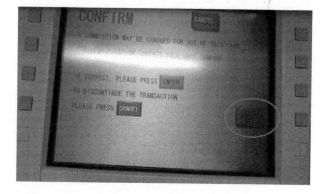

STEP SIX

Type in your name and phone number, which should match the name and phone number registered on the bill.

I LOST MY CREDIT CARD. NOW WHAT?

Here's what to do if you lose your credit card while in Japan for a long-term visit.

STEP ONE: Cancel your credit card.

Once you have searched for your credit card and are 100% sure it cannot be found, call the number of your credit card company's customer service department and request to cancel the card.

You can check online for the most recent Customer Care Services numbers, but here's a quick reference guide.

American Express (Japan): 0120-974990

(https://business.americanexpress.com/jp/en/program-administrator/customer-service)

Discover (outside U.S.): 1-801-902-3100

(https://www.discover.com/credit-cards/help-center/contact-us/index.html)

MasterCard (Japan): 00531-11-3886

(http://www.mastercard.com/global/_assets/docs/GlobalServiceTollfreeNumbers.pdf)

VISA (Japan): 00531-11-1555

(http://www.visa.ca/en/personal/lostcard.jsp)

You will need to give your name, billing address, home phone number, and possibly your Social Security Number. If you know your full credit card number, this information will expedite the reissuing process.

STEP TWO: Wait.

This is the tricky part.

Hopefully you have enough cash to last a few days as the credit card company mails your credit card to your original billing address.

Some credit card companies might FedEx your card directly to your hotel, but if your family members will be forwarding your credit card to you, make sure they use an overnight or express service. Depending on the length of your stay in Japan and the urgency of your need, the credit card might not arrive in time if sent by regular post.

If you need money right away, try asking a friend or family member for a digital money transfer at **Western Union** (http://www.westernunion.co.jp/en) which has locations all throughout Japan.

STUDY

Study abroad is an amazing opportunity to live like a local, explore with the freedom of a tourist, and make Japanese friends, all without the hassles or long-term commitment of securing employment. A few weeks of in-country experience can jumpstart both your Japanese language skills and your understanding of Japanese culture. The following sections offer advice on studying in Japan and advice on effective studying resources you can use, wherever you are, to improve your Japanese.

STUDY ABROAD

There are a myriad of summer and semester programs in Japan available to the adventurous traveler, such as the programs listed below. Study abroad programs and their requirements are constantly changing, so the Internet is the best place to begin your study abroad research.

Go Overseas (http://www.gooverseas.com/study-abroad/japan) and Study **Abroad 101** (http://www.studyabroad101.com/countries/japan) organize a variety of study, volunteer, and teaching opportunities in Japan. You can search by term, city, and/or number of reviews. Keep in mind, though, that most people only take the time to review a program if they had either a 5-star or 1-star experience.

High School Study Abroad

High school students can participate in a variety of summer, semester, and/ or homestay programs that may or may not require Japanese language experience.

AFS USA (http://www.afsusa.org)

Ayusa International (http://www.ayusa.org/students)

Center for Cultural Interchange (CCI)
(http://www.cci-exchange.com/travelabroad/program.aspx?id=666)

Council on International Educational Exchange (CIEE)
(http://www.ciee.org/hsabroad)

Experiment in International Living (EIL)
(http://www.experimentinternational.org/japan.cfm#.UHwlq1EZ5Mo)

Youth for Understanding USA
(http://yfuusa.org/countries/japan-20.php)

I believe that a summer program is the best option for your first visit to Japan, especially if you are just beginning your studies of Japanese (i.e. you have studied Japanese for one full year or less). On a summer program, you'll get a whirlwind cultural experience, which will ease the transition should you decide to return to Japan in the future. Even if you are 150% sure you want to major in Japanese, study at a Japanese university, and/or spend the rest of your life in Japan, a few weeks in-country will help you make informed decisions before committing to a longer program.

> **TIP**: If you want to look at Japanese universities or travel with your parents while in Japan, it might be better to do this at the end of your summer program, instead of at the beginning. Your parents may look to you for help navigating Japan, which may be easier if you have already adjusted to the time zone and culture. (And seeing your competence in a foreign country may reassure your parents that you are ready for an extended study abroad experience.)

College Study Abroad

Some four-year Japanese colleges like **Temple University – Japan Campus** (http://www.tuj.ac.jp/index.html) accept direct enrollment from foreigners. This section, however, will focus on summer and semester programs available to those already enrolled in a non-Japanese academic institution.

Many American colleges and universities have pre-approved, "sister school" study abroad programs in Japan. Other American schools require you to find your own independent program, such as the programs listed below.

Antioch University (http://www.antioch.edu/aea/programs/japan-and-its-buddhist-traditions)
Antioch offers a program in Kyoto concentrating in Japanese language and Japanese religions and spiritual traditions, such as Buddhism and Shinto. Program participants live in a Buddhist temple for most of the program, so students must follow the five basic Buddhist laws of abstinence:

    1) Abstain from taking life.
    2) Abstain from theft.
    3) Abstain from sexual misconduct.
    4) Abstain from lying.
    5) Abstain from intoxicants.

Participants will also participate in meditation. No prior Japanese study required.

CIEE (http://www.ciee.org/study-abroad)

Earlham College (http://japanstudy.earlham.edu/study-japan/courses
   Earlham offers a unique year-long program at Japan's prestigious **Waseda University** (http://www.waseda.jp/top/index-j.html). During the winter break, study abroad students participate in interesting cultural programs throughout Japan, such as living at a Zen temple, assisting tsunami relief efforts, or working at a traditional Japanese inn. Having Waseda University, as well as internship experience, on your resume may impress future Japan-based employers.

IES Abroad (https://www.iesabroad.org)

Nanzan University (http://www.nanzan-u.ac.jp/English)
   As a personal disclaimer, I studied at Nanzan University through the IES Abroad program. Studying at Nanzan was a truly life-changing experience for me. Not only did my Japanese dramatically improve, I made lifelong friends with both Japanese and fellow international students. Nanzan offers many clubs and extra-curricular activities, as well as an intensive Japanese language program that allows you to take classes with Japanese students. I highly recommend Nanzan University to anyone interested in studying abroad.

Kansai Gaidai University (http://www.kansaigaidai.ac.jp/asp)

Ritsumeikan University
(http://www.ritsumei.ac.jp/eng/html/admissions/program_jp/skp)

Temple University Summer Program in Japan (http://www.temple.edu/
studyabroad/programs/semester_year/japan/index.html)
   Your major may require taking courses that are only offered during certain years or semesters at your home institution. This is especially true for science-related majors, since it is unlikely you will be able to take equivalent science or math courses while in Japan. Check with your major department, as well as your school's Study Abroad office, as soon as possible to map out an academic plan.

   Many American schools do not accept full credit for courses taken abroad. This is not necessarily a bad thing, as it means that your grades will show up on your transcript, but not count toward your GPA. You can focus on the cultural experience instead of stressing about minor grade fluctuations. Check with your home institution's Study Abroad office in advance.

For Japanese students, admission to most Japanese universities (junior/specialty colleges excepted) is based solely on entrance exam results. Interview skills and extra-curricular activities are irrelevant. Japanese high school seniors are pressured to get accepted into a name-brand college, thus the after school and weekend cram-school sessions, known as *juku* 塾 . These schools prepare their students for entrance exams, and often offer the intellectual stimulation the students do not receive in their normal school. Many students begin *juku* in middle or even elementary school. Unfortunately, some students burn out after years of *juku*. College becomes the relaxing reward for years of hard work.

If you're enrolled in a study abroad program at a Japanese university, the level of academic difficulty at a Japanese university might not equal that of your home institution. Japanese language classes, however, tend to be highly intensive. Expect late-night *kanji* cramming, as well as a more textbook-based teaching method than you may have experienced in America.

Which Semester?

I think the best time during college to study abroad is the summer after your freshman year and/or any time during your junior year.

1) JYA = Junior Year Abroad

Many colleges designate junior year as the time to study abroad. Your friends and classmates may also be studying abroad during this time, so you won't miss out on as much socially or academically.

After two years of Japanese language study, you will be in a much better position to take classes at a Japanese university. Higher language abilities may also make it easier to adjust to daily life in Japan—buying groceries, interacting with your host family/roommates, etc. The more Japanese you know before you go, the faster you will improve once you're in Japan.

2) Summer Programs = Best Directly Before/After Sophomore Year

If you can't go on JYA because of strict credit requirements, I highly recommend a month or two-month summer program. Many summer programs run from June to July, so you'll still have time in August to relax and recover before the new school year at your home institution.

Students on summer programs less than ninety days usually enter Japan on a ninety day tourist visa, no application required.

Getting a Student Visa

When applying for study abroad, you may have to provide a list of any prescription drugs you currently take. If you have a personal history of mental illness, such as depression and/or an eating disorder, this information may influence the hiring/admission decisions of Japanese schools and companies.

Although Japan currently has no HIV/AIDS entry restrictions, some Japanese universities require an HIV/AIDS test, as well as other medical information, with your deposit balance.

You cannot receive a Japanese visa if you have a criminal record involving illegal drugs. This includes even the smallest amount of marijuana use, and/or prostitution. Many celebrities, such as Paris Hilton and Paul McCartney, have been (temporarily) denied access to Japan due to their history of drug use. Though the power of fame triumphed over Japanese Customs in their situations, do not expect to be so lucky.

If you wish to pursue postgraduate education in Japan, your college's Fellowship Office may help you find a scholarship.

Mail all your applications via registered or certified mail and keep your tracking number safe.

Short-Term Study Abroad Programs

If you want to try a short-term study abroad program before committing to a full semester in a foreign country, try a short-term volunteer or homestay program.

Although you will have to pay your own way, a volunteer trip can be a great way to gain in-country experience and build up your resume.

Go Overseas (http://www.gooverseas.com) features some sample "voluntourism" itineraries.

Many short-term programs, like **Habitat for Humanity Japan** (http://www.habitatjp.org/contents_e/involved/index.html) may be geared towards people already living in-country.

Volunteer programs and their requirements, however, are constantly changing, so a quick Internet search will provide you with the most up-to-date information.

Student Life

Join a club! Interacting with other people and trying out new activities are great ways to both have fun and improve your Japanese.

Activity-based clubs, such as sports clubs or theatre groups, will give you constant topics for conversation, which can (ironically) be difficult in a "conversation club" filled with go-getting foreigners and Japanese students interested in practicing their English. Participating in an athletic or cultural club will give you unique experiences and allow you to develop friendships with Japanese students in a low-competition environment.

Your Japanese university's sports teams may let you train with them, but you will not get to compete in actual, ranked matches against other schools. This is not a comment on your abilities, but rather on your transient presence as a study abroad student. Some sports teams at famous schools, such as Waseda University's baseball team, are of near-professional caliber and reputation. Many Japanese college students train for years before being allowed to represent their school at a match.

Always carry your student ID. Many museums, shops, and movie theaters offer student discounts. Some movie theaters have drastically reduced prices for students on a special weekday each month—"Students' Day," "Ladies' Day," even "Foreigners' Day." It's worth checking in advance with your local theater's Box Office to see when these promotions take place.

Many movie theaters in Japan let you reserve a specific seat, much like a play or musical production would in the U.S. This eliminates the need to arrive early to get seats together as a large group. You can choose your seat when you purchase a ticket.

HOW TO ENROLL IN A
JAPANESE HIGH SCHOOL

There are two ways to get into a Japanese high school: studying abroad as a short term transfer student, or directly enrolling.

Short Term Transfer Student

High school age students can study abroad at a Japanese high school, even if you don't speak, read, and/or write native-level Japanese!

Many study abroad programs, such as **Ayusa** (http://www.ayusa.org/students/japan) and **AFS USA** (http://www.afsusa.org/study-abroad/high-school-abroad/japan-high-school-program), offer homestay programs that let you attend a Japanese high school as an international student.

> This is your best bet if you dream of attending a Japanese high school, especially since these programs also provide homestay families and visa sponsorship. (And yes, you get to wear a Japanese school uniform.)

Homeschooled students may have an easier time adjusting their school year to the Japanese academic calendar. Students from traditional schools may have to leave their home institution in the middle of the school year. It may be possible for you to get academic credit for this time spent abroad, so check with your school before making this major decision.

Directly Enrolling in a Japanese High School

Getting into a Japanese high school is not an easy task, even if you are Japanese. Japan does not guarantee its citizens a high school education, and even public high schools require entrance exams. If a third year middle school student does not get into a high school, that student does not attend high school.

There is a reason there are rarely, if ever, any non-Japanese students in Japanese high schools, by which I mean the private and/or public educational institutions of Japan not specifically geared towards the children of foreign residents.

To be accepted into a Japanese high school, you must take the same entrance exam as the other applicants. The exam will be entirely in Japanese. You will not receive extra time nor any other special accommodation for being a non-native Japanese speaker. You must take the same exam on the same day in the same place as everyone else, meaning that you will have to fly to Japan for the exam. Due to the competitive and serious nature of high school admission, Japanese students are highly encouraged to apply to a mix of safety and stretch schools.

The content and length of the entrance exam depends on the school and its requirements, but expect to be tested in the Japanese core curriculum: Japanese, Math, Science, English, and Social Studies. The other applicants will have formally studied these subjects in Japanese for the past nine years. A perfect English score will not compensate for lower scores in other subjects. If you cannot read and write about these subjects in native-level Japanese, directly enrolling in a Japanese high school is not an option for you.

Not a Problem?

If the above requirements pose no deterrent to you, you will need to find a place to live, as well as adults willing to serve as your guardians.
The blog **Education in Japan** (https://educationinjapan.wordpress.com) is geared toward ex-pat parents raising children in Japan, but offers detailed information on the specifics of enrolling in Japanese schools.

DORM VS. HOMESTAY

Dorm or homestay family? Where you choose to live can define your study abroad experience.

Dorm 寮 ^{りょう} *Ryō*

Most Japanese university students commute to school from their family home or personal apartment, but some internationally-minded colleges (such as some of those listed in "Study—Study Abroad") provide dorm housing to foreign exchange students and a select group of Japanese students.

BENEFITS

Relaxed Curfew
   Every dorm has different rules, but a dorm will have a higher tolerance level for early-morning and late-night activity than a homestay family. Your dorm might have a midnight curfew, or even no curfew at all.

Unrestricted Use of Utilities
   Need to wash your clothes a specific way? Want to take a morning and evening shower every day of the week? No problem! Your dorm's caretaker may grow upset if you go crazy with the utilities, but you will undeniably have more freedom in a dorm.

Uninterrupted Down Time
   You can spend your free time however you choose, without having to first consider the schedule or desires of your family.

Guaranteed Internet Access
   Dorms are not required to provide Internet access, but most do (for a set fee). If your study abroad experience in Japan would be ruined without regular Internet access, stay in a dorm.

DRAWBACKS

Roommates

You do not get to choose your roommates. Study abroad programs often pair roommates randomly, as opposed to by similar sleeping schedules and/ or personality.

Every school has a different style of accommodation, but many programs offer a single room with a communal bathroom and kitchen facility. You will never have to share direct living quarters with a member of the opposite gender (unless your roommate acquires a significant other).

"Gaijin Clump"

The dreaded "Gaijin Clump"—the other people in your dorm will probably be foreigners, which can make it hard to meet Japanese people. The Japanese students who do live in your dorm may be overwhelmed by the number of foreign students seeking their attention. You may have to make a concerted effort to make Japanese friends outside of the dorm.

Cooking and Cleaning

You will have to do your own cooking, cleaning, and grocery shopping. This may be to your advantage, depending on your skills and the quality of the closest restaurants.

Homestay ホームステイ *Hōmusutei*

Many study abroad programs, especially those geared toward high school students, only offer the homestay option, and for a good reason. Interacting with Japanese people is one the best ways to learn Japanese, and staying with a homestay family can be an amazing and life-changing experience.

BENEFITS

Authentic Japanese Experience

Perhaps the most obvious benefit to a homestay is that you'll get to learn about Japanese culture in a way that no classroom could ever recreate. The memories you make with your homestay family will be completely unique and may form the foundation of a lifelong friendship.

Supportive Environment

Your homestay family is directly responsible for your health and safety. If anything happens to you—homesickness, getting lost on the way to the train station—your homestay family will be there to help. That means that if you get sick, you can focus on getting better instead of stressing about finding a doctor and getting to the grocery store before it closes.

What To Do When You Arrive

Give a small gift to your homestay family the day you arrive.

Call your parents to let them know you arrived safely and send them an updated information sheet with your homestay family's mailing address, phone number, and the names of everyone in your homestay family. Your homestay coordinator should already have given this information to you and your (real) family, but it will reassure your family members if you send them the most up-to-date information.

Language Immersion

If you and your homestay family communicate with each other in Japanese, your language abilities will skyrocket. You will also have someone to write to in Japanese once your study abroad program ends, as well as a possible place to stay during future visits to Japan. If you're nervous about your Japanese, or super-excited about getting to practice, having a homestay family is a low-pressure and high-opportunity chance to meet new people and practice your skills.

Instant Socializing

You will not have to worry about making friends to practice Japanese. In fact, you will probably spend most of your time with your homestay family. You will always have someone to talk to, and you'll be able to ask someone for help if you ever have any difficulties or concerns.

No Cooking or Cleaning

Host families provide their student with breakfast and dinner. (Exchange students are often expected to purchase their own lunch while at school.) Sharing meals with your homestay family is one of the easiest ways to get better acquainted with your family and practice your Japanese.

The food you eat with your homestay family is more likely to be authentic Japanese home cooking than what you come across in the States. In a homestay family, you have the opportunity to try new foods, without the worry or cost of cooking and grocery shopping. You might even get to learn some new recipes!

Some families may insist on doing your laundry for you, partly out of hospitality and partly because they don't want to risk you breaking the washing machine.

DRAWBACKS

Free English Lessons

Some homestay families expect their international student to help the family practice their English. Though you should endeavor to be a gracious guest (and there's no harm in occasionally helping the kids with their English homework), you should not be expected to provide regular tutoring or childcare.

Most families are not so calculating. Some may simply be proud of their English ability, or wish to make things easier for you when you get frustrated or tired. If your goal is Japanese fluency, resist the temptation to speak in your mother tongue and make the most of your chance to communicate with native speakers.

No Internet

Homestay families are generally not required to provide their students with any sort of Internet access. Some families, especially those in rural areas, might not have wireless or even Internet access at all. Some families may worry if they see you on the Internet for an extended period of time, perhaps assuming that you are shy or homesick.

You can set up your own wireless Internet with a provider like Softbank or DoCoMo, but this might be expensive and hurt the family's feelings.

All Japanese Food, All the Time

There is a big difference between Japanese food in America and Japanese food in Japan. You will not be eating tempura and *sushi* every day (except for my friend who was lucky enough to homestay with a *sushi* chef, but that's another story). The chance to try "new" Japanese foods is a great opportunity, but it does mean you have to be polite and open-minded during mealtime.

One of the best parts about a homestay program is that you get an insider's look at everyday Japanese life and behavior. The homestay family should not have to alter their diet to accommodate yours. If you have strict dietary concerns (i.e. you are a vegetarian, a vegan, or do not eat fish, pork, and/or shellfish), a homestay program may not be the best option for you.

House Rules

Although your homestay family may encourage you to make yourself comfortable and "act like a member of the family," you are a guest. As a guest, it is your responsibility to graciously accept your family's customs, as well as their hospitality.

Utilities are expensive in Japan, so some host families get upset if their homestay students take multiple showers a day or use large amounts of electricity. Especially since the Tōhoku earthquake, the Japanese are trying hard to conserve natural resources and electricity.

In Japan, people shower and wash themselves before entering the bathtub. (The shower is separate from the bath in most homes.) Japanese families often reuse the bath water for the entire family. When you enter the bathing area, if you see a bath full of water, don't pull the plug!

Some American college students may have difficulty adjusting to the family's *mongen* 門限 , or "curfew." Most families will not approve of you going in and out of the house whenever you choose. (Unless you are a man.) You will have to ask permission before inviting a female friend home—and don't even think about bringing guys over. Trains in Japan stop at midnight, so don't plan on late night partying unless your family is okay with you spending the night elsewhere.

What To Do If You Want to Leave

Once you are placed in a homestay family, you should try to enjoy and make the most of the homestay experience. You might not like your family's curfew, or your homestay brother might keep his music too loud, but unless there's a serious safety or personal health issue, you should try—both for your sake and for the sake of the homestay family that volunteered to host you—to try and work it out.

Many "problems" will resolve themselves once you and the homestay family get better acquainted. That being said, if you feel unsafe in your homestay, contact your coordinator immediately. Your coordinator will mediate a solution for you and your homestay family.

Before your homestay begins, research the hotel closest to your homestay family's address. Keep this information handy, just in case, and make sure your (real) family also has a copy of this information. This is information you will most likely never have to use, except to ease the worries of your (real) parents.

Wild Card

The most important factor that determines the success of a homestay is the homestay family itself. An exchange student's positive attitude, openness to new experiences, and ability to communicate can improve any homestay experience. Ultimately, however the success of the homestay depends on the personality and effort of the homestay family.

Dorm or Homestay Quiz

Should you stay in a dorm or in a homestay? Take the quiz below to find out!

1) How do you like to relax in the evening?

   a. Watching TV or hanging out with friends. (1 pts.)

   b. I like quiet time and just want to chill or surf the Internet at the end of the day. (3 pts.)

   c. Partying! I am a night owl and want as much nightlife as possible. (8 pts.)

2) Which of the following most describes your eating preferences?

   a. I'm an adventurous eater. I like to try new foods. (1 pt.)

   b. I like to try new foods every now and then. (3 pts.)

   c. I have a strict diet. I have to eat ABC every day, or I'm deathly allergic to DEF. (10 pts.)

3) How much privacy do you need?

   a. As long as I have my own room, I'm fine. (1 pt.)

   b. At least an hour or so a day, just to decompress and relax. (3 pts.)

   c. I like to have at least a few hours of solitary peace and quiet every day. (8 pts.)

4) How much Japanese do you speak?

   a. I've never studied Japanese. I hope I will know at least one person who speaks English. (8 pts.)

   b. I've never studied Japanese before, but I'm excited to learn. (3 pts.)

   c. I can have basic or advanced conversations in Japanese. (1 pt.)

5) Which is your #1 priority during your stay in Japan?

   a. I want to have fun, learn about Japanese culture, and practice my Japanese. (2 pts.)

  b.   My only goal is to practice my Japanese. (1 pt.)

  c.   I want to explore new places in Japan on my own or with a few friends. (5 pts.)

6) How long does it take you to get ready in the morning?

  a.   I can get ready in under an hour. (2 pts.)

  b.   I need at least an hour of mirror time before I go out. (4 pts.)

7) My parents freak out if I don't call or email every day.

  a.   Yes (10 pts.)

  b.   As long as I call them once a week or so, they'll be fine. (2 pts.)

  c.   No (1 pts.)

8) I like being around kids.

  a.   Yes (1 pt.)

  b.   Sometimes (3 pts.)

  c.   No (20 pts.)

10-20 points = You are well-suited for staying in a homestay family.

21-39 points = You can be comfortable in either a homestay or a dorm. Lucky you!

40-55 points = You would thrive best in a dorm.

> You can have a great time in Japan whether you are in a homestay family or a dorm. If you are positive and proactive, you will be able to make Japanese friends and improve your Japanese no matter where you choose

THE JLPT

The Japanese Language Proficiency Test (JLPT) is called the *Nihongo-nōryoku-shiken* 日本語能力試験 in Japanese.
<ruby>にほんごのうりょくしけん</ruby>

JLPT certification is a prerequisite for many paid positions and Japan-related opportunities. JLPT certification can enhance your resume, and enable you to place out of certain undergraduate Japanese courses.

Studying for the JLPT is not necessarily the best way to improve your Japanese, but if you want to work in Japan in a non-teaching position, JLPT Certification at the N1 (Fluent) or, in some cases, the N2 (Near-Fluent) level is often required.

Registering for the JLPT

First, read the instructions on the JLPT website (http://www.jlpt.jp/e) and decide which level is right for you.

Although most Japanese employers in non-teaching professions require foreign applicants to have at least an N1 or N2 level Japanese ability, the N3, N4, or N5 tests can be useful for personal assessment. N3, N4, or N5 level certification is not necessary, but may enhance your application for a job as an English teacher in Japan.

The JLPT is held biannually in July and in December. Many testing locations outside of Japan only offer the exam once a year. There are no retake dates, and registration is required six months in advance. You may take the test in Japan or overseas, but you cannot register overseas to take the exam in Japan (or vice versa).

Taking the JLPT in Japan

If you wish to take the test in Japan, the in-country section of the JLPT website provides a list of Japanese bookstores that sell application packets for about ¥500.

The cost of the application packet should not be confused with the test registration fee, which is ¥5500. Most large bookstores in Tokyo sell JLPT application packets, often located at the front register. Ask one of the bookstore's employees for assistance if you're not sure.

Follow the application packet's instructions (which are written in Japanese, English, and a few other languages) in the application guide. You'll need to send your application by certified mail, provide a residential mailing address, and submit two identification photos. (See "Work—Writing a Resume in Japanese" for details on what types of photos to use.) If you take the registration envelope and your completed forms to the post office, there are instructions written on the envelope for the postal worker on how to process your form, in case you're not sure what to do.

Taking the JLPT Overseas

If you wish to take the JLPT outside of Japan, check the available testing locations on the "List of Overseas Institutions." As of printing, the available American locations are Atlanta, Chicago, Fayetteville, Honolulu, Los Angeles, New York, Seattle, San Francisco, Philadelphia, Boston, and Washington, D.C.

Bring a non-digital watch, non-mechanical pencils, a photo I.D., and your registration information.

The length of the exam corresponds to the level of the exam, with the N5 exam totaling 105 minutes and the N1 exam lasting 170 minutes. Check the JLPT website for further details on the length, content, and pass/fail criteria of each level of the exam.

ESSENTIAL STUDYING RESOURCES

After years of studying Japanese, both in the classroom and on my own, these are the most helpful resources I've found for learning Japanese.

All Japanese, All the Time (http://ajatt.com)

This website is the ultimate resource for the dedicated learner of Japanese. It has numerous articles on language-learning tips, techniques, and methods of self-motivation. All Japanese, All the Time also provides links to Japanese websites and other useful studying tools.

Anki (http://ankiweb.net)

Anki is a fantastic Spaced Repetition System (SRS) that makes memorization easy and convenient. You can make your own digital flashcards, or download pre-made sets for free. The PC/Mac Anki software is free, but the smartphone apps are worth every cent. Loading Anki onto your phone turns idle moments into valuable review sessions. Anki is a must-have for language learners of all levels.

だいじりん
大辞林 Daijirin Dictionary App (https://itunes.apple.com/jp/app/da-ci-lin/id299029654?mt=8&ign-mpt=uo%3D4)

For advanced learners of Japanese, a monolingual dictionary can provide better and more detailed word definitions than most online English/Japanese dictionaries. This app condenses Daijirin's three volume, 2125 page dictionary into a convenient and excellent resource for advanced learners.

This app lets you look up words by the *hiragana* or *kanji* reading, and also offers different categories, such as "Names of People," "Names of Places," "Names of Animals," for faster reference. Daijirin's definitions are more in-depth than most online dictionaries, and you can tap on a word within a definition to look up another word. I highly recommend this app to those pursuing graduate or technical studies in Japanese.

Daijisen Dictionary (http://dic.yahoo.co.jp)

Daijisen 「大辞泉」 is a monolingual dictionary similar to Daijirin.
Daijisen is accessible for free through Yahoo Japan's dictionary service.
Just search using the 国語 feature.

Denshi Jisho (http://jisho.org)

This extensive online Japanese-English dictionary is easy to use. You can
search by *rōmaji*, *hiragana*, or *kanji*.

合格できる日本語能力試験
Gōkaku Dekiru Nihongo-nōryoku-shiken

This JLPT review series compiles practice grammar and reading
comprehension questions. It comes with two CDs for listening
comprehension practice. Like *Kanzen Master*, *Gōkaku Dekiru* does not
offer English translations.

Japanese (http://www.japaneseapp.com)

This extensive Japanese-English dictionary app and Anki are the only
iPhone apps you need to further your Japanese studies. In my opinion,
these two apps alone justify buying an iPhone. (These apps are also iPod
touch compatible and do not require internet access.) If you enable
Chinese-language character input on your iPhone, you can draw and
look up unknown *kanji* using this app.

Japanese Online Institute (JOI) (http://japonin.com)

JOI offers private and small group Japanese lessons online
via webcam. Whether you're in New York or Narita, JOI can
accommodate your schedule and learning style. JOI's group classes,
known as "Flex Lessons," range from absolute beginner to intensive
JLPT prep. Private tutors are available for consultation and can
customize lesson plans to suit your personal goals and schedule.
If you're not sure about private tutoring, you can try Flex Lessons
first. JOI offers many topics and times for Flex Lesson students.
Through group lessons, you can experience many different teaching
styles before committing to a private tutor. JOI is an excellent way
to improve and maintain your Japanese, especially for advanced
students looking to further their progress outside the traditional
classroom.

JGram (http://www.jgram.org)

If you need to quickly look up a Japanese grammatical structure, visit JGram. Each grammatical structure is organized by JLPT level and is accompanied by user-submitted practice sentences.

> **TIP**: Never rely 100% on Japanese sentences created by other language learners. When I'm looking for example sentences, I copy the grammatical structure and run a Google search to find Japanese sentences created by native speakers.

Jim Breen's WWWJIDC (http://www.edrdg.org/cgi-bin/wwwjdic/wwwjdic?1C)

Another fantastic online English-Japanese dictionary, especially for beginners and intermediate students. Many online English-Japanese dictionaries take their definitions from this source.

Kanji and Kana
Wolfgang Hadamitzky & Mark Spahn
Tuttle Language Library
ISBN: 978-0-8048-2077-6

This easy-to-navigate book contains all the kana and *jōyō kanji* 常用漢字 —the *kanji* you need to be considered literate—as well as their reading and stroke order. *Kanji and Kana* also lists the *jinmei-yō kanji* 人名用漢字 , which are used in Japanese names. This book is an indispensable *kanji*-learning resource, and a required text for many undergraduate Japanese courses.

Kanji Writer (http://japanese.nciku.com)

A *kanji* recognition website. Draw a *kanji* in Kanji Writer's "Handwriting Recognition" box to see its *hiragana* reading and English definition. This is a great tool for looking up unknown characters.

KeyholeTV (http://www.v2p.jp/video/english)

Keyhole TV is an easy, legal way to watch live Japanese TV on your computer at home. The resolution is not great, but the Keyhole TV download gives you live, free access to major Japanese television channels.

Natalia Doan

Lang-8 (http://lang-8.com)

This free online journal site can help you make Japanese friends and improve your Japanese writing skills. Write a journal entry in the language of your choice and have it corrected by a native speaker. Premium subscriptions give your account a variety of additional features, such as the ability to download PDF files of your corrections.

My Language Exchange (http://www.mylanguageexchange.com)

My Language Exchange can help you improve your conversational skills in any language. Find penpals and Skype conversation partners using this free service, which lets you refine your search by age, gender, location, and native language. Only Gold Members can initiate contact, but English speakers are enough in demand that, even with a free account, you should have no difficulty finding a partner. As always, proceed with caution when communicating with strangers online.

日本語総まとめシリーズ（語彙、漢字、文法、読解、聴解）
Nihongo Sōmatome Shirīzu (Goi, Kanji, Bunpō, Dokkai, Chōkai)

The *Nihongo Sōmatome* series works well as a training-for-the-test type of study aid. There is one book per level (N5 through N1) and per topic: Vocabulary (*Goi*), *Kanji*, Grammar (*Bunpō*), Reading Comprehension (*Dokkai*), and Listening Comprehension (*Chōkai*). Translations and definitions are provided in English, Chinese, and Korean.

Read the Kanji (http://readthekanji.com)

Read the Kanji boosts your reading vocabulary and *kanji* recognition using a system of color-coded flashcards and detailed statistics, which organize your progress by level of difficulty. Read the Kanji provides stroke order animations, detailed *kanji* readings, and a variety of customizable study settings. This is one of the easiest and most effective *kanji* studying tools I've used. Free trial access is available for the JLPT N5 and *hiragana/katakana* decks. Unlimited access subscriptions are $5 a month. Internet access required.

Rikai-chan (http://www.polarcloud.com/rikaichan)

Download the free Rikai-chan toolbar onto your Internet browser and simply scroll over any Japanese word to see the definition in English. Hit "C" and the word entry will be copied for easy transfer to a vocabulary list and/or Anki, or hit "S" to save it to a word entry file on your computer. Rikai-chan is an indispensable resource for anyone who regularly browses Japanese websites. Rikai-kun is a version of Rikai-chan for users of Google Chrome.

しんかんぜん
新完全マスター
Shin Kanzen Masutā

There is no official study guide for the JLPT, but many JLPT teachers and prospective test-takers rely on *Shin Kanzen Masutā*. There are five types of *Shin Kanzen Masutā* workbooks, one per topic for the N1 and N2 levels: Grammar, *Kanji*, Vocabulary, Listening Comprehension, and Reading Comprehension. These guides do not offer English translations. The *Bunpō* (Grammar) and *Dokkai* (Listening Comprehension) guides are essential, but you can study *kanji* and vocabulary without the aid of the *Shin Kanzen Masutā* series.

Doublecheck that you're buying Shin *Kanzen Masutā*, and not a regular edition of *Kanzen Masutā* published before 2010. (The character shin
しん
新 means "new.") The JLPT was modified in 2010 with the creation of the N3 intermediate level.

For the most up-to-date JLPT textbooks, visit Amazon Japan and type
にほんごのうりょくしけん
in your target level and 日本語能力試験 .

Space ALC (http://alc.co.jp)

This online Japanese/English dictionary is intended for native Japanese speakers, but can be a great translation tool for difficult, scientific, and/or technical terms. If you will be looking up Japanese words on an office computer, this is the dictionary I recommend, as many other online Japanese dictionaries have "Meet Asian Singles" ads in the sidebar.

Tagaini Jisho (http://www.tagaini.net)

Tagaini Jisho is a free, downloadable Japanese/English dictionary that should cover your basic word-lookup needs. Denshi Jisho is a better choice, especially if you're looking up slang terms, names, and/or verbs not in dictionary form, but Tagaini Jisho does not require Internet access. Tagaini Jisho is not my first-choice dictionary, but it is a helpful piece of software to have on your computer.

Tofugu (http://www.tofugu.com)

Tofugu is an English-language blog that features interesting articles about Japan and the process of learning Japanese. This website is a fun way to expand your knowledge of Japanese culture.

Zokugo Dictionary (http://zokugo-dict.com)

Zokugo 俗語 , or "slang," is an integral part of the Japanese language. If you come across an unfamiliar word, especially in *manga* (漫画、

Japanese comics) or *anime* アニメ , this Japanese-language website might help you find the definition.

CITING YOUR SOURCES IN JAPANESE

English Paper

Here is the MLA-approved method of citing Japanese language sources in an English paper:

Last Name, First Name. <u>Title of Book in Rōmaji [Translation in Brackets]</u>.
    City Published: Publishing Company, Year.

Last Name, First Name. "Title of Newspaper Article [Translation in
    Brackets]." <u>Name of the Newspaper [Translation in Brackets]</u>
    Date of Publication, edition name: Section in Newspaper.

Last Name, First Name. "Title of Magazine Article [Translation in
    Brackets]." <u>Name of Magazine [Translation in Brackets]</u> Date of
    Publication: Page Numbers.

Last Name, First Name. "Name of Article on Website in Rōmaji [Translation
    in Brackets]." <u>Title of the Internet Site</u>. Name of the Editor of the
    Site (if given). Date of electronic publication/last update. Date
    when the researcher accessed the source <URL of the source>.

For examples, please refer to the "Endnotes" chapter in the back of the book.

Japanese Paper

If you are writing a paper in Japanese, cite your sources in the following order.

(*Furigana* is provided in this example, but a normal citation should not include *furigana*.) The omission of punctuation is intentional.

Books

Last Name First Name (Year of Publication) 『Title』 Name of Publisher

Pages Referenced.

小島美津子（2012）『採用される履歴書職務経歴書はこう書く』日本実業出版社 10 pp.

Collections of Academic Papers, Magazines

Last Name First Name (Year of Publication)「Title of Article」『Title of Magazine』Volume Number (Year and Month of Magazine Publication) Pages Referenced. Publisher Name

綱島理友（2013）「綱島理友の物語：新ユニフォーム」『ベースボール週刊』Vol.3199（2013 年 10 月 12 日号）pp. 62. ベースボール・マガジン社

Newspapers

『Name of Newspaper』Date of Newspaper Article「Title of Newspaper Article」

『読売新聞』2013 年 8 月 27 日「オリジナル本の作成も」

Websites

Name of Website Creator「Name of Website」＜ Website Address ＞ (Date of Access)

土肥達磨寺「だるまの色について」＜ http://toi-daruma.jp/?mode=f2 ＞（2013/12/27 アクセス）

OUT AND ABOUT

Take every opportunity you can to enjoy and explore Japan, whether that means strolling around Shikoku or surveying the local supermarket:

BICYCLES AND TAXIS

In Japan, as in England, cars drive on the left side of the road.

Bicycles

Bicycling is an easy and cheap way to get around your hometown. Visit your local bike store, or search online for local Sayonara Sales to get the best deals.

> **TIP**: If you will be bicycling at night, buy a clip-on light attachment for your bike. You might be able to see without a light, but oncoming traffic might not be able to see you.

If you bicycle to work, a raincoat with a hood will protect you from the elements better than an umbrella. Screw-on umbrella holders (available and attached on-site at your local bike store) may jostle the umbrella when you pedal and might also block your vision.

> **TIP**: Keep your bicycle basket dry by covering it with a large garbage bag. Always carry a small plastic bag to cover your seat, in case you get caught in a sudden storm.

The "bike paths" you may see on the street are irrelevant; people and bicycles travel on both sides and in both directions. Buy a bell for your bike to avoid getting jostled.

Though bicycle parking is usually free and first-come-first-serve, some bike garages in high-traffic areas may have parking garages or meters. The meter will lock the bike in place. You will need to pay a small fee (usually ¥100-¥200) to retrieve your bike.

An example of bike parking in Shibuya, Tokyo.

Japanese mothers often bike their children to and from day care on bikes with child-friendly seats and baskets for groceries. These bikes are known as *mama-chari* ママチャリ , or "mama chariots."

The grooved yellow brick road you may see on the streets is a guide for blind people using canes.

Taxis

Unless you are going to a famous sightseeing location, it will help your driver if you can provide a Japanese address. Ask the concierge at your hotel or your homestay family to write out an address to give to your driver.

My first time in Tokyo, I was trying to go to the well-known conference facility and hotel "The International House of Roppongi." I brought the Japanese address, but the Tokyo taxi driver did not recognize the name of the hotel. This worried me. I tried translating the name of the hotel, but to no avail. It wasn't until we pulled into the parking lot that he said, in Japanese, "Oh, you meant the *Kokusai-Bunka-Kaikan!*" Lesson learned—the English name of a Japanese place might not be the same as the Japanese name! Bring both to ensure you arrive at your location on time and unstressed.

Japanese taxis can be expensive (fares usually start at ¥660), but most taxi drivers won't start the meter until they're sure they know where they're going.

TIP: Japanese taxis have doors that automatically open and close, so no need to shut the door behind you.

Most Japanese taxis will have a small tray in between the driver seat and the passenger seat. This is where you place your money when it comes time to pay.

Many, but not all, Japanese taxis accept credit cards.

THE METRO

Japan's rail system is clean, affordable, and convenient. Major stations provide English-language maps, but when in doubt, ask a station attendant for help.

Japanese Trains			
ふつうでんしゃ 普通電車	*Futsū-densha*	Local	Stops at Every Station
かくえきでんしゃ 各駅電車	*Kakueki-densha*		
かいそくでんしゃ 快速電車	*Kaisoku-densha*	Rapid	Stops at Selected Stations
きゅうこうでんしゃ 急行電車	*Kyūkō-densha*	Express	Stops at Fewer Stations than Rapid Trains
とっきゅうでんしゃ 特急電車	*Tokkyū-densha*	Limited Express	Major Stations Only

Japanese trains stop running around midnight. If you miss the last train, you will have to get either a taxi or a hotel room. Check your local train schedules on the English-language website **Hyperpedia** (http://www.hyperdia.com) before making plans.

If you or a friend will be visiting Japan, get a pre-loaded metro pass, such as ICOCA, Pasmo, or Suica. A preloaded pass will save time, money, and make your friend feel in the know! For a longer trip, apply for a **Japan Rail Pass** in advance. (See "Out and About—The Japan Rail Pass" for details.)

Some trains have swivel-around seats, which are great when traveling in groups. Look for seats with handle bars at the top, then press the foot pedal underneath the seat, and turn the seats so you can face each other during the ride.

Keep your metro pass in an easy-access location. Metro card wallets/pouches allow for easy scanning and are available in a variety of styles at any department store.

> **TIP**: Your school or company may provide a commuting pass, but get an ICOCA or SUICA pass, essentially a preloaded, reusable metro pass, for personal use. These passes eliminate the frantic coin-counting and

route tracking required for individual ticket purchases. Metro passes can be used like Edy electronic money in some stores. (See "Bills, Bills, Bills—Money" for details.)

If you're living in Tokyo, get an English-language metro map that lists the train stations in alphabetical order on the sidebar. These maps are free in major stations. Japanese daily planners often have subway maps of all the major Japanese systems, but the small typeface can make looking up stations difficult. Even if you can read Japanese, it can take some time to figure out where you want to go, especially since the Tokyo subway system links over 100 stations. Keep an English map with you for easy station lookup.

There is no such thing as "maximum capacity" on Japanese trains. If you're commuting during rush hour in Tokyo, prepare yourself for the "people pushers." These gloved station employees ensure that all appendages are safely in the train car before the doors close.

> **TIP**: If you want to listen to music on the train during rush hour, insert your headphones before boarding the train. Once you enter the train, you might have no space to lift your arms.

Girls-only cars operate during rush hour in an effort to alleviate the problem of groping, known as *chikan* 痴漢 . These cars are usually designated by bright pink signs.

> **TIP**: New Japanese cameras and camera phones are required to make a noise before taking a picture.

Japanese trains have special seats, called *yūsen-seki* 優先席 , for the elderly, handicapped, and pregnant. Do not sit in those seats when the train is full.

> **ETIQUETTE TIP**: If you offer your seat to a Japanese person on the train, that person may politely refuse. This does not necessarily mean they are uninterested in the seat. If the person refuses more than three times, it is possible that they prefer to stand. Otherwise, insist!

> **ETIQUETTE TIP**: Keep your bag on your lap or the floor of the train, not on the seat beside you, to make room for others to sit.

Japanese train stations have coin lockers where you can pay a nominal fee (usually ¥100—¥300) to store your baggage safely while you walk around. Coin lockers in train stations near sightseeing areas, like Shibuya, tend to fill up quickly, so plan ahead if you will be toting heavy luggage.

If you lose something on the metro, report it to the station attendant as soon as possible. There is actually a high likelihood that your lost item will be returned to you.

> **NOTE**: Umbrellas are the most commonly lost (and least reclaimed) items in Japanese train stations. Lost and Found stores these abandoned umbrellas, just in case. In 2002, over 330,000 umbrellas were lost and left in Tokyo metro stations.

Many train stations and sightseeing locations leave out an inkpad and special stamp for visitors to stamp their journals. *Kinen-sutanpu* 記念スタンプ "memorial stamps" and *kankō-sutanpu* 観光スタンプ, "sightseeing stamps," are especially popular with children. Carry a journal to keep a record of the places you've been!

Eating and drinking are not allowed on the metro, but feel free to bring refreshments on longer-route trains, such as the Shinkansen.

THE SHINKANSEN

The Shinkansen 新幹線 is the Japanese bullet train.

The Shinkansen				
Nozomi	のぞみ	Express	Major Station Stops Only	Approx. 2½ hours from Tokyo to Osaka
Hikari	ひかり	Semi-Local	Major Station Stops Some Smaller Stations	Approx. 3 hours from Tokyo to Osaka
Kodama	こだま	Local	All Stops	Approx. 4 hours from Tokyo to Osaka

There are three types of Shinkansen cars: Nozomi, Hikari, and Kodama.

Nozomi cars are the fastest and most expensive. Hikari trains are the next fastest, and stop at all major stations. Kodama trains stop at every station. Check with your local JR ticket booth for details.

There are three types of Shinkansen tickets:

Midori みどり Green Car—1st Class Seats

Shiteiseki 指定席 Reserved Seats

Jiyūseki 自由席 Non-Reserved Seats.

Non-Reserved Seats are the least expensive, but if you are traveling with cumbersome baggage, pay extra for a Reserved Seat. On heavy commuting days in a Non-Reserved car, you could wind up standing for the whole trip!

Although your tickets will normally be printed in Japanese, you can order tickets in English. Just ask the person at the counter for an English ticket: *Eigo-hyōki-no-kippu-de-onegaishimasu* 「英語表記の切符でお願いします。」

You might have to reserve tickets in advance (or wait an extra 30-40 minutes), but if you are traveling from Tokyo to Osaka, get a window seat on the right-hand side of the Shinkansen. You will be able to see Mt. Fuji. If you're traveling from Osaka to Tokyo, sit on the left-hand side to see Mt. Fuji.

When transferring from a JR line to the Shinkansen, give the person at the JR ticket booth your local ticket or ICOCA ticket pass. The station attendant will combine the fare charges so that you can walk through the gates using only your Shinkansen tickets.

When entering the train platform for the Shinkansen, insert both tickets into the ticket machine at the same time. Keep your tickets close, as you will need to present them to the train attendant if you booked a reserved seat. When leaving the train station, insert both tickets into the machine.

The Nozomi Shinkansen from Shin-Osaka to Tokyo (and back) has wireless Internet access, but it is not free. You have to buy a wireless plan in advance from a service provider, such as DoCoMo. DoCoMo offers two Shinkansen-accessible plans, one for ¥1500 a month or another plan for ¥500 each time you use the wireless service. Don't forget to close your account before leaving Japan. At this time, DoCoMo does not offer English-language support for this service.

On the Shinkansen Non-Reserved and Reserved Nozomi trains, there's one electric outlet per row. If you need power, snag a window seat to secure the outlet for yourself. It might be worth buying a Reserved ticket for a window seat, just in case.

TIP: You will need an adaptor if you want to use an American laptop. (The outlet is the Japanese two-prong style.)

Arrive at the platform at least ten minutes before boarding. When the Shinkansen timetable board says "Train Departs at 3:50 pm," what it means is that at 3:50 pm, the train will leave the station for its next destination.

If you have time before your train departs, buy a *bentō* lunch box for
your trip. Train station *bentō* are known as *eki-ben* 駅弁 <ruby>駅弁<rt>えきべん</rt></ruby>, and are available
throughout major stations. Eki-ben come in all different flavors and price
ranges, but pick one up before boarding the train. The kiosks in the main
area offer more variety than the mini-convenience stores on the platform,
and the Shinkansen snack cart only sells snacks and drinks.

When Japanese people travel, they often buy *omiyage* お土産 —souvenir
gifts, often small food items—for their coworkers and friends. Bringing
back *omiyage* will go a long way to fostering goodwill amongst your
coworkers, especially if you took time off work for your trip. In case you left
souvenir shopping to the last minute, *omiyage* shops sell a variety of edible,
individually-wrapped snacks in all major train stations and airports.

THE JAPAN RAIL PASS

The **Japan Rail Pass** (http://www.jrpass.com), often called the JR Pass, is a great value option for non-Japanese citizens who are visiting Japan. If you travel from Tokyo to Kyoto and back again even just once, the JR Pass makes up for itself in cost.

Available in 7-day, 14-day, and 21-day increments, the JR Rail Pass allows you unlimited use of any JR-operated train, including the Shinkansen, as well as local buses all over Japan.

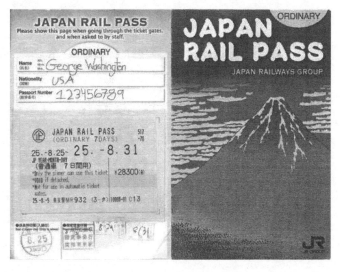

The JR Pass is available to foreigners who apply in advance, as long as they are entering Japan on a tourist visa.

> **NOTE**: You may not use the JR Pass to travel on the Nozomi (the fastest of the Shinkansen) or Mizuho (a limited-stop train between Shin-Osaka and Kagoshima) Shinkansen trains, but if you plan on extensive travel across Japan and don't mind spending an extra hour or two on the

train, the JR Pass is a great way to save money.

If you have specific travel plans and already know which Shinkansen trains you'd like to take, you can reserve all your tickets in advance.

TIP: Keep your JR Pass receipt. It may come in handy if you lose your JR Pass.

If You Lose Your JR Pass

Even if you have all your Shinkansen reservations preprinted in advance, few station attendants will let you slip through the gates after failing to present the required JR Pass.

You can try presenting your JR Pass receipt, but unfortunately, as indicated in the JR Pass Terms & Conditions, the JR Pass cannot be replaced if lost or stolen.

If you lose your JR Pass in a train station, report this loss to the nearest station attendant. There is a high likelihood that your JR Pass will be found, especially since the pass has your name on it. You will have to show your passport to reclaim your found JR Pass.

VISITING A JAPANESE TEMPLE OR SHRINE

Temple Etiquette

There are over 80,000 temples and shrines (*o-tera* お寺 and *jinja* 神社, respectively) in Japan.

Visiting a temple or shrine is not the same as attending church. As one of my Japanese friends likes to say, "Japanese people are born Buddhist, marry Christian, and die Shinto."

Some temples offer lodging, known as *shūkubō* 宿坊, and meals for respectful tourists. Visit **Koyasan** (http://eng.shukubo.net/index.html) a website sponsored by the Koyasana Tourist Association and Shukubo Temple Lodging Association, for more details and a list of temples that offer *shūkubō* lodging. Staying at a temple might not be cheaper than a hotel, but it will definitely be a unique experience. Guests are expected to respect the temple's rules and to abstain from photography during ritual meditation.

Temple & Shrine Etiquette

In case you get the chance to visit a Japanese temple or shrine, here's a quick introduction to proper temple/shrine etiquette.

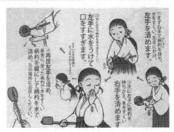

A helpful explanation of shrine etiquette displayed at Hōgyoku Inari Temple in Kumagaya

STEP ONE

Before you enter the temple, put your hands together and bow once.

STEP TWO

Temples and shrines have an area with water near the entrance. Purify yourself by grabbing the ladle, known as a *hishaku* ひしゃく, and pouring water over your left hand, then your right. You can also ladle water into your hands then use that water to rinse your mouth. Don't drink directly from the ladle or let water that has entered your ladle fall back into the main well.

STEP THREE

When you walk into the temple, there may be an area with incense and candles. If you'd like, you can buy one of these candles and light it along with your prayer.

Omikuji — Temple Fortunes

Japanese shrines offer *omikuji* 御神籤 , written paper fortunes, for about ¥500. Only the most popular sightseeing shrines have English translations, so here's a quick guide to the different levels of luck you may receive in your *omikuji*.

Omikuji Fortunes		
大吉	*Daikichi*	Excellent Luck
吉	*Kichi*	Good Luck
中吉	*Chūkichi*	Okay Luck
小吉	*Shōkichi*	A Little Luck
凶	*Kyō*	Bad Luck
大凶	*Daikyō*	Very Bad Luck

If your fortune is not favorable, tie your omikuji to the taut wire near the shrine. The wire is easily distinguishable by its rows of fluttering strips of white paper.

Omamori — Protective Charms

Omamori お守り , protective charms, make great souvenirs and are available at any shrine. *Omamori* can range from ¥500–¥1000, and are often used as cell phone straps.

You can purchase *omamori* for all sorts of protective powers—for test taking success, academic success (interesting how the two are separate), safe driving, romantic success, successful conception, and wealth, among others. Major Kyoto and Tokyo shrines may have signs in English explaining the *omamori*, but here's a quick guide, just in case.

Omamori Charms		
恋愛成就	*Renai-jōju*	Romantic Success
学業成就	*Gakugyō-jōju*	Academic Success
縁結び	*En-musubi*	Marriage
家内安全	*Kanai-anzen*	Safety of One's Family Peace and Prosperity in the Home
安産	*Anzan*	Safe and Successful Childbirth
子宝	*Ko-dakara*	Children
厄除け	*Yaku-yoke*	Warding Off Evil
商売繁盛	*Shōbai-hanjō*	Business Success
交通安全	*Kōtsū-anzen*	Safety while Driving

At the beginning of the year, bring your old *omamori* back to the temple to be burned. If you can't make it back to the temple, burn the *omamori* (safely) at home—don't throw it in the trash!

Ema—Wishes for the Future

Ema 絵馬 are small wooden plaques upon which people write their wishes and hopes for the futures. *Ema* are left hanging near the temple, where the gods will listen and grant the requests.

Many people write ema for test-taking success, romantic happiness, and for the health of their loved ones.

TOKYO SHORT GUIDE

Tokyo. It's the capital of Japan and famous for its fashion, fast-paced life, and blend of foreign culture and Japanese tradition. Just like how most of America is not like New York City, nowhere in Japan is quite like Tokyo.

I strongly recommend purchasing city-specific guidebooks, especially if you plan to visit Tokyo or Kyoto.

The DK Eyewitness *Travel Guide* provides full color, detailed illustrations and information on all of Japan's major sightseeing spots. If you can only purchase one guide to major sight-seeing spots, I would recommend this one, especially since this book is the most portable Japan travel guide available.

The *Lonely Planet* and *Rough Guides* to Japan tend to focus on budget travelers, but they are both good resources for those spending extended time in Japan.

If you can read Japanese, a Japanese-language travel guide (available in all Japanese bookstores, and many convenience stores) will introduce you to all sorts of places off the foreign tourist radar, just check online before making concrete plans.

A Tokyo-specific guidebook will provide more details on what to see and do in Japan's capital, but here's a quick look at some Tokyo Must-Sees.

Akihabara 秋葉原

Akihabara is famous as the *otaku* お宅 , or "nerd" mecca of Japan. Arcades, anime stores, and maid cafés surround the station. There are actually a few train stations labeled "Akihabara," but if you want to get straight to the heart of Akihabara, take the JR line to the Akihabara Electric Town exit.

The **Yodobayashi Camera** (http://www.yodobashi.com) in Akihabara has floors and floors of electronics, as well as a basement-level post office where you can ship your purchases domestically or internationally.

TIP: Longing for hot pretzels and the flavors of home? Visit the **Auntie Anne's** (http://www.auntieannes.jp/main.html) at Tokyo Metro Exit 5 of Akihabara Station. (There is a five pretzel limit per person.)

The **Gundam Café** (http://g-cafe.jp), a tribute to the "world of Gundam," is located directly outside of JR Akihabara Station and an interesting stop for fans of the Gundam Series. Next door is the world-famous **AKB48 Theater** (http://www.akb48.co.jp/theater), which features a rotating performance of members of Japan's chart-topping girl group, AKB48. Reservations are required, but the gift shop is open to the public.

> Anime-lovers across the world have embraced the word *otaku*, which literally means "in the house," as a stamp of pride. In Japan, however, being an *otaku* is not cute or trendy. The stereotypical *otaku* eschews modern hygiene, sleeps at night with a pillow in the shape of his (and *otaku* are almost always male) favorite anime character, and waits in line to order custom figurines of scantily-clad high school girls from popular anime. An *otaku* has limited social skills and spends most of his free time playing video games. While there's certainly nothing wrong with being an an anime aficionado, don't call someone an *otaku* unless you are close friends.

Densha Otoko 「電車男」, literally "Train Man," is a romantic comedy based on the true story of a shy but brave *otaku* who falls in love with a beautiful, non-*otaku* girl he defends on a train. With the support of his online *otaku* community, he sets out to woo the girl of his dreams and improve himself in the process. The movie is a one-of-a-kind romantic comedy available with English subtitles. *Densha Otoko* was also made into a TV show.

A *hikikomori* 引き篭もり, which literally translates as "pulling inside", is someone, usually a teenager, who withdraws into his/her room and does not leave the house. *Hikkikomori* give up on school, jobs, and social relationships. Some teenagers become *hikkikomori* after social or academic problems at school. The recent rise in *hikikomori* cases has become a problem for Japan.

Ghibli Museum 三鷹の森ジブリ美術館 *Mitaka-no-mori-jiburi-bijūtsukan* (http://www.ghibli-museum.jp/en/info)

This museum is a must-see for fans of *Totoro*, Spirited Away, and any other Studio Ghibli productions. The museum only allows a certain number of people inside each day. Reserve tickets (¥1000 each) in advance for a specific date and time.

> **TIP**: You can purchase tickets while still in the U.S. through the JTB website (http://www.jtbusa.com/en/other/o-ghibli.asp).

> **TIP**: Visit the **Lawson** website (http://www.lawson.co.jp/ghibli/museum/ticket/english.html) for detailed English instructions on how to purchase Ghibli Museum tickets while in Japan.

Although no recording devices or cameras are allowed inside the museum, you can take pictures with a large Totoro plushie in front of the museum.

There is a charming café on the museum grounds for light snacks and ice cream.

Ginza 銀座

Ginza is famous as an upscale shopping district in Tokyo. There are lots of fantastic (and expensive) restaurants in this area.

If you love *tenpura* 天ぷら , battered and deep fried vegetables and seafood, treat yourself to a meal at **Ten-ichi** 天一 (http://www.tenichi.co.jp). Ten-ichi is one of the most well-renowned *tenpura* restaurants in the world. The *tenpura* at Ten-ichi is deliciously light and fresh, with each piece cooked á la carte for the customer. If one-at-a-time *tenpura* is not your style, Ten-ichi also sells set meals with *tenpura* that change depending on the season. (I personally always order a set meal, especially since you can always order extra pieces á la carte if you're still hungry.) Prices vary depending on location, but Ten-ichi is an excellent experience in luxury dining. The main branch is in Ginza, but there are multiple branches of Ten-ichi throughout Japan.

There is a Ten-ichi in the Tokyo branch of the **Imperial Hotel** (http://www.imperialhotel.co.jp/e/tokyo). This luxury hotel is excellently located— less than a five minute walk from Ginza station, which gives you a direct train to the popular sightseeing spots of **Asakusa**, **Shibuya**, and **Omotesandō**. It is also walking distance from the Imperial Gardens of the

Tokyo Imperial Palace
(http://sankan.kunaicho.go.jp/english/guide/koukyo.html).

Jimbōchō 神保町

Rare book lovers may enjoy the quiet neighborhood of **Jimbōchō**. If you're searching for a specific book, check the town's website in advance: http://jimbou.info (Japanese only).

Pokémon Center ポケモン・センター

Pokémon enthusiasts may wish to visit a **Pokémon Center** (http://www.pokemon.co.jp/gp/pokecen/about). If you bring your Japanese Pokémon game with you, you can unlock special events and Pokémon only available at the Pokémon Center. The recent Pokémon games are region-locked, meaning you can only play Japanese games on a Japanese console, but you can still battle and trade with other trainers in the center. There are currently Pokémon Centers located in Sapporo, Tokyo, Sendai, Yokohama, Nagoya, Osaka, and Fukuoka.

Sensō-ji 浅草寺

Tokyo's most impressive Buddhist temple is located on the **Asakusa** stop of the Tokyo Metro Ginza Line. The road leading up to the shrine is packed with souvenirs. (Restaurants around the station tend to be overpriced, but street stalls leading the way to **Sensō-ji** sell all sorts of traditional Japanese sweets and street food.)

A *daruma* だるま is a red, wish-making figurine that you can buy at temples. All different kinds of daruma are sold in the stalls leading up to Sensō-ji. When you purchase a *daruma*, both eyes will be blank. Concentrate on your wish and color in the *daruma*'s left eye. When your wish comes true, draw in the other!

Daruma can only help with dreams that require effort and dedication on your part, such as passing an exam or becoming a world-famous pianist. If you want to win the lottery, you're better off praying at a shrine.

A traditional *daruma*

Daruma are traditionally red, but recently, some people, especially *daruma* manufacturers, believe that *daruma* can have different powers depending on their color.

Daruma Colors and Powers	
Red	Safety of One's Family Certain Victory
Orange	Generations of Prosperity
Yellow	Fame and Fortune
Green	Good Health Improvement at Sports
Blue	Success in Life
	Independence
	Promotion
Purple	Harmonious Relations with Others Spiritual Stability
Pink	Love
Silver	Change
	Continued Improvements
Gold	Winning 1st Place in a Competition
White	Passing Tests
	Success at School
	Longevity
	Safe Childbirth
Black	Protection from Disasters
	Getting "In the Black" Financially

Oedo Onsen Monogatari 大江戸温泉物語

A great bathhouse located in **Odaiba**, Tokyo. (Details in "Out and About: *Onsen*—Japanese Hot Springs" section.)

Roppongi 六本木

Roppongi is popular with foreigners. It is famous for its nightlife, which can, occasionally, be dangerous. Some bars in Roppongi only accept cash.

Roppongi Hills 六本木ヒルズ *Roppongi Hiruzu*
(http://www.roppongihills.com)

Roppongi's most famous
shopping center. Easily identified
by the large spider statue nearby,
known as "Maman." Roppongi
Hills has a movie theater, lots
of gourmet cafés and boutiques,
and a sky view observation deck
(accessible for ¥1500). Admission
to the observation deck also
includesadmission to the **Mori Art Museum**.

The Mori Art Museum 森美術館 Mori-bijutsukan
(http://www.mori.art.museum/eng)

This art museum features rotating exhibits of modern art.

Shinjuku 新宿

Shinjuku boasts many amazing restaurants, as well as perhaps Tokyo's
most concentrated nightlife scene. Keep alert in this entertainment district,
especially around **Kabuki-chō** 歌舞伎町.

Shibuya 渋谷

Shibuya is Tokyo's trendiest shopping district, like Japan's equivalent of
Times Square.

Shibuya 109 is the symbol of Shibuya and the department store of choice
for many Japanese teenage girls. Known affectionately as *Ichi-maru-kyū*,
literally "one, zero, nine" １０９. **Shibuya 109** is immediately visible
upon exiting Shibuya Station on the Hachiko Exit side.

TIP: If your Softbank phone runs out of batteries, the Softbank store in
Shibuya has adaptors you can use to charge your phone for free.

TIP: Nothing tastes quite like a **Krispy Kreme** (http://krispykreme.jp/
index.html), and fortunately for donut-lovers everywhere, Krispy Kreme
branches are expanding across Japan. There's one with comfy booths
near the Shibuya train station.

Shibuya is packed with all sorts of shops, restaurants, and karaoke places. Shibuya is about a thirty minute walk from **Omotesandō** 表参道, a popular date destination for the upwardly mobile. Omotesandō is the Champs-Élysées of Japan, and is immediately recognizable by the designer stores and expensive restaurants that line the streets.

Between Omotesandō and Shibuya is **Harajuku** 原宿, an area famous for the teenagers who flock to it and the unusual clothes they wear. There are lots of crepe stalls and fast-food places in the Harajuku area, as well as **Maisen** (http://mai-sen.com), the flagship restaurant of one of Japan's most famous chains specializing in *ton-katsu* 豚カツ, fried pork cutlet. Maisen products are often available in the bottom-floor food section of department stores.

If you're already in the Omotesandō/Harajuku area, stop by the **Design Festa Gallery** (www.designfestagallery.com). It's a small art gallery that features a rotating exhibit of independent artists. Entrance is free, though the artists' works are all on sale, in case you see something you like. This gallery is a great stop and conversation starter if you are on a date. There's a café and an *okonomiyaki* restaurant in the back. (For more details on *okonomiyaki*, see the following chapter, "**Osaka Short Guide**.")

Tōgō Shrine 東郷神社 *Tōgō-jinja* (http://www.togojinja.jp) is a quiet place of serenity in the otherwise bustling Harajuku area. There's a koi pond, a little bridge, and a relaxing view.

Sumida-Gawa River Cruise 東京都観光汽船 *Tōkyō-to-Kankō-Kisen*

Don't let jetlag slow your sightseeing. Take a waterbus down the Sumida River, known as the *Sumida-gawa* 隅田川, for a relaxing and inexpensive view of Tokyo. There are multiple options, the most popular being the Sumida River Line and the Asakusa-Odaiba direct line. A leisurely cruise is a great activity for the somewhat fatigued sightseer. Visit **Tokyo Cruise Ship** (http://www.suijobus.co.jp) for more details.

Tokyo Imperial Palace 皇居 *Kōkyo*
(http://sankan.kunaicho.go.jp/english/guide/koukyo.html)

The **Tokyo Imperial Palace** is surrounded by large, park-like grounds, and is about a fifteen minute walk from Tokyo Station. Strolling the grounds can be a relaxing way to end the afternoon. If you would like a tour, you will need to apply in advance.

Tsukiji 築地

Tsukiji is famous for the **Tsukiji Fish Market** 築地市場 *Tsukiji-Ichiba* (http://www.tsukiji-market.or.jp), where you can see all sorts of fish and marine life for sale. Stop by the market and its surrounding restaurants before 8 am for some of the freshest *sushi* in Tokyo.

> **TIP**: If you decide to buy a fish from the market, keep in mind that the vendors do not provide ice for off-the-street purchases. You'll have to carry the fish with you in the plastic bag the stall provides, so get your fish to a refrigerator as soon as possible.

> **TIP**: Fish are charged by the kilogram, so the fish you see may cost more than the price listed.

Yoyogi Park 代々木公園 *Yoyogi-kōen*

Many Tokyoites go to **Yoyogi Park** to escape the hustle of urban life. You may bring alcohol—and many picnic groups do—but take your garbage with you when you leave. On the weekends, vendors sell snow cones and *yakisoba* 焼きそば , fried noodles, around the entrance.

OSAKA SHORT GUIDE

> "*Kyō-no-kidaore, Ōsaka-no-kuidaore.*"
> 「京の着倒れ、大阪の食い倒れ」
> "Kyotoites go broke spending all their money
> on *kimono*, Osakans spend it all on food."

Tokyo has 160,000+ restaurants (compared to New York City's 23,000+), but although Tokyo beats out the rest of Japan in terms of quantity, Osaka is considered by many to be Japan's culinary capital.

Osaka is, personally, my favorite Japanese city. It's not as traditional as Kyoto or as modern as Tokyo, but the people are friendly, the food is fantastic, and there is always a lot to do.

Dōtonbori/Namba 道頓堀・難波

Leave from Subway Exit #14 (of the public subway, not the JR Line), and you'll be smack-dab in **Dōtonbori**, the center of Osakan nightlife. This long stretch of covered shopping and dining can provide hours of entertainment. There's always something interesting going on in **Namba**—whether it's an impromptu Celtic street performance or a bunch of pro-wrestlers shouting down the streets. If you're living in Osaka, Namba at night is an absolute must. Around the Dōtonbori Bridge (*Dōtonbori-bashi*, 道頓堀橋), you can see two famous symbols of Osaka—the flagship branch of the Dancing Crab Restaurant, **Kani Dōraku** 「かに 道楽」 (http://douraku.co.jp), and the Glico "Running Man" sign.

Kani Dōraku is easily recognized by the large moving crab sign above its front door. You can order from the set menu or à la carte. Nearly every dish in the restaurant contains crab. The Japanese menu is full

The flagship Kani Dōraku's storefront sign.

of glossy pictures, so this is a great place to eat, even if you don't speak Japanese. The staff here are accustomed to serving foreigners and often have English menus available. The Japanese menu is more frequently updated and full of glossy pictures. Kani Dōraku is a great place to eat, even if you don't speak Japanese.

If you walk far enough, Namba, Dōtonbori, and Shinsaibashi 心斎橋 merge into one another. The shopping and restaurants in these areas are some of Osaka's best. The streets are packed at night, especially on the weekends.

Okonomiyaki—Osaka's Specialty

Different regions of Japan often have different accents. For example, an Osakan may have a completely different accent than a Tokyoite. Different regions of Japan also have regional specialities or famous dishes, known as *mei-butsu* 名物.

One of Osaka's *mei-butsu* is *okonomiyaki* お好み焼き. *Okonomiyaki* is a fried mixture of egg, cabbage, and whatever meat toppings (often shrimp, squid, and/or beef) you desire, covered in a delicious sweet and salty sauce.

Though popular all across Japan, *okonomiyaki* and *takoyaki* たこ焼き are Osakan specialties. *Takoyaki* is an octopus dumpling/biscuit, served with mayonnaise and *katsuobushi* 鰹節, the flakes of a smoked skipjack tuna.

Okonomiyaki may sound strange, but it is delicious and fun. Choose your ingredients, mix the batter, and fry on both sides, then drench in sauce and serve.

Host Clubs ホストクラブ *Hosuto-kurabu*

There are clubs in Japan called "host clubs" where women pay to get flattered and served alcoholic drinks by attractive Japanese men.

A Japanese host club's ranking list of its top-ranked hosts.

See those guys in Namba with chunky belts and flat-ironed hair trying to pick up girls (an act, coincidentally, called *nanpa* ナンパ). Those are the newbie hosts, assigned the difficult task of recruiting customers off the street and leading them back to the club. When the women arrive at the club, they are presented with a photo album of the club's hosts. Once you choose a host, he will be your host for the rest of the evening and any future visits to the club. There are certain events, like the "champagne call" (*shanpan-kōru* シャンパンコール), in which you order a few bottles of expensive champagne and all the hosts gather to your table. Otherwise, there's no "host-hopping" allowed. If you tire of your host, you will have to find a new club. A night at a host club can cost upwards of $200, with some patrons spending as much as $1000 (or more) in one night.

There's presumably no sex involved, but many girls return to the host club multiple times in hopes of eventually becoming the girlfriend of their favorite host. As a host from Kobe told Time magazine, "If [women] just wanted a drink, they could go to a liquor store. If they wanted sex, they could call a gigolo. What they want and we provide is caring. Kindness. The knowledge that someone is thinking of them."

If you're interested in learning more about host clubs and their patrons, there's an excellent English-subbed documentary about the life of hosts called "The Great Happiness Space."

There's also a popular and delightfully unrealistic manga and anime series called "Ouran High School Host Club," *Ouran Kōkō Hosutobu* 「桜蘭高校ホスト部」, which has also generated a live-action drama, CDs, and even a video game.

Hostess Clubs ホステス・クラブ *Hosutesu-kurabu*

Hostess clubs are the female-version of host clubs. They are also known as キャバクラ *kyabakura*, short for "cabaret clubs."

Though the offered services differ, the basic concept is the same: hostesses smile, flirt, and entertain their clients for a set fee. Hostesses, also known as *kyaba-jo* キャバ女 , earn commission on the number of drinks and reservations they can sell.

Like working at a host club, being a hostess is not without its dangers. Besides the physical risk of excessive alcohol consumption, there are numerous horror stories of both foreign and Japanese hostesses who are mistreated and/or physically harmed by overzealous clients.

Osaka Castle 大阪城 *Osaka-jō*

Osaka Castle (http://www.osakacastle.net) is a must-see if you're in Osaka. The museum is almost entirely in Japanese, but English brochures are available. Bring your camera for the view from the top.

> **TIP**: As dear as Osaka is to my heart, if you can only see one Japanese castle, make it **Himeji Castle** 姫路城 *Himeji-jō* (http://www.himeji-castle.gr.jp/index/English). Himeji Castle is perhaps the most famous and awe-inspiring of all Japanese castles, and is a UNESCO World Heritage Site. **Himeji** 姫路 is approximately an hour from Osaka by Rapid Service train.

Osaka Aquarium 大阪海遊館 *Osaka-Kaiyūkan*

The **Osaka Aquarium** (http://www.kaiyukan.com/language/eng/index.htm) is one of the largest aquariums in the world, and is famous as one of Japan's best. The aquarium offers a free listening tour (Japanese only) that can be accessed on your Japanese DSi.

NOTE: Most exhibits in Japanese museums do not have English descriptions.

The Osaka Aquarium has many claims to fame, one of which is being the first place in the world to successfully exhibit the Spinetail Mobula. The Spinetail Mobula, or *itomakiei* イトマキエイ, is a large stingray native to Japan that can grow to sizes of over eight feet. Also make sure you see Osaka Aquarium's Whale Shark.

The aquarium can be a nice daytrip if you live in Osaka. There's a shopping center with a food court only a five minute walk from the aquarium, in case you get hungry. Like many aquariums, Osaka Aquarium has an excellent gift shop.

Takarazuka 宝塚

Takarazuka (http://kageki.hankyu.co.jp) is a form of all-women's musical theatre unique to Japan. Women perform all the roles in these fantastic, sequin-studded musicals. Takarazuka plays are often adapted from Western books and plays, as well as from Japanese legends, *manga*, and video games. Examples of past musical performances include F. Scott Fitzgerald's *The Great Gatsby*, Oscar Wilde's *The icture of Dorian Gray*, Shakespeare's *Romeo and Juliet, Casablanca, Sabrina*, and Charles Dickens' *Great Expectations, and Oklahoma!*.

Takurazuka Ongaku Gakkō 宝塚音楽学校 ("Takarazuka Music School") (http://www.tms.ac.jp) prepares some of Japan's most talented young women for a life on the stage, with classes in acting, ballet, traditional Japanese dance, modern dance, voice, piano, and chorus.

Anyone who wants to be in the Takarazuka Company must attend this school. Auditions are rigorous, with only forty openings a year. Only girls with "attractive face and figure" between the ages of fifteen and eighteen can apply. There are two types of Takarazuka actresses—*otoko-yaku* 男役 ("men's part") and *musume-yaku* 娘役 ("girl's part"). Otoko-yaku generally have more fans and are the true stars of Takarazuka.

As in the professional Takarazuka company, you are either an otoko-yaku or a musume-yaku; there is no switching back and forth.

If you're in Osaka (where the Takarazuka theatre is based) or in Tokyo, I highly recommend seeing a Takarazuka performance. Even if you can't understand Japanese, the costumes alone make the trip worthwhile. Daily performances occur at 11 am and 3 pm. Book tickets well in advance.

Nara Park 奈良公園 *Nara-kōen*

Nara is less than an hour from Osaka, and a fantastic place for a day trip. The official mascot of Nara is "Sento-kun" せんとくん.

Deer are the unofficial mascots of Nara. You will find deer-themed goods, as well as actual deer, throughout Nara, and especially in Nara Park. Legend has it that long ago, one of the Japanese gods descended to Earth and a deer offered himself as transportation. Since then, the deer of Nara are protected spiritual symbols and favorites of the gods.

TIP: Wear pants—sometimes the deer bite!

The temples and shrines of Nara collectively form a UNESCO World Heritage Site. While

Sento-kun waits to greet guests at Nara Station.

you're in Nara Park, stop by the famous Great Buddha, known as the *Daibutsu* 大仏 at the Buddhist temple **Tōdai-ji** 東大寺. Tōdai-ji's Great Buddha Hall is the largest wooden building in the world.

TIP: While in the Great Buddha Hall, try to squeeze your way through the hole in one of the support pillars. According to local legend, if you can wiggle yourself through, you are guaranteed a spot in heaven!

KYOTO SHORT GUIDE

No visit to Japan, however short, is complete without a trip to Kyoto. The longer you live in Japan, the more often people will ask if you've ever been to Kyoto. It's like living in New Jersey and having never been to New York. The list of Must-Sees in Kyoto is long, so I recommend purchasing a guidebook for Kyoto.

I also recommend, at least for your first trip to Kyoto, joining a tour bus or sightseeing group that can provide reliable transportation to each temple/shrine on your itinerary. Navigating from place to place on your own can be frustrating and time-consuming.

There is a Tourist Information Center staffed with English speakers in JR Kyoto Station. This is a great place to stop in Kyoto to sign up for a tour and get sightseeing information. There is another Tourist Information Center inside Kyoto Station that mostly has maps and guidebooks. Either Tourist Information Center will be able to direct you to an English speaker who can help you make plans for your Kyoto sightseeing experience.

The City of Kyoto has made it a priority to preserve their cultural and historical heritage, thus all new businesses in historical districts must conform to the traditional look of the city.

Kiyomizu Temple 清水寺 *Kiyomizu-dera*
(http://www.kiyomizudera.or.jp)

Kiyomizu Temple is one of Kyoto's most famous temples, and is a Must See by itself, but romantics might want to stop by **Jishu Shrine** (http://www.jishujinja.or.jp), or *Jishu-jinja* 地主神社 on the way. Jishu Shrine is dedicated to the god of love and matchmaking. Many come to Jishu Shrine to pray for good luck in romantic endeavors. You can find many love-themed *o-mamori* for sale.

The Love Fortune Stones: There are two prominent stones in Jishu Shrine, known as the "Love Fortune Stones" or *Koi-uranai No Ishi* 恋 占

いの石<ruby>石<rt>いし</rt></ruby>. Walk from stone to stone with your eyes closed. If you make it to the opposite stone without opening your eyes, you will find true love. If someone helps you find the stone, you will need someone to help you find true love.

Wishes and Curses: Write your love troubles on one of the people-shaped pieces of paper, known as *Hitogata-barai* 人形祓い. After paying the ¥200 donation, drop your paper doll into the bucket of water and watch your concerns or curses melt away as they prepare to be granted.

How to Solve Your Love Troubles Using Paper Dolls

1. Fill out the paper doll as in the example shown. Pay the token offering to the gods.

2. Blow on the doll three times.

3. Place the doll into the water.

4. Go to the main shrine and pray. The god in this shrine works to prevent misfortune.

Fushimi Inari Shrine 伏見稲荷大社 *Fushimi Inari Taisha*

This shrine is another Kyoto Must See.

Although foxes are normally considered trickster spirits in Japanese culture, the foxes at **Fushimi Inari Shrine** are servants and messengers of Inari, the God of the Harvest. Many of the foxes have different expressions or different things in their mouths.

BALL
The ball in the fox's mouth symbolizes the spirits of the deceased.

GRAIN
The fox holding a head of rice symbolizes the prayers for a good harvest.

NOTHING
Some foxes don't hold anything! They are very special.

KEY
This fox holds the key to Inari's treasure.

SCROLL
This fox carries the scroll that holds the key to Inari's power. It is composed of divine virtues.

Torii Gates 鳥居

Perhaps one of the most iconic images of Kyoto, the *torii* gates at Fushimi Inari are as beautiful as they are breath-taking. The bright color of the over 10,000 *torii* gates is supposed to deflect magic and evil. Many companies sponsor a *torii* gate. Look on the opposite side of the gate for the business or benefactor's name (in Japanese) and the date the gate was donated.

Omokaru-Ishi 重軽石

Towards the end of the path, atop two pillars shaped like pagaodas, you will see two round stones, known as the "Heavy or Light Stones,"or *Omokaru Ishi*.

Look at the two stones and think of a wish or desire you have. Choose one of the stones and try to lift it up. The weight of the stone depends on your wish! If the stone is heavier than you imagined, it means your wish will not come true. If the stone is lighter than you thought, fortune will be in your favor.

Golden Pavilion 金閣寺 *Kinkaku-ji*

The **Golden Pavilion** is one of the most iconic symbols of Kyoto. This temple is completely covered in gold leaf, thus the name.

The formal name of this Zen Buddhist temple is *Rokuon-ji* 鹿苑寺 , literally "Deer Garden Temple," named in honor of "the Deer Park, or Magadaava, where Buddha gave his first sermon. The Golden Pavilion was originally built in 1397 as a villa for Yoshimitsu Ashikaga, the third shogun of the Ashikaga shogunate.

Unfortunately, the original Golden Pavilion was burned down in 1950, an event later fictionalized by Yukio Mishima in *The Temple of the Golden Pavilion*. The reconstruction was made in 1955, where it continues to awe and inspire its visitors.

Famous Kyoto Foods

Kaiseki-ryōri 会席料理 is a traditional type of Japanese cuisine that includes multiple courses. *Kaiseki-ryōri* usually consists of small samplings of different types of vegetables, pickles, *tenpura*, noodles, rice, fish, and includes a traditional Japanese dessert. Though *kaiseki-ryōri* is available in most Japanese cities, the traditional atmosphere of Kyoto makes the perfect backdrop for a traditional meal. Many *ryokan* in Kyoto serve especially delicious *kaiseki* meals in a traditional Japanese atmosphere. *Kaiseki* meals can often be arranged either in-room or in a larger dining area to accommodate big groups.

Kyoto is famous for its traditional Japanese sweets, known as *wagashi* 和菓子. *Wagashi* are often made with rice flour and *anko* 餡子, a type of sweet bean paste. *Wagashi* are a delicious and uniquely Japanese treat that can be purchased individually or enjoyed at a teahouse. I highly recommend trying *wagashi* while attending a Japanese tea ceremony. There are many teahouses in Kyoto that perform tea ceremony for the public—a quick inquiry at your hotel should point you towards the teahouse closest to you. (For more on tea ceremony, see "Culture and Language—Japanese Tea Ceremony.")

One famous Kyoto *wagashi* is *yatsuhashi* 八橋.

These small, taco-shaped Japanese sweets are made from rice flour, sugar, and cinnamon. *Yatsuhashi* are an acquired taste for some, but make great omiyage souvenirs for family and Japanese friends.

Kimono and *Yukata*

Kimono 着物 and *yukata* 浴衣 are types of traditional Japanese clothing.

Yukata are usually made of cotton, and are worn in the summer to casual events, such as festivals. *Kimono* are made of silk and worn on formal occasions, such as weddings and tea ceremonies. There are different types of *kimono* and *yukata* for men and women, and diifferent patterns and accessories depending on both the age of the wearer and the season.

All *kimono* are essentially the same size. Depending on the size of the person wearing the *kimono*, the length of the *kimono* can be adjusted using cloth ties called *koshi-himo* 腰紐 . The versatility and high quality of *kimono* allow a properly taken care of *kimono* to be passed down for generations.

For sample pictures of *yukata* and *kimono*, visit the online store **Yukata Kimono Market Sakura** (http://www.kimono-yukata-market.com). This website offers a variety of authentic *yukata* and vintage *kimono*, and ships internationally.

Many Japanese people enjoy wearing *kimono* or *yukata* when visiting Kyoto. If you would like to experience walking around Kyoto in a *kimono*, ask your hotel or search online for a company that offers *kimono* rental, or *kimono-rentaru* 着物レンタル . Rental *kimono* are also available for men and children. If you decide to wear *kimono* while sightseeing, budget a little extra time for your travel plans; it can be difficult to move quickly in a *kimono*. Most *kimono* rental companies also offer help putting the *kimono* on correctly as an additional service.

You will need a Japanese friend (or YouTube tutorial) to show you how to properly wear a *yukata* for the first time. If you would like to learn how to put on a *kimono* by yourself (which is more complicated), I recommend taking classes. Being able to properly dress yourself in *kimono* requires practice. If you are living in Japan, you can find a teacher online at **Shuminavi** (http://shuminavi.net), though most lessons do require advanced Japanese language ability.

Ladies, if you get a chance to wear a *kimono*, wear footless leggings and a camisole top underneath your *kimono*. The slimmer the silhouette, the more comfortable you will be in your bulky *kimono*. (If you are especially petite, you may need to use a hand towel underneath your *obi* to even out your lines.)

If you will be wearing a *kimono* during especially cold weather, you might want to rent or purchase a *haori* 羽織 jacket. *Haori* are specifically designed to be worn with *kimono*. However, if it is raining, a full-length raincoat will better protect the silk of your *kimono*.

If you decide to purchase a *kimono*, I highly recommend also buying a *kimono* bag, or *wasō-baggu* 和装バッグ . A full *kimono* set, including undergarments, the cloth ties, the socks, and all the little accessories that make wearing a *kimono* so much fun, is a significant purchase, and can take up a lot of space. *Kimono* require special preservation and should not be casually stuffed into a backpack or tote bag. A *kimono* bag makes transporting and storing your *kimono* much easier. A *kimono* bag can be found for around $35 online, and include special compartments for your *geta* and all the other pieces of a *kimono*.

Though you can find *yukata* in any price range, it's possible to get a complete *yukata* set—*tabi* 足袋 socks, the *koshi-himo* cloth ties, *obi*, and everything except the *geta* 下駄 shoes—for around $50. If you are in Japan and don't have the time (or inclination) to go *yukata* shopping, **Rakuten** (http://rakuten.jp) offers *yukata* sets at a range of prices.

The Book of Kimono: The Complete uide to Style and Wear, by Norio Yamanaka, is an excellent reference for those interested in the history and physical components of the *kimono*.

Geisha and Maiko

Geisha 芸者 are perhaps some of the most famous and misrepresented symbols of traditional Japan. Real *geisha* are skilled musicians, dancers, and conversationalists who train for many years before reaching *geisha* status. (The word *geisha* literally means "art person.") They are entertainers bound by a strict hierarchy and code of conduct. Unfortunately, the misrepresentation of *geisha* in the West is largely a result of the U.S. occupation of Japan after World War II. Many Japanese women pretending to be *geisha* would "entertain" the American soldiers, who would bring back tales of "the Japanese *geisha* girls" to their home country. True *geisha* are increasingly rare, but still embody the spirit of tradition and the city of Kyoto.

> For more information on *geisha*, I recommend the book *Geisha*, by Liza Dalby. This book provides unparalleled historical analysis and insight into the world of the *geisha*. Dalby trained as a *geisha*, and her research, insights, and personal experiences are both riveting and revealing.

The **Gion District** 祇園 in Kyoto was and is famous for its *geisha*, who refer to themselves as *geiko* 芸子 . You may see a few "*geisha*" while strolling during the day around Kyoto, but real *geisha* are usually seen only at night. *Geisha* are hired to entertain businessmen and politicians at parties, and are rarely seen in public during the day, except on special occasions. Attending a party with a *geisha* often requires money and/or connections.

There are many places in Kyoto that will, for a fee, dress you as a *maiko* 麻衣子 , an apprentice *geisha*. *Maiko* traditionally have brighter *kimono* and bigger hair accessories than *geisha*, which is why most women prefer to be dressed as *maiko*. (However, "*geisha* experiences"

A picture of the author on her first trip to Kyoto.

芸 者 体 験 are also available.)
<ruby>げいしゃたいけん</ruby>

   During a "*maiko* experience" or *maiko-taiken* 舞妓体験 (also known as
a *maiko-sutajio-satsuei* 舞妓スタジオ撮影), you will receive a professional
application of *maiko* makeup and a *maiko kimono* to wear during a
professional photo shoot.

   You can also walk around outside in your *maiko* attire for an additional
fee. The whole experience costs around $150, less or more depending on the
package you choose.

   The makeup application and photo shoot take at least an hour and a half,
and advance reservation is required. (Your hotel or inn can do this for you.)
"*Maiko* experience" photos make great souvenirs and postcards to send back
home.

ONSEN—JAPANESE HOT SPRINGS

Onsen 温泉 are communal bathing facilities located over geothermally heated hot springs.

Onsen trips are popular with Japanese and foreign tourists alike. Men and women's facilities are kept separate, as visitors enter the *onsen* completely naked.

> **NOTE**: Some *onsen* offer co-ed bathing facilities for couples and families to enjoy together, but these are rare. Co-ed *onsen* always provide body wraps or towels for people to wear while in the *onsen*, thus preventing accidental exposure. Wearing a swimsuit or other body covering is only appropriate if you are at a co-ed *onsen*. Otherwise, check your modesty at the door!

Depending on which *onsen* you visit, you may be the only foreigner present. Soaking in an *onsen* is a quintessential Japanese experience.

Many *onsen* locations also offer *sentō* 銭湯 , artificial, indoor "springs," or *roten-buro* 露天風呂 , outdoor *onsen* in which you can soak under the stars and enjoy the cool night air. Large *onsen* facilities may offer spa services and/

or overnight lodging.

Onsen Guidelines

These standard guidelines apply to *onsen* across Japan.

1. No tattoos!

Japanese gangsters—known as *yakuza* やくざ —are covered in tattoos, and instead of saying "no *yakuza* allowed," (although some places are that straightforward) the staff simply say "no tattoos" and thus avoid offending the yakuza.

You can probably get away with having a tattoo if the tattoo is small or if you are obviously non-Japanese. Keep your tattoo covered, just in case.

2. Change into a *yukata*

Upon entering the *onsen*, the person at the counter may give you a *yukata*, a light, cotton robe. (This *yukata* is not the same as the light, cotton *yukata* often worn in the summer, especially during festivals.) After getting your *yukata*, you will also choose an *obi*, the sash that keeps the *yukata* in place. Once you've chosen your *yukata* and your *obi*, the counter attendant will give you a large bath towel and a small washcloth.

> **NOTE**: Even if you are a man going to the men's *onsen*, the counter attendant may be a woman.

Small lockers will be provided for you to check your belongings.

Some *onsen*, especially small, local facilities, will not have *yukata*. Instead, check your belongings in a small locker and proceed straight to the showering area.

3. Shower before entering the *onsen*

Before entering the *onsen*, you must shower.

> **TIP**: The *onsen* will provide shampoo, conditioner, and soap. I recommend bringing deodorant from home. Hair dryers should be provided in the changing room.

> **TIP**: Ladies, don't bother applying makeup before or after going to an *onsen*. You have to be clean to enter the *onsen*, and post-soak, makeup

may clog your freshly-steamed pores.

Take the small washcloth with you into the *onsen*. The rest of your belongings should remain in your locker. (Women on TV sometimes enter the *onsen* completely wrapped in a bath towel, but this is only because they are on television.)

Ladies, please don't go into the *onsen* if you're having your period. If you are in a private *onsen* in a private room, that's fine, but if you are in a public facility, please be considerate of the other guests who have come to relax and feel clean. It might be okay if you have a light flow and thoroughly wash yourself beforehand (standard *onsen* procedure anyway). Some women wear tampons in the *onsen*, but many consider this poor form.

4. Enter the *onsen*

Relax, and enjoy!

> ### *Oedo Onsen Monogatari* 大江戸温泉物語
> English website: www.oom.cn
> Japanese website: www.ooedoonsen.jp

Though there are plenty of fantastic *onsen* in Japan, one of my favorites—*Oedo Onsen Monogatari*—is located in Odaiba 大台場 , less than an hour from Shibuya, Tokyo.

Want to have the *onsen* experience without having to get naked in front of a whole bunch of strangers? *Oedo Onsen Monogatari* offers many non-naked activities, along with a dining area and indoor performances that you can enjoy with friends. This *onsen* is also foreigner-friendly, with lots of signs and menus with pictures (though little English). Feel free to bring a camera, though obviously not in the bathing parts of the facility.

If you're a videogame lover, visit **Sega Joypolis** (http://tokyo-joypolis.com). This multiple-floor arcade has lots of games and exhibits, and is only a ten minute walk from *Oedo Onsen Monogatari*. On the opposite side is a shopping center in **Palette Town** (http://www.palette-town.com). Although there are currently no starter Pokémon available in Palette Town at this time, there are lots of restaurants and shops, as well as an open area for outdoor performances.

After checking in at the front desk, you get to choose a colorful *yukata*.

Don't worry, you keep your underwear on underneath, at least until you enter the baths.

You can easily spend three to four hours in this theme-park like *onsen*. They have hotel options in case you lose track of time, with separate "men only" lodgings available as well.

One way to get to *Oedo Onsen Monogatari*, take the JR Yamanote line from Shibuya to Osaki, then take the Rinkai Line to Tokyo Teleport Tower. From there, a free shuttle bus will take you to the bathhouse. There are many other ways to get there, so visit the *onsen*'s website for details.

Non-Naked *Onsen* Activities

(Additional Fee Required)

Doctor Fish Pedicure *Fisshu Serapi* フィッシュ・セラピー

Dip your feet into a pool of warm water and have the Doctor Fish nibble down your calluses. The fish only eat dead skin, but don't get a Doctor Fish pedicure if your feet have large blisters or cuts.

> **TIP**: This is more of a "foot bath" than a pedicure, so for best results, get a traditional pedicure before arriving. With the easy-to-sluff-off dead skin already removed, the fish will be able to work their magic.

Outdoor Foot Bath *Ashi-yu* 足湯

Leisurely relax outside with your feet in warm water—great for kids and large groups. No fee required.

Beauty Treatments *Esute* エステ

As at a regular spa, there are many beauty treatments available, including different types of facials and massages. Some massages, such as foot massages, are performed in a communal room, whereas other massages are performed in private. Make a reservation upon arrival to minimize potential waiting time.

Salt Stone Sauna *Ganen-yoku* 岩塩欲

Thirty minutes in the Salt Stone Sauna will open your pores and help your skin sweat out impurities. Change into the cloth *yukata* the sauna will provide. (This *yukata* is different from the brightly colored one provided upon entering the *onsen* facilities. You should not wear underwear while in this *yukata*.) The sauna attendants will give you a towel to lay, beach-style, atop the warm salt stones. You will be given a water bottle to keep yourself hydrated. Private showering facilities are available for use after the sauna treatment.

Sand Bath *Suna-buro* すなぶろ砂風呂

The Sand Bath is a great option for people who don't want to get wet. After changing into your Sand Bath *yukata*, you will be wrapped in blankets. Nestled inside this warm cocoon and with only your face exposed, you will be buried in hot sand and left to relax.

Remove your jewelry and any metal piercings before entering the Sand Bath. The sand gets hot!

The Sand Bath is a great option for people who don't want to get wet, although you may need to take a shower afterwards to rinse off the sand.

If you have long hair, pull it back before entering the Sand Bath. You may need to take a shower afterwards to rinse off the sand.

FOUR DAYS WITH MOM

Mom coming to visit you in Japan? Here is a sample four day itinerary.

Day One

Arrive at Narita Airport in the morning. Take your jetlagged mother to Tokyo for lots of walking to keep her awake. Stroll around **Asakusa** and see Sensō-ji. Take the Ginza Line directly to **Shibuya** for evening shopping and dinner. (Or visit **Akihabara** to shop for some high-tech electronics.)

Day Two

Have a quick breakfast and take the Shinkansen down to **Kyoto**. Sign up for a sightseeing tour and enjoy a full day of temples and shrines. Share a room in a *ryokan* 旅館 りょかん, a traditional Japanese inn. Eat a traditional dinner at the *ryokan*, then enjoy a late-night soak in an outdoor *onsen*.

Try the website **Japanese Guesthouses** (http://www.japaneseguesthouses.com) for clear photos and English explanations of various *ryokan* throughout Japan. This website lets you search for *ryokan* with *onsen*, and distinguishes between "standard *ryokan*," that are simple and almost more like hotels, "modern *ryokan*," that look like hotels on the outside, but look traditional inside, and "traditional *ryokan*," which pride themselves on their traditional, Japanese atmosphere.

> **NOTE**: Families and groups of friends usually rent one room when they visit a *ryokan*. Everyone in the group sleeps in the same room, on individual futon that the inn staff will roll out of the way during the day.

For an exquisite, luxury *ryokan* experience, I recommend **Tawaraya** 俵屋旅館 (http://www.kyoto-club.com/tomaru/rkn/tawaraya.html).

Tawaraya deserves its reputation as Japan's most famous *ryokan*, and has been run by the same family since the 1700s. The atmosphere is serene, the service is superb, and the food is spectacular. Tawaraya embodies the best of Kyoto. It is traditional, tranquil, and meticulously beautiful. Staying at Tawaraya is both a privilege and a pleasure. It may be difficult to make reservations, so plan in advance.

Bookings are available at **JAPANiCAN.com** (http://www.japanican.com/en/hotel/ detail/6232046/?pn=2&sn=2&rn=1&ref=TripadvisorMETAB16). JAPANiCAN (http://www.japanican.com) is run by the Japan Travel Bureau, and is a a great places to get hotel/train packages, sightseeing tours, and sumo tickets.

Day Three

While you're in **Kyoto**, sign up for a mother-daughter *maiko/geisha* photo session. After some last-minute sight-seeing, take an afternoon train to Osaka and walk around **Namba/Dōtonbori** at night. Have a late dinner at **Kani Dōraku**, the Dancing Crab Restaurant.

Day Four

See a **Takarazuka** performance in the morning. Visit **Osaka Castle** in the afternsoon and take the evening train back to **Tokyo**.

FOUR DAYS WITH DAD

Day One

Arrive at **Narita Airport**. Stroll around **Asakusa** (see **Sensō-ji**) and attend a baseball game at **Tokyo Dome** (http://www.tokyo-dome.co.jp/e) in the evening.

There is nothing in the world like a Japanese baseball game. Imagine Super Bowl-level excitement, except that each player on each team has his own, personalized "cheer song," which is sung every time he is up to bat. Some baseball stadiums charge different rates depending on which teams are playing. (Yomiuri Giants and Hanshin Tigers games sell out quickly.) Book in advance to score the best deals.

> **TIP**: For more information on baseball in Japan, read *You Gotta Have Wa* by Robert Whiting. His books capture the excitement and magic that is Japanese baseball.

Purchase tickets in advance. I recommend first researching which game you would like to attend online, then buying tickets at your local convenience store. (You use the same machine that also sells bus tickets and movie tickets, located near the ATM.) The menu will be entirely in Japanese, so if you come prepared with the date and time of the baseball game you would like to see, someone from behind the counter should be able to help you. A list of Giants games and times is available in Japanese at the **Yomiuri Giants**' official website (http://www.giants.jp/G/ticket). You could also ask your hotel for assistance, or go in person to the Tokyo Dome ticket booth a few days before the game.

The **Tokyo Yakult Swallows** (http://www.yakult-swallows.co.jp/english) are also based in Tokyo, and might be easier to get tickets for than the Giants.

Day Two

Take advantage of the jetlag and make your way to **Tsukiji** before 6 am for a stroll around the **Tsukiji Fish Market** and a *sushi* breakfast. Shower back at the hotel and then take the Shinkansen to **Kyoto**. (Set your phone alarm so you don't fall asleep and miss your stop!) Spend the afternoon sightseeing.

Day Three

Take a daytrip to **Nara**. See **Tōdai-ji** and walk around **Nara Park**. Return to **Kyoto** for the evening.

Day Four

Take the train to **Himeji** to see **Himeji Castle**, then continue to **Tokyo**. Enjoy a late dinner and walk around **Shibuya**.

FUN, FUN, FUN

The following chapters will give you advice on ways to have fun and save money while shopping, dining out, and making friends in Japan.

SHOPPING

Department Stores

If you buy something with a credit card, the clerk may ask if you'd like to have your card swiped once. Some people prefer to divide their payment over multiple credit cards, which incurs a small transaction fee. If you'd like to pay in full on one card, say "*Ikkai, onegaishimasu*"「一回お願いします」.

Sometimes in department stores, people will queue in front of what look like bingo dispensers. If you have time, get in line! These type of promotions—called *chūsen-kai* 抽選会 or, more casually, *fukubiki* 福引き —let you turn the dispenser handle for free. If a marble of a certain color comes out, you may win a large prize. Usually everyone who waits in line gets something. The consolation prizes are often magnets, hand warmers, or candy.

Many Japanese women save the shopping bags from stylish stores and reuse them as totes. If you buy something from a name-brand store—or even just a store with a cute bag, save the bag and use it in your daily life! *Oshare-ne!*「おしゃれね〜！」 ("Stylish!")

Buying Japanese Books

Before going to a bookstore to buy a specific volume of *manga* 漫画 , or Japanese comics, write down the name of the *manga*'s publisher and the *kanji* reading of the author's name. New releases are displayed in the front, but bookstores usually arrange older releases based on the publisher, then alphabetically by author's last name.

BookOff (http://www.bookoff.co.jp) sells used manga for about ¥200 each. They also sell used video games, DVDs, and CDs. BookOff is not the place to find latest releases (although sometimes they do turn up), but BookOff's prices and vast collection make it a great place to stock up on books. Unlike most bookstores, BookOff does not shrink wrap its merchandise, so lots of people stand and read the manga in front of the shelves. (This is called *tachi-yomi* 立ち読み).

> **TIP**: You can sell your used books, *manga*, CDs, and/or DVDs to BookOff. You won't get much money, but selling your used books is a great way to clear out your bookshelves before leaving the country. BookOff also accepts popular foreign-language titles.

Bookstores (with the exception of used bookstores like BookOff) will ask if you want your book covered with a brown paper wrapper, for privacy's sake. This service is free of charge.

Renting and Buying Japanese Movies

Geo (www.geo-online.co.jp) offers inexpensive movie, *manga*, and CD rentals, as does Tsutaya (www.tsutaya.co.jp), which also sells new-releases in some locations. These chains have locations all throughout Japan. You will need to provide proof of address, such as your Resident Card, in order to receive a rental card.

> **TIP**: Most Japanese rental stores require you to return the DVDs in store, but Tsutaya offers a pre-paid envelope service (à la Netflix) for ¥100.

When you rent movies, the counter clerk will give them to you in a black cloth bag, so no need to feel embarrassed about whatever you decide to rent.

Before going to a store to rent a non-Japanese DVD, double-check the movie's Japanese title. English titles are often different from their Japanese counterparts.

> Sometimes the Japanese titles of Western movies are close enough to guess. For example, "Ratatouille" becomes "Remy's Delicious Restaurant," *Remī-no-oishii-resutoran* 「レミーのおいしいレストラン」. "Legally Blonde" is "Cutie Blonde," *Kyūtei-Burondo* 「キュウティ・ブロンド」. However, guessing is not always reliable. In my local DVD store, both "American Pie" and "8 Mile" were located in the aisle labeled "Lovey-Dovey Romances."

> **TIP**: Establishing common interests is a great way to connect with the people you meet. Learn the Japanese names of your favorite TV shows and books, even those that are Japanese. (For example, the Japanese movie called "Kamikaze Girls" in English is actually called "*Shimotsuma Monogatari*" 「下妻物語」 in Japanese.)

Most movie stores organize movies by genre, then in Japanese alphabetical order. Japanese alphabetical order starts with the first row, "A," "I," "U," "E," "O," and continues to the next row starting with "KA" and so on, until ending with "N." For example, if you're looking for the drama *Hana Yori Dango*「花より男子」, look under the は section.

Japanese Alphabetical Order				
あ A	い I	う U	え E	お O
か KA	き KI	く KU	け KE	こ KO
さ SA	し SHI	す SU	せ SE	そ SO
た TA	ち CHI	つ TSU	て TE	と TO
な NA	に NI	ぬ NU	ね NE	の NO
は HA	ひ HI	ふ HU	へ HE	ほ HO
ま MA	み MI	む MU	め ME	も MO
や YA		ゆ YU		よ YO
わ WA				を WO
ん N				

All DVDs are region-encoded, meaning that you can watch Japanese DVDs, which are Region 2, in Region 2 DVD players. DVDs in the U.S. and Canada are Region 1, so DVDs you purchase in Japan might not work on your laptop or American DVD player. You can purchase an inexpensive, portable DVD player at any Japanese electronics store.

Samurai Swords

There are many places in Japan where you can buy "samurai-style" swords, or wooden swords for the purposes of martial arts practice. If you are interested in an antique, authentic samurai sword, visit **Unique Japan** (http://new.uniquejapan.com/home) for detailed information on owning, choosing, and registering an antique samurai sword. If you are interested in purchasing one of their samurai swords, Unique Japan will take care of sword registration for you.

Japanese swords are classified as fine art, not weapons. To preserve the swords' cultural heritage and rarity, Japanese sword makers may produce only a limited number of swords a year, thus the reason for Japan's excellent knife industry.

Unlike gun laws in the U.S., in order to legally own a sword in Japan, the sword must be registered—not the owner. This Japanese law applies to antique swords as well as modern creations. The sword registration certificate must accompany the sword at all times. Illegal possession of a sword, like illegal possession of a firearm, is a criminal offense punishable by up to three years in prison and/or a $3500 fine. The exceptions to this rule include blades under 15 cm (5.9 inches), as well as decorative and/or training swords that cannot be sharpened.

The easiest and safest way to ship a sword to or from Japan is via FedEx. Wooden and/or plastic swords can be shipped through the Japanese Post Office. Specify on your customs/shipping form that the sword is a toy, and not an actual weapon.

If, for some reason, you need to take a sword into Japan, there is a limit of three swords per person.

DINING

The best website for finding restaurants in Japan is **Gurunabi** (http://www.gnavi.co.jp). You can search for restaurants and bars by cuisine type, atmosphere, price, style of restaurant, number of people accepted per reservation, and proximity to a specific train station. Gurunabi is free, and, if you can read Japanese, a great way to discover new restaurants in Japan. (Gurunabi also offers a reduced version of its website in English.) Many of the restaurants listed on Gurunabi offer special discounts to those who make reservations online.

If you can read Japanese, free coupon magazines, such as ***Hot Pepper*** (http://www.hotpepper.jp/index.html), are available in all major metro stops. These magazines are great ways to find new restaurants and salons at discounted prices. ***Coupon Land*** (http://www.c-pon.com) focuses exclusively on Tokyo.

For even deeper discounts on restaurants, beauty treatments, and more, try the daily-deal site **Groupon Japan** (http://groupon.jp). **Rurubu** (http://www.rurubu.com) can help you plan trips and get discounted lodging. Both these websites are entirely in Japanese.

Types of Restaurants

Many ramen stalls near train stations offer standing room only, and reduced prices to go with it. Look for huddles of business men slurping noodles in front of a counter. Don't be offended by the noises around you. Slurping is considered proper noodle-eating etiquette.

The Japanese fast-food chain Yoshinoya (http://www.yoshinoya.com) serves a dish called *gyūdon* 牛丼 , which is basically meat over rice. This chain is popular with men.

A *famari-resu* ファミリレス , or "family restaurant," is an inexpensive, often Western-style restaurant popular with families. For an American equivalent, think of an Olive Garden or Applebee's.

Many restaurants in Japan are located on the upper floors of buildings. These restaurants usually do not have English menus, but if you are feeling adventurous, you can often find great restaurants simply by taking an elevator to one of the less-frequented floors in a restaurant complex building. (The added bonus of this strategy is that if the restaurant you wanted to go to is booked full, you can simply stop at a restaurant on a different floor for a quick change of plans.)

In the evening hours, many restaurant employees advertise their menus on the street using signs and loud voices. These employees often work for restaurants on the upper floors of buildings, which often do not get as much foot traffic as first-floor restaurants. The restaurant staff try to usher customers upstairs and often offer great deals for large groups. However, these restaurant employees rarely approach foreigners because of the language barrier. If you speak Japanese and want an all-you-can-eat or all-you-can-drink experience for a party of five or more, this is a great way to make sudden plans for a large group. (Especially since many of these employees usually carry a walkie-talkie or phone to instantly communicate with the restaurant's front desk before letting you know how soon you can get a table.)

Many restaurants serve set meal options, known as *teishoku* 定食. These come with a drink—usually a selection of sodas, coffee, and/or tea. Even if you would prefer a water, order one of the drinks on the set menu.Some waiters will try to explain to you that the teishoku includes a free drink. Save time by just ordering from the menu, then asking for water on the side.

Nomihōdai 飲み放題 means that for a flat fee (usually ¥2000-¥4000), you can drink as much and as many different types of alcohol as you want. As you can imagine, *nomihōdai* courses are popular at bars and restaurants.

CAUTION: The legal Japanese blood alcohol level is 0.03% (America's is 0.08%), which means that if you drive after eating a dessert made with even the smallest amount of alcohol, you could be arrested for drunk driving. DUI penalties are the same in Japan whether you are driving a car or a bicycle, so if you're going to drink, plan on alternate modes of return transportation.

Dining Etiquette

Say *Itadakimasu* 「いただきます」 before eating and *Gochisōsama-deshita* 「ごちそうさまでした」 afterwards. These phrases don't have an exact English translation, but basically express appreciation for the meal.

Don't point your chopsticks at people or leave your chopsticks standing straight out of your bowl of rice. When helping yourself to a communal dish, use the opposite ends of your chopsticks, the ends that have not touched your mouth, or a separate, clean pair of "serving only" chopsticks that may be provided with the meal.

If you know you're going to be eating *soba* そば , *udon* うどん , or *rāmen* ラーメン noodles, don't wear a white top! Noodle-based dishes can speckle the shirts of even the most careful eaters. Slurping is considered polite noodle-eating etiquette in Japan.

NOTE: Soba noodles are thin and made of buckwheat. *Udon* noodles are made of wheat flour. *Rāmen* noodles, the kind you get at a restaurant, not the prepackaged kind that comes in a cup, are made of wheat. All are tasty, but soba is the healthiest of the three.

It is considered rude to eat and walk on the street at the same time. Most ice cream stands offer bench seating.

MAKING FRIENDS AND MEETING PEOPLE

There are numerous English magazines and online websites geared toward foreigners in Japan. Refer to your city's local magazines for the most up-to-date info on local events.

If you're in Tokyo, I recommend ***Metropolis*** (http://metropolis.co.jp) and ***Time Out Tokyo*** (http://www.timeout.jp/en/tokyo).

If you're in the Kansai region, I recommend ***Kansai Scene*** (http://www.kansaiscene.com).

If you can speak and read Japanese, the website **Shuminavi** (http://shuminavi.net) has a huge listing of interest groups and classes that you can join. You could also try your local community center or ward office to learn more about events in your local community.

> **NOTE**: An activity club at a school is called (club activity)-*bu* ~ 部 .
> (For example, tennis club would be called *tenisu-bu* テニス部 .) A club/ interest group outside of school is often called a "circle," or *sākuru* サークル .

Meetup (http://meetup.com) can help you find nearby interest groups and/or social clubs in the language and country of your choosing. If you don't see a group that interests you, start one!

One of the easiest ways to meet people is to stop listening to your iPod on the subway. Many people are excited to meet foreigners and practice their English, if given the chance.

> **TIP**: Ladies, when strangers ask where you live—for safety's sake—tell them about your two Japanese roommates.

Always carry a small notebook with you when teaching or meeting up with people who don't speak a high level of English. Drawing is an easy way to explain things, and spelling out words and names can help surpass the language barrier.

If improving your Japanese is one of your main goals during your stay in Japan, avoid what I call the "Gaijin Clump." It can be tempting (and fun!) to hole up at **Outback Steakhouse** (http://www.outbacksteakhouse.co.jp/en/index.html) with your fellow ex-pats once in a while, but if you spend all your time with foreigners, you will miss out on many language-learning and cultural opportunities.

Ladies, feel like having a girls' night out? Many travel companies and restaurants offer special rates for *joshikai* 女子会 , a relatively new word meaning "all-girl parties." Groups of women can sometimes receive discounts on lodging, food, and other travel experiences.

Most people in Japan usually party outside of the home, but if you do get invited to someone's place, bring a gift. (And before you give it to them, say *Tsumaranaimono-desukedo*… 「つまらないものですけど …」. This set phrase is used when giving gifts, and roughly means "This is a boring thing, but…").

When entering someone else's home, it is polite to say *O-jama-shimasu* 「お邪魔します」 , literally "I'm intruding."

If you're interested in going over to the house of someone who is more than a friend, keep in mind that about 49% of unmarried Japanese people between the ages of 20-34 live with their parents. Most young Japanese people wishing to engage in intimate activity go to a "love hotel," *labu-hoteru* ラブホテル . Over half the sex in Japan takes place in love hotels. (Yes, someone actually conducted a study on this. Check the Endnotes at the back of the book if you don't believe me.)

Love hotels rent rooms by the hour, and sometimes have a theme, such as "Hello Kitty," "subway station," or even "Christmas." Rates depend on the type of hotel, any provided extras (such as toys and/or costumes), and the duration of one's visit. Overnight "stays" will obviously be more expensive than hour-long "rests."

NOTE: Some love hotels even have notebooks in each room, where guests can write (and read) accounts of their…visit.

What's Your Type?

There are many ways to positively describe someone's appearance, and it is not uncommon for an acquaintance to straight out ask "What type of girls/guys do you like?" Understand your friends' preferences using the guide below. The magazines mentioned below are listed in the Resource List section.

What's Your Type?		
The Word	The Meaning	Magazines
かわいい *kawaii* cute	*Kawaii* girls are cute, feminine, and have a touch of innocence—think skirts, bows, and floral prints. *Kawaii* is sometimes spelled in *kanji*: 可愛い.	*non-no* *Steady* *AneCam* *CanCam*
格好いい *kakkōii* cool	*Kakkōii* boys are cool, strong, and attractive—the Alpha males of Japan. This term usually applies to boys, but girls are sometimes described as *kakkōii*. *Kakkōii* is often spelled in *hiragana*.	Most male pop stars, musicians, and athletes featured in women's magazines.
美人 *bijin* beautiful	Literally "beautiful people," *bijin* are naturally beautiful, model types. *Bijin* has a more mature connotation than *kawaii*.	*25ans* *Miss* *Oggi* *AneCam* *CanCam*
美少年 *bishōnen* pretty boy	A word for cute, somewhat feminine-looking boys. Often used to describe characters in BL *manga* (guy×guy romance geared towards women), so don't use this word to describe guys you like.	Anime Manga
ギャル *gyaru* gal type	Girls with tanned skin, dyed hair, and tight clothes. *Gyaru* are rarely seen without rhinestones.	*vivi* *Egg* *Happie nuts* *I Love Mama*
イケメン *ikemen* hot	Similar to *kakkōii*, except only used to describe guys.	Most male athletes featured in women's magazines.
お姉ちゃん *one-chan* big sister	The Japanese equivalent of the "girl next door." Girls who look and act like "big sisters." Kind, friendly, and naturally beautiful.	*non-no* *Steady* *AneCam*
ホスト *hosuto* host type	Men with bleached, flat-ironed hair. Often seen wearing pointy-toed shoes and expensive accessories. May or may not work in a host club.	*Men's Egg* *Host Magazine*

JOINING A GYM IN JAPAN

Gym memberships first require a "New Member Registration Fee," *Nyūkaikin* 入会金 , of about $150, possibly more. Add that to your monthly payments (about $150 a month), and you're making a serious investment in the club, especially if you have a short term visa and have to pay a year's of dues in advance. Recently-opened clubs may offer discounted new membership plans and/or waive the registration fee..

Konami Sports Club (http://www.konamisportsclub.jp) has large facilities and an equally large monthly fee, but most branches offer reduced-expense plans, such as "Only Weekdays" or "Only Mornings."

Some **Gold's Gym** (http://www.goldsgym.jp) locations will accept Gold's Gym membership plans from the U.S., but I wouldn't count on this. If you're already a Gold's Gym member, it wouldn't hurt to try.

For those of you residing in Tokyo, I recommend **Tip-X Gym** (http://tip.x-tokyo.jp) in Shibuya. Tip-X has excellent facilities, group fitness classes, Power Plates, weightlifting and cardio machines, and an indoor pool and sauna, not to mention that Tip-X is located in the hubbub of excitement and shopping that is Shibuya. (There is also a branch located in Shinjuku.)

Some gyms do not admit people with tattoos, or require tattoos to remain covered when using the facilities. The gym will inform you of this in advance.

> When signing up for a gym membership, I was asked a series of questions, including: "Do you have a tattoo?" and "Are you a member of an organized crime syndicate?"

Many community centers in Japan have public gyms and swimming pools that you can use for a nominal fee per visit. Many local parks are free and jogger-friendly.

Japanese fashion magazines are often wrapped in rubber bands and enclose a free giveaway, like a tote bag or pouch. Some women use these bags in the gym to carry their face towels and water bottles.

CULTURE AND LANGUAGE

The following chapters offer a detailed explanation of several components of Japanese culture, including honorific suffixes, blood typing, Japanese holidays, New Year's cards, and tea ceremony.

HONORIFIC SUFFIXES

In Japan, calling someone by his/her first name is a sign of intimacy. When addressing someone in Japanese, it is important to use the appropriate honorific suffix, depending on the nature of your relationship.

There are many honorifics in Japanese, especially in regards to martial arts and political positions, but the following suffixes are the most common. Honorific suffixes are only for referring to other people. Do not apply one of the following suffixes to the end of your own name.

～ちゃん *chan*

USED FOR: female children, female teenagers, female subordinates
FORMATION: first name + *-chan*

The suffix "*-chan*" implies a close level of intimacy, such as a parent/child or best friend relationship.

This suffix has a cute image, so many teenager girls refer to their friends using *-chan*. Sometimes very young boys are called *-chan*, but this suffix usually only applies to girls.

～くん *kun*

USED FOR: male children, male teenagers, female subordinates
FORMATION:
  Male → first name + *-kun*
  Male → last name + *-kun*
  Female → last name + *-kun*

This suffix is generally used for male children, male teenagers, and sometimes male adults. This suffix can also be used by a male superior to refer to a female subordinate.

～さん *-san*

USED FOR: basically everyone
FORMATION: last name + *-san*

This is the default honorific suffix. It is gender-neutral, polite, and used between equals.

This suffix is often affixed to professions. For example, someone who works at a *sakana-ya* 魚屋 (literally "fish store") would be called a *sakana-ya-san* 魚屋さん .

後輩 *-kōhai*

USED FOR: underclassmen
FORMATION: never used to address someone

Kōhai is the word for underclassmen, but it is not actually a suffix. Use *-san* to refer to underclassmen.

～先輩 *-senpai*

USED FOR: upperclassmen
FORMATION: last name + *-senpai* OR by itself

This suffix is used by underclassmen to address upperclassmen. *Senpai*, unlike *kōhai*, can be affixed to a name or used by itself a title.

Senpai/kōhai relationships are very important in Japanese culture. Even after graduation, underclassmen continue to call their former upperclassmen *senpai*.

～先生 *sensei*

USED FOR: upperclassmen
FORMATION: last name + *-sensei* OR by itself

The term *sensei* is used for highly educated and respected authority figures, such as teachers, doctors, lawyers, and artists/craftsmen who have achieved a certain degree of mastery.

Even after you are no longer a student or your former teacher is no longer a teacher, you should continue to address your former teacher as *sensei*. Once a *sensei*, always a *sensei*.

USED FOR: people much higher in rank than oneself
FORMATION: last OR first name + *~sama*

This is the highest honorific suffix and is most often used to refer to customers, or *o-kyaku-sama* お客様 .

Although the imperial family of Japan has its own set of honorifics, Japanese media often refer to the emperor and his relations using *~sama*.

Many celebrities, as a show of affection, are referred to by their first names, plus *~sama*.

CULTURE NOTES

In Japan, four (*yon* or *shi*) and nine (*ku* or *kyū*) are considered unlucky numbers, because they sound the same as the characters for "death" (死 *shi*) and "pain" (苦 *ku*), respectively.

If someone gives you a five yen coin, it means that person wishes you happiness and success in all future endeavors. The word for five yen, *go-en* 五円 , sounds the same as the word for destiny: *go-en* ご縁 .

In 1950, most Japanese women got married at 23. In 2011, that number rose to 29. Traditionally, Japanese women stay at home after getting married. They may receive intense pressure from those around them to quit work and focus on raising children.

There's an unfortunate slang term for unmarried Japanese women over the age of 25. In Japan, Christmas is a romantic holiday shared with your significant other. Couples and families eat "Christmas Cake" *Kurisumasu-kēki* クリスマス・ケーキ together. A woman over the age of 25 who isn't married is called "Christmas Cake" since, theoretically, no one wants it after the 25th.

Rock-Paper-Scissors, known as *Janken-pon* じゃんけんぽん (or *janken*, じゃんけん, for short) is popular in Japan. *Janken* is the fastest way to make decisions in a large group, and a perennial hit in classroom games.

<u>Non-Competitive Variation</u>: *Gūpā* ぐう・ぱあ is like Rock-Paper-Scissors, except with no Scissors and no winner. *Gūpā* is used to divide a large group into two smaller groups: the *gū* "rock" group and the *pā* "paper group."

<u>Group Janken</u>: Rock-Paper-Scissors can also be played in groups. If three people make rock, one makes paper, and one makes scissors, there is no winner. If during the next round, three people make rock and two make paper, the two who chose paper are the winners. This continues until only one person remains. Some elementary school teachers use this version of Rock-Paper-Scissors to decide which kids received seconds during lunch.

It's illegal in Japan for political candidates to campaign over the Internet. Around election time, cars and even parades of bicycles blare campaign ads. A candidate driving a car and reading his/her speech at the same time is not unusual.

Someone who can't read the mood of a situation is called a "KY," short for *Kūki-yomenai* 空気読めない , or "can't read the atmosphere."

Don't say "Bless You" after someone sneezes. Just pretend it didn't happen.

Japanese Era Years

Besides the conventional, Western method of counting time (6/1/2016, for example), Japan also delineates time using Common Era years. A new Common Era begins on the first day after the death of the reigning Japanese Emperor. The current era, Heisei 平成 , began on January 8th, 1989. (The Shōwa Era 昭和 lasted from 1926 to January 7th, 1989). Official Japanese papers, such as diplomas and government documents, always give the date using the era year calendar.

Heisei Calendar			
しょうわ 昭和63	1998	へいせい 平成13	2001
しょうわ 昭和64	1/1→1/7/1989	へいせい 平成14	2002
へいせい 平成1	1/8→12/31/1989	へいせい 平成15	2003
へいせい 平成2	1990	へいせい 平成16	2004
へいせい 平成3	1991	へいせい 平成17	2005
へいせい 平成4	1992	へいせい 平成18	2006
へいせい 平成5	1993	へいせい 平成19	2007
へいせい 平成6	1994	へいせい 平成20	2008
へいせい 平成7	1995	へいせい 平成21	2009
へいせい 平成8	1996	へいせい 平成22	2010
へいせい 平成9	1997	へいせい 平成23	2011
へいせい 平成10	1998	へいせい 平成24	2012
へいせい 平成11	1999	へいせい 平成25	2013
へいせい 平成12	2000	へいせい 平成26	2014

The *kanji* for Heisei is often abbreviated to "H," so "2013" would be written as "H25."

NOTE: "H" on its own, however, is an abbreviation for *ecchi* エッチ , which means "sex."

Wedding Gifts

If attending the wedding of a Japanese friend or relative, you will be expected to bring a cash gift of ¥20,000-30,000 (roughly $300 dollars). If you are not very close to the couple, ¥10,000 is okay, just make sure that whatever amount you give cannot be split in half. If you give the couple ¥20,000 (that's two ¥10,000 bills), the money can be divided equally, with one bill per person. Now that the couple is starting their life together as a team, they should share the money, not divide it straight between themselves. Give the couple an odd number of bills, like ¥15,000 (one ¥10,000 bill and one ¥50,000 bill) or ¥30,000 (three ¥10,000 bills), which cannot be divided equally.

The money you give to the couple should be crisp and unmarked. Ask your bank teller for clean bills, *shin-satsu* 新札 . (If you don't have time to go to the bank, you can use an iron to press the money.)

If giving the couple a cash present would be a hardship for you, order a separate (ideally Western-style) gift. Write a message explaining the gift and how it will be delivered to the couple. Put the message in the wedding envelope and give the envelope to the reception desk when you enter. This "gift swap" is only acceptable because you are a *gaijin* and do not understand Japanese culture. If you are on a tight budget, make the most of your *gaijin* status!

Ask the sales clerk at the stationery store for a wedding envelope, or a *shūgi-fukuro* 祝儀袋 . Even if you see an envelope you like, ask for assistance before making a purchase. You do not want to give the couple a funeral or "Get Well Soon" envelope by mistake! A general guideline to choosing an envelope: the fancier the envelope, the more money should be inside it.

A stationery store's selection of envelopes. As to be expected, the more colorful envelopes on the left are for weddings, and the somber envelopes on the right are for funerals. Some of the brightly colored envelopes are all-purpose celebration envelopes

If you can, use a brush or calligraphy pen to address the wedding envelope. Addressing the letter in a ballpoint pen gives it an ordinary, "just a letter" feel, and *kanji* written by a brush pen tend to look more elegant.

Brushes and calligraphy pens are usually sold near these envelopes, as well as in many convenience stores. If you won't be writing in *kanji*, I recommend using a thick gel pen (0.7 or greater) for the best effect.

BLOOD TYPES IN JAPAN

ABO blood type, or *ketsueki-gata* 血液型 , is to Japan what astrology is to the Western world. A person's blood type is believed to be linked to one's personality. Blood type information is often included in descriptions of characters in TV shows and celebrity interviews.

Blood Typing

There are many ways to categorize blood. ABO blood grouping divides blood into four basic types: A, AB, B, and O.

The connection between blood type and personality has no scientific support beyond the debatable research of Masahiko Nōmi, but the idea of a relationship between blood type and personality is still popular in Japanese culture today.

Japanese Blood Type Personalities		
Blood Type	Characteristics	Examples
A	Considerate	
	Loyal	Britney Spears
	Calm	Madoka Kaname/"Madoka Magica"
	Punctual	Richard Nixon
	Shy	Light Yagami/"Death Note"
	Perfectionist	Ringo Starr
	Self-Conscious	Ichigo Kurosaki/"Bleach"
	Stubborn	
B	Creative	
	Passionate	Leonardo DiCaprio
	Curious	Naruto Uzumaki/"Naruto"
	Cheerful	Akira Kurosawa
	Unpredictable	Miley Cyrus
	Self-Centered	Paul McCartney
	Vain	Gon Freecss/"Hunter x Hunter"
	Irresponsible	
AB	Rational	
	Controlled	Thomas Edison
	Talented	Sasuke Uchiha/"Naruto"
	Sensitive	Marilyn Monroe
	Critical	Jackie Chan
	Unforgiving	John F. Kennedy
	Cautious	Cloud Strife/"Final Fantasy 7"
	Indecisive	
O	Outgoing	
	Active	Elvis Presley
	Expressive	Sailor Moon/"Sailor Moon"
	Goal-Oriented	Hayao Miyazaki
	Independent	Mizuki Ashiya/"Hana Kimi"
	Carefree	Queen Elizabeth II
	Clumsy	John Lennon
	Greedy	Giovanni/"Pokémon"

JAPANESE HOLIDAYS

Japanese National Holidays			
January 1st	New Year's Day	*O-shōgatsu*	<ruby>お<rt>しょうがつ</rt></ruby>正月
2nd Monday of January	Coming of Age Day	*Seijin-no-hi*	成人の日
February 11th	Foundation Day	*Kenkoku-kinen-no-hi*	建国記念の日
Late March	Vernal Equinox Day	*Shunbun-no-hi*	春分の日
April 29th	Showa Day	*Shōwa-no-hi*	昭和の日
May 3rd	Constitutional Memorial Day	*Kenpō-kinenbi*	憲法記念日
May 4th	Greenery Day	*Midori-no-hi*	みどりの日
May 5th	Children's Day	*Kodomo-no-hi*	こどもの日
3rd Monday of July	Marine Day	*Umi-no-hi*	海の日
3rd Monday of September	Respect for the Elderly Day	*Keirō-no-hi*	敬老の日
Around September 23	Autumnal Equinox Day	*Shūbun-no-hi*	秋分の日
2nd Monday of October	Health and Sports Day	*Taïku-no-hi*	体育の日
November 3rd	Culture Day	*Bunka-no-hi*	文化の日
November 23rd	Labour Thanksgiving Day	*Kinrō-kansha-no-hi*	勤労感謝の日
December 23rd	The Emperor's Birthday	*Tennō-tanjōbi*	天皇誕生日

January *Ichi-gatsu* 一月 <ruby>いちがつ</ruby>

> Though the lunisolar month names are often used on calendars, these terms may be unrecognizable to many Japanese people. When speaking Japanese, refer to the months using the name ending in *-gatsu*.

January is known as *Mutsuki* 睦月 , or "Harmonious Month," on the traditional Japanese Lunisolar Calendar.

1/1: New Year's *O-shōgatsu* お正月

The New Year's season, which generally runs from December 29th to January 3rd, is referred to as *O-shōgatsu*, and is perhaps the most important holiday in Japan. New Year's Day itself is called *Ganjitsu*, 元日 . Families spend the end of December preparing for New Year's, with *O-sōji* お掃除 , "mass house-cleaning," the preparation or purchase of a special New Year's *bentō*, known as *O-sechi* 御節 , and the mailing of New Year's cards, *nengajō* 年賀状 . (See the next chapter, "*Nengajō*—Japanese New Year's Cards," for more details.)

Traditionally, *O-sechi* were prepared in advance so that, after weeks of hurried cleaning and cooking, the women of the house could finally enjoy a well-deserved break. Nowadays, most people order *O-sechi* from grocery stores or department stores, which take reservations up to three months in advance.

2nd Monday in January: Coming of Age Day *Seijin-no-hi* 成人の日

Seijin-no-hi celebrates those who are twenty, the age of adulthood in Japan. Young women visit shrines and temples in beautiful *furisode* 振袖 , a type of *kimono* only worn when one is twenty years old. *Furisode* are distinguishable by their bright colors and long, swinging sleeves.

February *Ni-gatsu* 二月

February is traditionally known as *Kisaragi* 如月 , the archaic Chinese word for "February." A less common, Japanized-spelling of *Kisaragi* is 衣更着 . The origins of this spelling are unclear, but one theory is that the combination of the characters "cloth," "getting closer" (presumably to the cold) and "to wear," reflects the temperature of February—still cold enough to wear thick layers.

Another theory is that the name *Kisaragi* came from the plants, *kusaki* 草木 , that are once again growing, *kōsei* 更生 , during this time. According to this theory, the name *Kisaragi* comes from an archaic abbreviation of this plant rebirth: *kisaragi* 生更ぎ .

2/3: *Setsubun* 節分

Setsubun is a ritual that occurs the day before the beginning of spring. Beans are thrown, a ritual known as *mame-maki* 豆撒き —to ward off evil spirits, and to cleanse away all the evil of the former year. *Setsubun* has its roots in the Lunar New Year.

2/11: Foundation Day *Kenkoku-kinen-no-hi* 建国記念の日

Foundation Day is a national holiday with no long-standing traditions.

2/14: Valentine's Day *Balentain-dē* バレンタインデー

On Valentine's Day in Japan, girls give chocolate to the boys they like.

Starting in late January, stores display tiers of chocolate-making supplies and brightly-wrapped chocolates for Valentine's Day. This can be as simple as melting down some cheap chocolate bars and mixing in toppings, or as complicated as following gourmet recipes.

Types of Valentine's Day Chocolate			
Friend Chocolate	友チョコ	*Tomo-choko*	The chocolate female friends sometimes exchange with each other. Does not possess romantic connotations.
Obligation Chocolate	義理チョコ	*Giri-choko*	The chocolate women give to their male coworkers out of obligation. Possesses no romantic connotations.
Normal Chocolate	普通チョコ	*Futsu-choko*	Regular, store-bought chocolate. May or may not possess romantic connotations.
Gourmet Chocolate	高級チョコ	*Kokyu-choko*	Expensive, high-quality chocolate. An adult woman would give this to a man she was interested in romantically. Some adult women buy this for their parents.
True Feelings Chocolate	本命チョコ	*Honmei-choko*	The ultimate confectionary expression of romantic affection. *Honmei-choko* is homemade, attractively packaged, and given only to the object of one's romantic affection.
White Day (March 14th)	ホワイト・デー	*Waito-dē*	If the (male) recipient of *Honmei-choko* reciprocates the giver's feelings, he will give the girl marshmallows, cookies, or some other (ideally white) sweet exactly one month after Valentine's Day. (Not all men celebrate White Day but it's a neat idea.) There are no established rules for White Day gifts, but some men will give gifts twice the approximate cost of the *giri* or *futsu choko* they received.

March *San-gatsu* 三月

March is traditionally known as *Yayoi* 弥生 . There are many theories on the origin of this name. One theory is that the character iya 弥 , which means "more and more," combined with the *o* 生 from *oishigeru* 生い茂る, which means "to grow abundantly," is a reference to the growth of new plants in March. Yayoi is also an abbreviation of the archaic name Kusaki Yaohi Tsuki 草木彌生月 —"the month when plants grow."

3/3: Girls' Day *Hina-matsuri* 雛祭り

Starting in mid-February, families display a set of ornamental *Hina-matsuri* dolls representing the Emperor, the Empress, and the courtiers of the Heian Period (794—1185 ACE). Antique Hina-matsuri collections are annually displayed in museums.

Hina-matsuri dolls are popular gifts from grandparents to their granddaughters, but don't leave the dolls out too long! If the dolls are still on display after *Hina-matsuri*, superstition has it that the young girls in the family will never get married.

3/14: White Day *Waito-dē* ワイト・デー

Men who received chocolate on Valentine's Day give reciprocal candies/ cookies on this day.

Around 3/20: Vernal Equinox Day *Shunbun-no-hi* 春分の日

Vernal Equinox Day is a national holiday with no current traditions.

April *Shi-gatsu* 四月

April is traditionally known as *Uzhuki* 卯月. The character "*u*" 卯 is a type of bean plant, and April is the month when this plant begins to flower. This character is also read as *bō*, which means "hare," the fourth sign in the Chinese zodiac.

4/29: Shōwa Day *Shōwa-no-hi* 昭和の日

Shōwa Day is a national holiday honoring the birthday of the late Emperor Shōwa (4/29/1901—1/7/1989).

May *Go-gatsu* 五月

May is traditionally known as *Satsuki* 皐月. The satsuki is a pink mountain

azalea. Fans of the Miyazaki classic "Totoro" *Tonari No Totoro* 「隣のトトロ」
will recognize that the film's two main characters, "Satsuki" and "Mei",
are both named for the 5th month.

April 29th, May 3rd - 5th: Golden Week *Gōruden-wiku* ゴールデンウィーク

"Golden Week" is a week of consecutive national holidays. This is perhaps
the most popular and expensive time in Japan to travel.

5/3: Constitution Memorial Day *Kenpō-kinenbi* 憲法記念日

Constitution Memorial Day commemorates the day Japan's post-World
War II constitution took effect (May 3rd, 1947).

5/4: Greenery Day *Midori-no-hi* みどりの日

Greenery Day is a national holiday with no current traditions.

5/5: Children's Day *Kodomo-no-hi* こどもの日

Children's Day was originally known (and is still thought of) as "Boys'
Day." To celebrate children, families (with sons) fly koi streamers, known as
koi-nobori 鯉幟 .

2nd Sunday in May: Mother's Day *Haha-no-hi* 母の日

Families celebrate and honor the mothers in their lives.

June *Roku-gatsu* 六月

June is traditionally known as *Minazhuki* 水無月 , or "month of water."
June is the beginning of Japan's humid monsoon season, so the characters
for "water" 水 and "nothing" 無 , which functions in this context as a no
particle indicating possession —combine with "month" 月 to refer to how
quickly the water evaporates after the monsoons. June is also the month of
rice planting, an agricultural feat that requires a great deal of water.

3rd Sunday in June: Father's Day *Chichi-no-hi* 父の日

Father's Day has not yet been completely adopted into the Japanese tradition, but many people celebrate fathers and fatherhood on this day.

July *Shichi-gatsu* 七月

Traditionally known as *Fumiduki* 文月, which means "Book Month." This month's name is a phonetic abbreviation, since July was the month of the farming of a wetland rice known as *fufumiduki* フフミヅキ. (This rice is now known as *fumiduki*.)

7/7: *Tanabata* 七夕

The Japanese star festival Tanabata celebrates the Chinese legend of two celestial lovers who are only allowed to meet once a year, on Tanabata. On Tanabata, people write their wishes on small pieces of paper and hang them on decorative bamboo trees. There are Tanabata festivals all across Japan.

<u>**THE LEGEND:**</u> There once was a Star Princess named Orihime who wove beautiful cloth for her father by the bank of the Milky Way. She loved weaving and would work without stopping from sunup to sundown. Her father, the Star King Tentei, grew worried that if she kept working so hard, she might become sick. Orihime told her father not to worry and kept working.

Concerned for his daughter, the Star King decided that he wanted her to get married. He searched the Milky Way for nice young stars for her to meet. He arranged for her to meet Hikoboshi, the Cow Herder Star, who lived on the other side of the Milky Way. When Hikoboshi and Orihime met, it was love at first sight. They got married right away.

However, once they got married, Orihime stopped weaving. Hikoboshi let his cows stray all over the sky. Angry, Tentei forbade the two to meet and separated them across the Milky Way. Orihime fell into despair. She cried and cried, and begged her father to let them meet again.

Tentei decided to let the two of them meet on the seventh day of the seventh month, as long as she worked hard at her weaving during the rest of the year. When the seventh day of the seventh month finally came, Orihime had no way to cross the Milky Way and meet Hikoboshi. She cried so much that a flock of birds came to her and made their wings into a bridge for her to cross. If it rains on Tanabata, the birds cannot come and Orihime and Hikoboshi must wait yet another year to meet.

7/15 (8/15 in the *Kantō* region of Japan): *Obon* お盆

Somewhat like "The Day of the Dead" in Mexico, on *Obon*, people light paper lanterns and float them down the river, a symbolic signal of their ancestors' spirits returning to the world of the day. The *Obon* festival lasts three days, but begins at different times in different regions. Historically, Obon was celebrated according to the solar calendar. There are often fireworks, folk dances, and carnival games around Obon. Many people wear *yukata*.

3rd Monday in July: Ocean Appreciation Day *Umi-no-hi* 海の日

Ocean Appreciation Day is a national holiday with no current traditions.

August *Hachi-gatsu* 八月

August is traditionally known as *Haduki* 葉月 . *Ha* 葉 means "leaf." August is when the leaves of the rice plant spread out. Some scholars believe that this month's name instead refers to the leaves lost by trees during this month.

September *Ku-gatsu* 九月

September is traditionally known as *Nagatsuki* 長月 , "long month."

3rd Monday in Sept.: Respect for the Elderly Day *Keirō-no-hi* 敬老の日

Some people try to spend this national holiday with their grandparents.

Around Sept. 23rd: Autumnal Equinox Day *Shūbun-no-hi* 秋分の日

Autumnal Equinox Day is a national holiday with no current traditions.

October *Jū-gatsu* 十月

October is traditionally known as *Kannaduki* 神無月 , "month of the gods." Some scholars have concluded that October is the "month of no gods" because of the character *na* 無 , which usually means "no" or "none." However, recent scholars believe that the *na* in this month's name is actually meant to be a no sound, making *Kannaduki* "the month of the gods." Either way, the gods of Japan are rumored to gather in October at Izumo Temple in Shimane to drink a special type of gods-only alcohol, known as *shinshu* 神酒 , and discuss important matters, such as matchmaking.

2nd Monday in October: Health and Sports Day *Taiiku-no-hi* 体育の日

Health and Sports Day is a national holiday with no current traditions, though many schools hold their Sports Festivals in October.

November *Jūichi-gatsu* 十一月

November is traditionally known as *Shimotsuki* 霜月 —"Frost Month." The first frost of the year often occurs in November.

11/3: Culture Day *Bunka-no-hi* 文化の日

Culture Day commemorates the announcement of Japan's post-World War II constitution, which set up a constitutional monarchy on November 3rd, 1946. The 3rd of November is also the birthday of Emperor Meiji (11/3/1852—7/30/1912), a theoretically unrelated coincidence.

11/15: *Shichi-Go-San* 七五三

A traditional rite of passage that celebrates children who are three, five, or seven years old. Many parents dress their children in *kimono* on *Shichi-Go-San* and take them to a nearby temple.

A family visits a temple to celebrate *Shichi-Go-San.*

11/23: Labor Thanksgiving Day *Kinrō-kansha-no-hi* 勤労感謝の日

Labor Thanksgiving Day is the former date of an imperial harvest festival known as *Niiname-sai* 新嘗祭 . Despite the English translation of this national holiday, Labor Thanksgiving Day bears no resemblance to Thanksgiving Day in America.

December *Jūni-gatsu* 十二月

    December is traditionally known as *Shiwasu* 師走 —"Teachers Run." Those of you teaching will consider December an aptly-named month! This month's name comes from the busy monks—depicted by the *kanji* for "teachers"—in the Heian Period. During December, the monks were so busy that it would look like they were running in circles around the Buddha statues.

12/23: The Emperor's Birthday *Tennō-tanjōbi* 天皇誕生日

    The reigning Emperor's birthday is always an annual holiday. Upon the Emperor's death, the holiday changes to the date of the incoming Emperor's birthday.

12/25: Christmas *Kurisumasu* クリスマス

    Christmas is a romantic (not national) holiday in Japan. It is often incorrectly abbreviated as "X'mas."

    Many couples get together and eat Christmas Cake and **Kentucky Fried Chicken** (http://www.kfc.co.jp/xmas). KFC takes reservations for fried chicken buckets throughout December.

NENGAJŌ—JAPANESE NEW YEAR'S CARDS

One of the most important Japanese holiday traditions is the sending of *nengajō*, New Year's cards. Instead of Christmas cards, Japanese families send New Year's postcards to their family, friends, and colleagues. The postcards are delivered on New Year's Day.

Most *nengajō* feature a traditional New Year's greeting and a picture of the current Chinese zodiac animal, which changes every year. The zodiac sign *kanji* differ from the *kanji* for the animals themselves.

Due to the volume of *nengajō* families must send, many people opt for pre-printed cards, much like Westerners do in the U.S. for Christmas cards. For a personalized touch, stationery stores sell stamps, colored inks, pens, stickers, and other personalization options for *nengajō*. Many people enjoy making and embellishing their own cards. Photo printers are also popular around this time of year, and many couples share family photo *nengajō* with their loved ones. Designate homemade postcards as *nengajō* by writing 年賀 *nenga* in red below the stamp.

Date the *nengajō* with the date it will be received, January 1st. Write 元旦 *gantan*, which means "the morning of January 1st."

Zodiac Sign Order and *Kanji*			
Rat	子	*Ne*	2020
Ox	丑	*Ushi*	2021
Tiger	寅	*Tora*	2022
Rabbit	卯	*U or Bō*	2023
Dragon	辰	*Tatsu*	2024
Snake	巳	*Mi*	2025
Horse	午	*Uma*	2014
Sheep	未	*Hitsuji*	2015
Monkey	申	*Saru*	2016
Rooster	酉	*Tori*	2017
Dog	戌	*Inu*	2018
Pig	亥	*I*	2019

Those of you living in Japan can mail *nengajō* anytime in mid-December before the 26th. The post office will hold your cards until New Year's Day.

International mail will not be held by the post office, even if it contains the *nenga* stamp. Any *nengajō* mailed after the 26th will be delivered on the 3rd of January.

Do not send New Year's cards to those who are in mourning. This is considered bad luck and bad form.

On New Year's Day, Japanese children receive *otoshidama* お年玉 "New Year's money." The amount given depends on the giver and the age of the child, but at least ¥1000 is customary.

Nengajō produced by Japan Post have a raffle number on the back, also called *otoshidama*. Check Japan Post's website up to fifteen days after New Year's to see if you've won something. *Otoshidama* prizes range from a commemorative set of postage stamps to a trip to Hawaii. Japan Post *nengajō* are sold both at the post office and in stationery stores. Look for a preprinted stamp in the top right-hand corner. You will need to add additional postage if you want to send prepaid *nengajō* overseas.

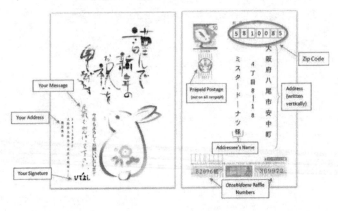

Nengajō are traditionally written vertically. When writing vertically, long vowel sounds and hyphens are written as | to distinguish them from the *kanji* for one, 一 .

Write the addressee's name last name first. If you're addressing a letter in Japanese to someone in Japan, include the formal suffix 様 *sama* after his/ her name. Never affix *sama* to your own name.

New Year's Greetings

Happy New Year! (Casual)

あけましておめでとう！

Akemashite-omedetō!

Happy New Year! (Polite/Normal)

あけましておめでとうございます！

Akemashite-omedetō-gozaimasu!

Happy New Year (Formal)

きんがしんねん
謹賀新年

Kinga-shinnen

Thank you for all your kind help this past year. (Formal)

さくねんちゅう　たいへん　せ わ
昨 年 中 は大変お世話になり、ありがとうございました

Sakunenchū-wa-taihen-o-sewa-ni-nari-arigatō-gozaimashita.

I hope for your continued favor this year. (Formal)

ほんねん　　　　　　　　　　　ねが
本年もどうぞよろしくお願いいたします。

Honnen-mo-dōzo-yoroshiku-onegai-itashimasu.

Wishing everyone good health. (Formal)

みなさま　　　けんこう　　　いの　もう　あ
皆様のご健康をお祈り申し上げます。

Mina-sama-no-go-kenkō-o-o-inori-mōshiagemasu.

Hope you have a great year! (Casual)

ことし　　げんき
今年も元気でね！

Kotoshi-mo-genki-de-ne!

Let's hang out again this year! (Casual)

今年もまた遊ぼうね！

Kotoshi-mo-mata-asobō-ne!

If you receive a *nengajō* from someone you did not send one to, send that person a friendly note by January 7th.

Thank you for your New Year's Card. (Polite)

早々の年賀状ありがとうございました。

Sōsō-no-nengajō-arigatō-gozaimashita.

I apologize for the late New Year's Card. (Formal)

年賀状が遅くなって申し訳ありません。

Nengajō-ga-osokunatte-mōshiwake-arimasen.

ROKUYŌ—LUCKY AND UNLUCKY DAYS

The Japanese calendar designates some days as "lucky" and some days as "unlucky" through a system called *rokuyō* 六曜 <ruby>ろくよう</ruby>. *Rokuyō* are derived from the Chinese calendar, and are generally ignored in day-to-day life, except when planning weddings and funerals. Should you decide to get married in Japan, it is often cheaper to get married on an "unlucky" day.

Rokuyō Calendar		
Kanji	*Rōmaji*	Meaning
先勝	*Senshō*	Good luck in the morning, bad luck in the afternoon. It's a good idea to hurry in everything you do today.
友引	*Tomobiki*	Good luck in the morning, bad luck in the afternoon, amazing luck in the evening. On this day, you will take misfortune away from friends. This is a good day for business deals, but a terrible day for funerals. A friend may try to pull you (the literal meaning of the *kanji*, though this was simply for spelling purposes in Chinese) into hell, which is why crematoriums are traditionally closed on *Tomobiki* days. Though not ideal for funerals, *Tomobiki* days are great for sharing fortune with friends. Many wedding favors are shipped on this day.
先負	*Senbu*	Bad luck in the morning, good luck in the afternoon.
仏滅	*Butsumetsu*	"Luck so bad it can even destroy Buddha." This is the worst day in the *rokuyō* calendar. Avoid holding weddings and celebrations on this day (unless you want to take advantage of heavy discounts).
大安	*Taian*	The luckiest day of the calendar. You'll succeed in whatever you do. This is the most popular day for weddings.
赤口	*Shakkō*	There is luck on this day only between 11 am and 1 pm. The rest of the day is very unlucky.

Natalia Doan

Determining the order of lucky and unlucky days requires the use of Japan's Lunisolar Calendar. For accuracy's sake, check the Japanese site **AJNet** (http://www.ajnet.ne.jp/dairy).

JAPANESE TEA CEREMONY

Japanese tea ceremony, known as *sadō* 茶道 (さどう), is a traditional art still practiced today. Here's a quick etiquette guide in case you're invited to an *Urasenke* 裏千家 (うらせんけ) style Japanese tea ceremony.

Getting Ready

Tea ceremonies are held in traditional Japanese teahouses or tearooms, known as *cha-shitsu* 茶室 (ちゃしつ). *Cha-shitsu* have floors made of *tatami* mats, so no shoes are allowed inside of a tearoom. You must wear socks in a teahouse. Ideally bring a clean pair of socks you can change into before entering the *cha-shitsu*.

Ladies, do not wear lipstick or heavy lip gloss to tea ceremony. The tea cups, *chawan* 茶碗 (ちゃわん), are, in many types of tea ceremony, reused by the other members of your party. Due to the porous clay the *chawan* are made of, *chawan* are usually lightly washed only with water. (This is not true for public tea ceremony demonstrations, such as at a local temple or garden.)

Do not wear jewelry to Japanese tea ceremony. This includes earrings, rings, and watches. Tea ceremony is supposed to be an escape from worldly, material concerns, and a time for internal peace and reflection.

Entering the Teahouse

Seating order in the teahouse or tea room is determined by rank. The highest-ranking member of your party should sit closest to the hanging wall scroll, the *kakemono* 掛物. The lowest ranking member should sit closest to the door.

As a foreign guest, you may be given the seat of honor. If at all possible, try to have at least one person sit ahead of you. Not only will you appear humble and polite, being second in line allows you to copy the behavior of the person ahead of you.

Upon entering the teahouse, you should sit with your legs under your knees, in a position called *seiza* 正座. However, even Japanese people sometimes find *seiza* painful, so most hosts will invite their guests to sit in a more relaxed position.

The Ceremony Begins

There is a beautiful, highly ritualistic aspect of tea ceremony that can be a joy to watch. Tea ceremony is usually conducted in contemplative silence, allowing the guests to enjoy the relaxed atmosphere of the teahouse and a period of introspective reflection.

The *O-temae-san* お手前さん —the person conducting the tea ceremony—will, at a certain point in the ceremony, say "*O-kashi, o-dōzo*"「お菓子、おどうぞ。」This indicates that it's time for the person ahead of you to take a traditional Japanese sweet, known as *wagashi*, from the provided plate.

Formality dictates that the highest-ranking (thus first served) guest turn and say *O-saki-ni*「お先に」, which means something along the lines of "you first," to the lower-ranking person at his or her side.

The lower-ranking person must decline. The higher-ranking person will then take one sweet. When that person receives a cup of tea, he/she will also offer it to you first, but you must decline.

Time for Tea

When it's your turn, first offer a sweet to the person next to you. When he / she declines, say "*O-kashi-o-chodō-itashimasu*" 「お菓子をちょうどいたします。」.

Using the chopsticks, place the sweet on your sweet paper, known as *kaishi* 懐紙 . Afterwards, wipe the end of your chopsticks off on the edge of your sweet paper before placing the chopsticks back on top of the bowl.

> The tools and sweets used in tea ceremony change depending on the season. The sweets might be shaped like summer flowers in the summer, and the *kaishi* might have faint images of falling snow in winter.

Soon you will be presented with a cup of *matcha* tea.

First, lift the cup of tea, and give a short bow, as if to the heavens, then bring the cup towards you and rotate it two times clockwise. This is so that the pretty, main side is facing outward.

Ideally, you should finish your tea in three gulps.

After you've finished the tea, use the tips of your fingers to wipe the area where your mouth was. You can wipe these on the used sweet paper, which should then be folded (dirty side inwards) and set behind you. You should take this with you when you leave the teahouse.

Examine the teacup's beauty, then rotate it back two times and place it on the *tatami* in front of you for the *O-temae-san* to collect. Lean forward and examine the cup once more.

The *chawan* examining step may seem excessive, but many *chawan* and tea ceremony accessories are true works of art. There are museums dedicated to antique *chawan*, and chawan made by master craftsmen can easily cost in the hundreds or thousands of dollars. (Don't worry, you can buy a good chawan for under $100.) Authentic *chawan* are made by hand, so no two are exactly the same. Real *chawan* should have the artist's seal on the bottom. That's one of the reasons you examine a *chawan* after finishing your tea, to get a closer look at a piece of art.

If you want a detailed, picture-filled guide to tea ceremony, I recommend *Urasenke Chanoyu Handbook One* and *Urasenke Chanoyu Handbook Two* by Soshitsu Sen XV the 15th Grandmaster of the School of Urasenke Tea

Ceremony. The process and procedure of Urasenke Tea Ceremony is depicted using pictures and concise English explanations.

For information on the history of tea ceremony, there are multiple texts available, one of which is *Cha-No-Yu: The Japanese Tea Ceremony* by A.L. Sadler, which provides a thorough history of tea ceremony in Japan.

SAYŌNARA—LEAVING JAPAN

Here are the last few things you need to take care of before leaving Japan.

1. Thank You Notes

Write thank you notes to all the people who made your stay in Japan special. (See the next chapter: "How to Write a Thank You Note in Japanese.") Thank you notes can also be sent from your home country. If you can, include a small souvenir gift from your country.

2. *Sayōnara* Sale

I recommend liquidating your unnecessary possessions one to two months before your departure. Give away as much stuff as possible, keeping in mind that shipping items home can be expensive, as can the airline fee for oversized luggage.

Pay the oversized garbage fee in advance if you will be disposing of anything large (ask your apartment manager for details).

If you're a JET, your apartment may be inherited by the incoming JET. You can leave useful things (such as teaching supplies) for the next generation.

3. Return Your Health Insurance Card

Return your health insurance card to your local ward office. Some companies require you to submit your health insurance card directly to HR or your supervisor when terminating employment.

4. Close Accounts

Close your bank account and cancel your cell phone plan.

Make sure that all your utility bills have been paid. If you're leaving in the middle of the month, you may still have to pay utilities and rent through the next month.

Communicate with your company in advance so that they can wire your last month's salary to your American bank account via an international money transfer. (There may be a small foreign transaction fee.)

5. Return your Alien Registration/Resident Card

Return your Alien Registration or Resident Card to Japanese Customs when you leave the country. Keeping your Resident Card (even if just for your scrapbook) may cause problems when you next visit Japan.

6. Reclaim Your Pension Money

If you've been employed more than six months during your time in Japan, you can reclaim a substantial amount of your retirement pension simply by filling out a few forms.

You must apply for your pension reimbursement within two years of leaving Japan. You cannot apply for it while still living in Japan. You must not be a Japanese citizen or have already received any pension payment.

If you wish to reclaim your payment, complete and mail the **Japan Pension Service**'s form (http://www.nenkin.go.jp/n/www/english/detail.jsp?id=10), along with your pension booklet and a copy of your passport, after leaving Japan.

7. Tickets and Transportation

Most bus tickets to the airport require a minimum of 24 hour advance notice.

An easy way to arrange bus tickets is to call the local hotel that manages the bus stop from which you would like to depart. You can learn more about bus times and bus stations at the **Airport Limousine Bus** official English website: http://www.limousinebus.co.jp/en . If you can read Japanese, you can buy your ticket using one of the ticket machines at your local convenience store.

Double-check your plane's departing terminal. If your return flight departs from Narita International (http://www.narita-airport.jp/en/guide/ t_info/index.html), check which terminal you will be leaving from on the airport's terminal list before boarding your taxi. And pack a snack for the flight home!

HOW TO WRITE A THANK YOU NOTE IN JAPANESE

If you stayed with a host family during your time in Japan, send them a thank you note once you return to your home country. Your host family will appreciate your gratitude and may feel more inclined to stay in touch.

If you have just begun to learn *kanji*, feel free to write your letter entirely in *hiragana*. Remember, it really is the thought that counts.

The following sample thank you note is written in polite Japanese, with formal and seasonal greetings omitted. Use the line-by-line explanations to customize your thank you note, or flip to the end of this chapter for a complete sample thank you note.

Thanking Your Homestay Family

(Names of Family Members) さんへ、

お元気ですか？

 How are you?

ご無沙汰していますが、お元気ですか？

 It's been a while, but how are you?

 If it's been more than a month since you saw your homestay family, write ご無沙汰していますが. Otherwise "how are you" お元気ですか is fine.

<u>3ヶ月間</u>、ありがとうございました。

 Thank you for the past <u>three months</u>.
 2 週間 = two weeks
 6ヶ月間 = six months
 1 年間 = one year

とても楽しかったです。

> It was a lot of fun.

皆さんと<u>カラオケをする</u>のはとても楽しかったです。

> It was really fun <u>going to karaoke</u> with everyone.

観光する = sightseeing

祭りへ行く = going to the festival

京都へ行く = going to Kyoto

神社へ行く = going to the shrine

映画を見に行く = going to see a movie

テレビゲームをする = playing video games

<u>Yuko さんの料理</u>はとてもおいしかったです。

> <u>(Yuko's) cooking</u> was very delicious.

天ぷら = *tenpura*

焼肉 = *yakiniku*

焼き鳥 = *yakitori*

ラーメン = *ramen*

すき焼き = *sukiyaki*

お好み焼き = *okonomiyaki*

皆さんはいろいろなことを教えてくれました。

> You all taught me many things.

この<u>3 ケ月間</u>のこと、忘れません！

> I will never forget the past <u>three months</u>!

また<u>日本</u>へ行きたいです。

> I want to go to <u>Japan</u> again.

<u>アメリカ</u>に来てください。

> Please come to <u>America</u>.

私は<u>アメリカ</u>を皆さんに紹介したいです。

> I want to show you <u>America</u>.

(name of your home state) ＋ 州

(name of your home town) ＋ 町

また会いたいです！

I want to see you again!

皆さんによろしくお伝えください。

Please say "hello" to everyone for me.

これからも連絡を取り合おう！

Let's keep in touch!

Including your personal contact information will increase the chance of a reply.

If you didn't give your family a thank you gift before leaving Japan, send a thank you note from America and include a small, wrapped token of appreciation. A framed photo of you with your homestay family is an excellent choice.

For further details on formal and informal letter-writing styles, read *Writing Letters in Japanese* by Kikuko Tatematsu, Yoko Tateoka, Takashi Matsumoto, and Tsukasa Sato.

Yukoさん、Tomoyoさん、Makotoさんへ、

ご無沙汰していますが、お元気ですか？

3ヶ月間、ありがとうございました！とても楽しかったです。

皆さんとカラオケをするのはとても楽しかったです。

Yukoさんの料理はとてもおいしかったです。

皆さんはいろいろなことを教えてくれました。

この3ヶ月間のこと、忘れません！

また日本へ行きたいです！

アメリカにきてください！私はアメリカを皆さんに紹介したいです。

また会いたいです！

皆さんによろしくお伝えください！

これから連絡を会おう！

Alex

☆○△123@☆○. com

IN CASE OF EMERGENCY

Hopefully you'll never need this section, but here are a few tips and helpful phone numbers to have on hand in case of emergency.

Emergency Phone Numbers			
110	Police	けいさつ 警察	*Keisatsu*
119	Fire Department	しょうぼうしょ 消防署	*Shōbōsho*
	Ambulance	きゅうきゅうしゃ 救急車	*Kyūkyūsha*

Emergency phone calls can be made free of charge from any Japanese phone, including public pay phones.

The Tokyo Metropolitan Health & Medical Information Center (http://www.himawari.metro.tokyo.jp/qq/qq13enmnlt.asp) offers emergency medical interpretation by phone for non-Japanese speakers anywhere in Japan. (Their website lets you search in English for Tokyo hospitals by location and/or nearest train station.) For their Japanese interpretation services, call (03) 5285-8185 from 5-8 pm on weekdays and 9 am-8 pm on weekends and holidays. They can interpret English, Chinese, Korean, Thai, and Spanish. In non-emergency situations, you can dial 03-5285-8181 between 9 am and 8 pm to learn more about the Japanese medical and health insurance system.

Most police officers, firefighters, and/or emergency response teams in Japan do not speak English. English is a mandatory subject in Japanese schools, but the curriculum emphasizes reading and writing (a.k.a. test-taking), not speaking.

Include a Japanese contact on your emergency list, even if he or she is just a coworker you have only spoken to three times. Emergency response teams may feel more comfortable explaining your condition to a native Japanese speaker, and if your loved ones are a few time zones away, an in-country contact may more rapidly assist you in the event of an emergency. Japanese family friends and roommates are ideal emergency contacts.

If you do not speak Japanese, keep a *rōmaji* reading of your address in your wallet and by your telephone, in case of emergency. (See "Settling In— At Home" for more information about Japanese maps and addresses.) You should also carry a list in Japanese of any allergies you have, any medications you currently take, and your emergency contact information.

In Case of Fire

1) Call 119.
2) Speak to the operator.

「火事です。＿区（市）、＿町の＿番の＿号、住宅が燃えています。」
"Kaji-desu. (Give address). Jutaku-ga-moeteimasu."
"There's a fire at (address). My house is burning."

3. Stand outside so you can guide the fire trucks to the fire.

In Case of Medical Emergency

1) Call 119.
2) Speak to the operator.

「救急です。＿区（市）、＿町の＿番の＿号、…」
"Kyūkyū-desu. (Give address). (Give illness.)"
"It's a medical emergency. My address is_(address)_. I am suffering from _(illness)_."

「私の名前は＿。私は＿歳です。ケイタイ番号は＿。」
"Watashi-no-namae-wa_(name). Watashi-wa_(age number)_sai-desu. Keitai-bangō-wa_(cell phone number)."
"My name is_____. I am _____ years old. My cell phone number is_____."

3) Gather your passport, cash, health insurance card, and any medication you are currently taking. Ambulances operate for free, but you will be expected to pay the hospital in cash immediately after receiving medical attention. Many hospitals do not accept credit cards.

For reasons of speed and convenience, in non-life threatening situations, I recommend taking a taxi to the hospital. You will need to provide the driver with the name and (sometimes) the address of your hospital. In Japan, you register at a certain hospital and that specific hospital keeps all your data on file. If you just say "take me to the hospital," the driver may be unsure where to take you.

Visiting the Hospital

Always bring a Japanese-English dictionary with you when seeking medical attention. There is no guarantee that an English-speaking hospital will have an English speaker present at the time of your visit, or even that the "English speaker" on call can actually speak fluent English. (See "Study—Essential Studying Resources" for some great Japanese/English dictionaries you can load onto your phone.)

Use the following phrases in the event of a hospital visit.

To speak about yourself, say *Watashi-wa* 私は, before each sentence. To speak about a friend, say *Tomodachi-wa* 友達は.

I have a stomach ache. *Onaka-ga-itai-desu.*
おなかが痛いです。

I am having a heart attack. *Shinzō-hossa-ga-arimasu.*
心臓発作があります。

My chest hurts. *Mune-ga-kurshii-desu.*
胸が苦しいです。

I broke a bone. *Hone-ga-oreta.*
骨が折れた。

I feel queasy. *Onaka-o-kowashiteimasu.*
おなかを壊しています。

(He/She is) unconscious. *Ishiki-ga-shimasen.*
意識がしません。

I have a bad burn. *Hidoi-yakedo-desu.*
ひどい火傷です。

It is hard to breathe. *Kokyū-ga-kurushi-sōdesu.*
呼吸が苦しそうです。

My ____ is bleeding. ____ *kara-chi-ga-deteimasu.*
____から血が出ています。

Eye = *Me* 目
Ear = *Mimi* 耳

Arm = *Ude* 腕
Leg = *Ashi* 足

I suddenly collapsed. *Totsuzen-taoremashita.*
突然倒れました。

I can't move my____. ____*wo-ugokemasen.*

____を動けません。
Neck = *Kubi* 首
Hand = *Te* 手
Arm = *Ude* 腕
Leg = *Ashi* 脚
Feet = *Ashi* 足 ("Leg" and "foot" are pronounced the same in Japanese, but spelled differently.)

I've been having convulsions for the past ten minutes.
Jūppun-mae-ni-keiren-wo-okoshimashita.
１０分前に痙攣を起こしました。

I have a high fever. *Netsu-ga-takai-desu.*
熱が高いです。

I have a fever of 39°. *Netsu-ga-san-jū-kyū-do-arimasu.*
熱が３９℃あります。

The **Tanaka Clinic** has a comprehensive Japanese/English list (http://www.tanaka-clinic.net/eng/medical_terms.htm#RANGE!A105) of body parts and medical ailments.

If you have a fever, refer to your temperature in Celsius. Do 度, pronounced like "dough," means "degrees."

As mentioned in "Before You Leave," research the nearest hospital and the nearest English-speaking hospital to where you will be staying.

°F	°C	Japanese
104°	40°	*yon-jū-do*
102°	39°	*san-jū-kyū-do*
100°	38°	*san-jū-hachi-do*
98.6°	37°	*san-jū-nana-do*
96.8°	36°	*san-jū-roku-do*
95°	35°	*san-jū-go-do*
93.2°	34°	*san-jū-yon-do*

Hospital registration occurs at the time of your first visit, after which you will receive a plastic hospital card. Next time you visit the hospital, the staff will use your patient identification card to retrieve your medical information.

If you possess international or travelers' health insurance, hold onto your medical receipts after receiving medical treatment at a Japanese hospital. You will pay the full out-of-pocket expenses at the Japanese hospital, then file for a refund upon return to your home country.

Illegal Substances

Hopefully this goes without saying, but do not even think about bringing drugs into Japan. Possession of one marijuana joint equates to a five year sentence in *Japanese prison*. No, you cannot serve your time on U.S. soil. According to the U.S. Embassy, "bail [is] virtually unheard of for foreigners." Access to interpreters is not required under Japanese law, and inmates are not allowed access to personal medication of any kind. First-time substance offenders occasionally get a six month to three year sentence. For foreigners, this sentence is followed with deportation with no possible future re-entry to Japan.

You can be convicted of drug use based on a positive blood or urine test. About 25% of all U.S. citizens currently in Japanese prison were incarcerated because of a drug-related crime.

Though hopefully you will never have any legal trouble in Japan, the Japanese police are authorized to arrest and detain anyone for up to 48 hours on the suspicion of having committed a crime. You have the right to remain silent, the right to hire a lawyer at your own expense, and the right to notify your embassy of your arrest. According to the U.S. embassy, however, the Japanese police occasionally begin questioning before the lawyers arrive.

Embassy Information

The **U.S. Embassy**, *Amerika-taishikan* アメリカ大使館 , provides the most up-to-date safety information and assistance for Americans living in Japan. Non-Emergency Services, such as lost passports, are by appointment only. If you lose your passport, refer to the U.S. Embassy's website (http://japan.usembassy.gov/e/acs/tacs-passports-lost.html) for proper procedure.

Please visit the U.S. State Department's website (http://www.travel.state.

gov) for up-to-date safety information.

Regardless of your intended length of stay, print the Embassy's handy guide (http://japan.usembassy.gov/e/acs/tacs-emergency.html) for placing an emergency call before you leave.

American Embassies in Japan	
U.S. Embassy Tokyo べいこくたいしかん 米国大使館 Emergency Number = (03) 3224-5000 Appointments Online 1-10-5 Akasaka Minato-ku, Tokyo 107-8420 とうきょうとみなとくあかさか 東京都港区赤坂1-10-5	U.S. Consulate General Osaka-Kobe そうりょうじかん アメリカ総領事館 Emergency Number = (06) 6315-5912 Appointments Online 11-5-2 Nishitenma Kita-ku, Osaka 530-8543 おおさかふおおさかしきたくにしてんま 大阪府大阪市北区西天満11-5-2
U.S. Consulate General Naha べいこくそうりょうじかん 米国総領事館 Emergency Number = (03) 3224-5000* Appointments Only = (098) 876-4211 Appointments Online 2-1-1 Toyama Urasoe City, Okinawa 901-2104 おきなわうらそえとうやま 沖縄浦添当山2-1-1	U.S. Consulate General Sapporo べいこくそうりょうじかん 米国総領事館 Emergency Number = (03) 3224-5000* Appointments Only = (011) 641-1115 Kita 1-jo, Nishi 28-chome Chuo-ku, Sapporo 064-0821 ほっかいどうさっぽろちゅうおうくきた　じょうにし　　ちょうめ 北海道札幌中央区北1条 西28丁目
U.S. Consulate Fukuoka べいこくりょうじかん 米国領事館 Emergency Number = (03) 3224-5000* Appointments Only = (092) 751-9331 2-5-26 Ōhori 2 Chuo-ku, Fukuoka 810-0052 ふくおかけんちゅうおうくおおほり 福岡県中央区大濠2-5-26	U.S. Consulate Nagoya べいこくりょうじかん 米国領事館 Emergencies Only = (052) 581-4501 Appointments Only = (06) 6315-5912 Nagoya Int'l Center Bldg. 6th Floor 1-47-1 Nagono Nakamura-ku, Nagoya 450-0001 あいちけんなごやしなかむらくなごの 愛知県名古屋市中村区那古野1-47-1
*Emergency calls directed to the Tokyo Embassy.	

The following embassies and consulates are closed on all Japanese and American national holidays.

Tokyo Embassy
    Provides service to Americans in Tokyo, Chiba, Fukushima, Gunma, Ibaraki, Kanagawa, Nagano, Niigata, Saitama, Shizuoka, Tochigi, Yamagata, and Yamanishi.

Consulate General Osaka-Kobe
    Provides service to Americans in Osaka, Aichi, Ehime, Fukui, Gifu,

Hiroshima, Hyogo, Ishikawa, Kagawa, Kochi, Kyoto, Mie, Nara, Okayama, Shimane, Shiga, Tokushima, Tottori, Toyama, and Wakayama.

Consulate General Naha
 Provides service to Americans in Okinawa, the Amami Oshima Islands, and parts of Kagoshima.

Consulate General Sapporo
 Provides service to Americans in Akita, Aomori, Hokkaido, Iwate, and Miyagi.

Consulate Fukuoka
 Provides service to Americans in Fukuoka, Kagoshima, Kumamoto, Miyazaki, Nagasaki, Oita, Saga, and Yamaguchi.

Consulate Nagoya
 Provides emergency consular services for Americans living in Aichi, Gifu, and Mie. Limited consular services available on an appointment basis. (Overlap with Consulate General Osaka-Kobe.)

This book, like all travel guides, is a work-in-progress. I have provided the information in this book to the best of my ability, but feedback and suggestions are more than welcome.

If you would like your name and tips included in future reprints of this book, I would love to hear your comments, questions, and stories at feedback@worktravelstudyjapan.com.

I WISH YOU WONDERFUL TRAVELS.

Ganbatte!

RECOMMENDED READING

All the books previously mentioned are listed in this section, as well as some of my personal favorites on Japanese history, language, and culture.

Culture

The Book of Kimono: The Complete Guide to Style and Wear
Norio Yamanaka
ISBN: 978-0-87011-785-5, ISBN in Japan: 978-4-7700-1285-2

As mentioned in "Out and About—Kyoto Short Guide," this is a great book for those interested in the history and physical components of the *kimono*. This book alone will not teach you how to wear a *kimono*, but it can give you an introduction to traditional Japanese dress. There are many drawings and a few color pictures.

Cha-No-Yu: The Japanese Tea Ceremony
A.L. Sadler
ISBN: 978-0804834070

As mentioned in "Culture and Language—Japanese Tea Ceremony," this book provides a comprehensive history of Japanese tea ceremony.

Geisha
Liza Dalby
ISBN: 978-0-520-20495-9

As mentioned in "Out and About—Kyoto Short Guide," Dalby's book provides unparalleled historical analysis and insight into the often misrepresented "floating world."

Japanese Schoolgirl Inferno: A Tokyo Teen Fashion Subculture Handbook
Patrick Macias and Izumi Evers
Illustrations by Kazumi Nonaka
ISBN: 0-8118-5690-9

This humorous and well-illustrated guide to Japanese street fashion both past and present will interest any fans of Japanese fashion and pop culture.

Kimono
Liza Dalby
ISBN: 0-300-05639-7

Kimono is an excellent book on the history and cultural significance of the *kimono*.

Samurai Sushi
Bobby Suetsugu
ISBN: 0-7606-5933-2

This travel-sized volume has large pictures and detailed explanations on the origin, ingredients, and characteristics of many types of *sushi*.

The Story of Sushi: An Unlikely Saga of Raw Fish and Rice
Trevor Corson
ISBN: 978-0-06-088351-5

This book provides an interesting look at Japanese culture and the *sushi* industry, both in America and abroad, through a nonfiction account of America's first *sushi* chef training academy.

Tokyo Vice: An American Reporter on the Police Beat in Japan
Jake Adelstein
ISBN: 978-0-3074-7529-9

Tokyo Vice is a disturbing and fascinating account of the underside of Japanese culture, with an emphasis on the *yakuza* and their power in modern-day Japan.

Totto-chan: The Little Girl at the Window
Tetsuko Kuroyanagai
ISBN: 978-4-7700-2067-3

Totto-chan is a touching and uplifting memoir about a Japanese girl living during World War II and the elementary school that changed her life forever.

Urasenke Chanoyu: Handbook One & Two
Soshitsu Sen XV
Urasenke Foundation: 4th ed., 1993.

As mentioned in "Culture and Language—Japanese Tea Ceremony," these two books might be a bit tricky to get a hold of, but they are excellent guides for the serious student of tea ceremony.

Yakuza Moon: Memoirs of a Gangster's Daughter
Shoko Tendo
ISBN: 978-4770030863

Yakuza Moon is the memoir of a Japanese woman born into a yakuza family.

You Gotta Have Wa
Robert Whiting
ISBN: 0307455971

As mentioned in "Out and About—Four Days with Dad," this book is all about the history and culture of Japanese baseball.

Fiction

Botchan
Sōseki Natsume
ISBN: 978-4-770-00701-8

Botchan is a Japanese classic about a young man who moves from Tokyo to teach math in rural Japan.

Memoirs of a Geisha
Arthur Golden
ISBN: 978-0-739-32687-9

This best-selling novel is perhaps the most famous and controversial book about *geisha* in the English-speaking world. Arthur Golden's tale depicts the struggles and triumphs of a young, up-and-coming *geisha*. Though many debate the cultural accuracy of Golden's representation of *geisha*, the book itself is an enjoyable, fast-paced read that has entertained and inspired millions around the world.

Norwegian Wood
Haruki Murakami
ISBN: 978-0-375-70402-4

This book is considered a classic of modern Japanese literature. It is one of Murakami's most well-known novels, and has been translated into several languages.

Japanese Study

ビジネスメールものの言い方辞書 *Bijinesu Mēru Mono No Iikata Jisho*
["How to Say It" Business E-mail Dictionary]
シーズ者 *Shīzu-sha* [Cybernote Information System]
ISBN: 4-7741-2180-0

As mentioned in "Work—At the Office," this book is an excellent guide to writing business e-mails in Japanese.

Kanji and Kana
Wolfgang Hadamitzky and Mark Spahn
ISBN: 978-0-8048-2077-6

As mentioned in "Study—Essential Studying Resources," this book is indispensable to the *kanji*-learning student.

敬語すらすら便利帳 *Keigo Surasura Benrichō*
[Smoothly Use Keigo Reference Book]
今井登茂子 [Tomoko Imai]
ISBN: 978-4-8207-1756-0

As mentioned in "Work—At the Office," this Japanese-language book is an excellent reference for those who want to brush up on their *keigo*. Imai's explanations are clear and concise. She offers many practical examples and phrases that you can immediately apply in your daily life as a professional in Japan.

Oxford Beginner's Japanese Dictionary
Jonathan Bunt, with Gillian Hall
ISBN: 978-0-1992-9852-5

The *Oxford Beginner's Japanese Dictionary* is an excellent dictionary for the beginning student of Japanese. Its *hiragana* look-up index is convenient and gets you used to reading *hiragana*, while also providing the *kanji* for each entry. *Rōmaji* dictionaries may seem easier to use, but the sooner you switch to a *hiragana* dictionary, the faster you will be able to read Japanese. You can't go wrong with this basic dictionary.

Writing Letters in Japanese
Kikuko Tatematsu, Yoko Tateoka, Takashi Matsumoto, Tsukasa Sato
ISBN: 4-7890-0664-6

As mentioned in "*Sayōnara*—Leaving Japan: How to Write a Thank You Note in Japanese," this book gives samples and thorough translations of seasonal greetings, congratulation letters, health inquiries, condolence letters, and letters of request. Finding this book might require some Internet research, but this book is a great reference for those who anticipate extensive written correspondence.

Living in Japan

How to Get a Job in Japan: Get Hired and Get Here
Andy Fossett
ISBN: 978-1-4515-7669-3

As mentioned in "Work—The Job Search," this is a slim, but information-packed guide to getting a job in Japan.

Life After the B.O.E.
David Namisato
ISBN: 978-1466340725

Read this book after a few months of teaching in Japan, or when you're back in your home country and longing for some nostalgic memories of teaching in Japan. Namisato's comics humorously and poignantly capture the experience of the ex-pat English teacher. You can read *Life After the B.O.E.* for free online, but the print version comes with a few extra comics and makes a great memento.

さいよう りれきしょ しょくむけいれきしょ か
採用される履歴書・職務経歴書はこう書く [*Saiyō-Sareru Rirekisho Shokumu-keirekisho Wa Kō Kaku*]
[How to Write a Resume That Will Get You Hired]
こ じ ま み つ こ
小島美津子 [Mitsuko Kojima]
ISBN: 978-4-534-02598-1

As mentioned in "Work—Writing a Resume in Japanese," this Japanese language book is an excellent aid to resume writing.

The apan Health Handbook
Meredith Enman Maruyama, Louise Picon Shimizu, and Nancy Smith
Tsurumaki
ISBN: 4-7700-2356-1

As mentioned in "Before You Leave—Health and Medical," this book is a must for anyone on prescription medication who is planning an extended stay in Japan.

Tokyo on Foot
Florent Chavouet
ISBN: 978-4-8053-1137-0

This art book is one I recommend reading after returning from Japan. Chavouet's descriptions and illustrations of Tokyo's streets and people strike the perfect note of hilarious and poignant.

Travel

As mentioned in "Out and About—Tokyo Short Guide," I highly recommend the most recent edition of DK Eyewitness Travel Guide: Japan.

The *DK Eyewitness Travel Guide* is, in my opinion, the definitive travel guide to Japan. If you can only purchase one guide, I would recommend this one.

The Lonely Planet and Rough Guides to Japan tend to focus on budget travelers, but they are both good resources for those spending extended time in Japan. I also recommend purchasing specific city guides for Tokyo and Kyoto. Smaller city guides will offer more detail than their larger counterparts and can be carried around on a daily basis.

SNAPSHOT GUIDE TO JAPANESE

There are three alphabets in Japanese: *hiragana*, *katakana*, and *kanji*.

Hiragana	Katakana	Kanji	Rōmaji	Definition
がんばって	ガンバッテ	頑張って	Ganbatte	A frequently used Japanese phrase that means "good luck," "go for it," and "do your best!"
けいたい	ケイタイ	携帯	Keitai	Literally means "portable." A *keitai* is a cell phone.

Hiragana 「ひらがな」 is the first alphabet taught in Japanese schools.

There are 46 *hiragana* characters. Japanese children learn *hiragana* in first grade.

When *hiragana* appear over other Japanese characters, these *hiragana* are called *furigana* 振り仮名 or "ruby text." *Furigana* serve as a pronunciation guide to Japanese characters, and are often seen in books for Japanese children or next to unusual words. *Furigana* will be used throughout the rest of this book.

Hiragana are often used to convey cuteness, and many girls choose to spell their names in *hiragana* when writing notes to friends. However, a sentence entirely written in *hiragana* may be long and difficult for native Japanese speakers to read at one glance.

Many Japanese words that share the same *hiragana* spelling mean different things. For example, *ame* あめ can mean either "candy" or "rain."

Katakana 「カタカナ」 is the alphabet used to write foreign words.

There is one *katakana* for each *hiragana*. *Katakana* are used in place of *hiragana* to write words of non-Japanese origin, such as "computer" and "John."

Katakana is often seen as "cool," so many advertisements stylistically use *katakana* spellings of Japanese words to indicate emphasis or a foreign accent. For example, Fukuoka City, a city on the Kyushu island of Japan, has dubbed themselves "the Ward of Cute" 「カワイイ区」 in an effort to boost tourism. Spelling "cute," or *kawaii* かわいい, in *katakana* makes this word look more exotic and sophisticated. Many advertising campaigns use *katakana* to draw attention to certain words.

Katakana spellings of names, such as ジョージ・ワシントン ("George Washington") are often separated with a black dot • to indicate where the first word ends and the next begins.

Kanji 「漢字」 are Chinese characters adopted into the Japanese language.

Each *kanji* has two readings—the Chinese reading, known as the *on-yomi* 音読み, and the Japanese reading, known as the *kun-yomi* 訓読み. *Kanji* clear up the confusion between words with similar sounds. Using the example from before, "candy" is spelled 飴 and "rain" is spelled 雨, even though their *hiragana* reading あめ (*ame*) is the same.

Kanji generally pose the greatest difficulty for English-speaking learners of Japanese.

The Japanese sixth grade graduate should be able to read and write 1006 *kanji*. The adult Japanese citizen, 2136. There is also a special list of *kanji* for personal names, which includes characters and special readings not on the list of *kanji* one must know to be considered literate.

Japanese parents often select a child's name based on the meaning of the individual *kanji*. For example, the name "Misaki" can be written as 美咲, using the characters for "beautiful" and "bloom." "Ichirō" 一郎 uses the characters for "first" and "son." Many names, such as "Haruna" 陽菜 and "Hina" 陽菜 share the same *kanji*, but are pronounced differently. Just as in English, there are many different ways to spell and pronounce personal names in Japanese.

Kanji can have multiple pronunciations that change depending on each character's location in a word. For example, 女 is *onna* "woman" by itself, but goes by the *on-yomi* pronunciation *jo* when combined with the character for child, to make *joshi* 女子, or "girl." The *kanji* for child, 子 *ko*, also changes pronunciation depending on its location in a word.

女 *onna* woman	+	子 *ko* child	=	女子 *joshi* girl

Many foreign learners of Japanese want to spell their name in *kanji*, mistakenly thinking this will make their name "more Japanese," and thus easier to read. *Ma* 馬 and *ri* 離 may look like they could combine to make "Mary," but these *kanji*—*ma* meaning "horse" and *ri* meaning "to separate"—may be difficult for a Japanese speaker to read correctly when combined. Playing around with *kanji* can be fun, but when it comes to spelling your name, stick with *katakana*.

Most Japanese sentences have a mixture of *kanji*, *hiragana*, and *katakana*. For example, the sentence below says "I like orange juice." "I" and "like" are in *kanji*. "Orange juice," which is a foreign word, is in *katakana*. The other parts of the sentence are in *hiragana*.

Rōmaji「ローマ字」are the English transliterations of Japanese words.

Though not technically a Japanese alphabet, *rōmaji* are often used as a pronunciation guide to Japanese words.

Throughout the rest of this book, I will give the readings of Japanese words in both *kanji* and *rōmaji*.

This book spells Japanese words using the modified Hepburn style of *rōmaji*. Basically, that means that a word like "school," which would phonetically be spelled in English as *gakkou* 学校, will be spelled as *gakkō*.

This style of *rōmaji* makes pronunciation easier for those who have not studied Japanese. (Students of Japanese can refer to the *furigana* for each word's exact pronunciation.)

「 and 」 are the Japanese parantheses symbols.

RESOURCE LIST

Here's a list of all the stores, schools, and services mentioned in this book, listed alphabetically.

ABC Cooking Studio
> http://www.abc-cooking.co.jp
> A Japanese company specializing in cooking and baking classes.

Aeon   http://www.aeonet.com/aeon_index.php
> An *Eikaiwa* school in Japan.

AFS USA http://www.afsusa.org
> A nonprofit organization with international exchange programs in Japan.

Ageha   http://infor.co.jp/ladys_fashion_beauty/koakuma_ageha
> A Japanese women's magazine.

Agency for Cultural Affairs
> http://www.bunka.go.jp
> The Japanese government agency responsible for promoting and preserving Japanese culture and history.

Airport Limousine Bus
> http://www.limousinebus.co.jp/en
> A airport transportation company.

AKB48 Theater
> http://www.akb48.co.jp/theater
> The flagship performance hall of AKB48, the internationally-known Japanese girl J-pop group.

All Japanese, All the Time
> http://ajatt.com
> An excellent motivational and organizational resource for the dedicated learner of Japanese.

Altia Central
> http://recruiting.altmoot.com
> A dispatch English-teaching company in Japan.

Amazon
> http://amazon.com
> Online retailer of a variety of goods.

Amazon Japan
> http://amazon.jp
> Japanese online retailer of a variety of goods.

American Express
> https://www.americanexpress.com
> A major credit card company.

American Chamber of Commerce in Japan
> https://japan.careerengine.org/accj
> A job board site sponsored by the American Chamber of
> Commerce in Japan.

AneCam
> http://www.anecan.tv/index.html
> A Japanese women's magazine.

Anki   http://ankiweb.net
> Easy-to-use flashcard software.

Antioch University
> http://antioch.edu
> An American university with a Japan study abroad program.

Aoki Style
> http://www.eshop.aoki-style.com
> A Japanese suit company.

AU   http://www.au.kddi.com/english
> A Japanese cell phone company.

Ayusa   http://www.ayusa.org/students/japan
> A study abroad company that offers high-school programs in
> Japan.

Auntie Anne's Pretzels
    Japan
    http://www.auntieannes.jp/main.html
    An American soft pretzel company with branches in Japan.

Big Echo
    http://big-echo.jp
    A Japanese karaoke parlor company.

BookOff
    http://www.bookoff.co.jp
    Secondhand Japanese bookstore/entertainment retailer.

CanCam
    http://cancam.tv/index.html
    A Japanese women's magazine.

Career Cross
    http://www.careercross.com
    A Japanese job site geared towards bilingual professionals.

Center for Cultural Interchange
    CCI
    http://www.cci-exchange.com
    A non-profit, international exchange organization with programs
    in Japan.

Council on International Educational Exchange CIEE
    http://www.ciee.org
    A non-profit, international exchange organization with programs
    in Japan.

Citibank http://citibank.co.jp/en
    A major Japanese bank.

Country Code
    http://countrycode.org
    A list of the different country codes used when dialing
    international phone numbers.

Coupon Land
    http://www.c-pon.com
    A Japanese online and print discount magazine.

Crocs   http://www.crocs.com
             A shoe manufacturer popular in America and abroad.

Daijirin

             https://itunes.apple.com/jp/app/da-ci-lin/
             id299029654?mt=8&ign-mpt=uo%3D4
             A monolingual Japanese dictionary app.

Daijisen
             http://dic.yahoo.co.jp
             A monolingual Japanese dictionary accessible through Yahoo
             Japan's dictionary service.

Daijob   http://www.daijob.com
             A Japanese job board geared towards bilingual job-seekers.

Denshi Jisho
             http://jisho.org
             An extensive online Japanese-English dictionary.

Design Festa Gallery
             http://www.designfestagallery.com
             A small, independent art gallery in Harajuku, Tokyo.

Discover
             https://www.discover.com
             A major credit card company.

Docomo
             http://www.nttdocomo.co.jp/english
             A Japanese cell phone company.

Domino's Pizza Japan
             http://dominos.jp
             A pizza delivery company in Japan.

ECC   http://recruiting.ecc.co.jp
             An *Eikaiwa* school in Japan.

Education in Japan Community
             https://educationinjapan.wordpress.com
             An excellent resource for those interested in the details of the
             Japanese education system.

Edy http://www.edy.jp
  A Japanese digital money company.

Epipen http://www.epipen.jp
  The Japanese-language explanation of how to use an epipen.

Experiment in International Living EIL
  http://www.experimentinternational.org
  A non-profit, international exchange organization with summer
  programs in Japan.

Egg http://eggmgg.jp
  A Japanese magazine imprint specializing in gal and host fashion.

Face Mark
  http://www.facemark.jp/facemark.htm
  A Japanese directory of Japanese emoticons.

FBC Foreign Buyers' Club
  http://www.fbcusa.com
  An imported Western food product merchant.

francfranc
  http://www.francfranc.com
  A Japanese home furnishings store.

Fukuoka Now
  http://fukuoka-now.com
  A classifieds board and job guide for foreigners living in Fukuoka.

Gaijin Pot
  http://gaijinpot.com
  An online board featuring job opportunities, classified ads, and
  other resources for foreigners in Japan.

Geo http://www.geo-online.co.jp
  A DVD/manga/video game rental store.

Ghibli Museum

http://www.ghibli-museum.jp/en/info
The Studio Ghibli Museum in Tokyo.

Glico   http://www.glico.co.jp
A Japanese snack company.

Go Abroad

http://www.goabroad.com
A website featuring a variety of international study, work, and volunteer opportunities.

Go Overseas

http://www.gooverseas.com
A website featuring a variety of international study, work, and volunteer opportunities.

Gold's Gym Japan

http://www.goldsgym.jp
The Japanese branch of Gold's Gym.

Groupon Japan

http://groupon.jp
A Japanese daily deal site.

Gundam Café

http://g-cafe.jp
A Gundam-themed café located in Akihabara, based on the popular Gundam Series *anime*.

Gurunavi

http://www.gnavi.co.jp
A free online guide to restaurants in Japan. Features many special discounts and coupons.

Habitat for Humanity Japan

http://www.habitatjp.org
A volunteer organization specializing in short-term volunteer construction work.

Happie nuts

http://h-nuts.com/pc/index.html
A Japanese women's magazine.

Heart English School
> http://www.heart-school.jp/en/index.html
> A dispatch English-teaching company in Japan.

Himeji Castle
> http://www.himeji-castle.gr.jp/index/English
> The official website of Himeji Castle.

Host Magazine
> http://hostmagazine.jp
> A Japanese magazine catering to hosts.

Hot Pepper
> http://www.hotpepper.jp/index.html
> An online and print Japanese restaurant coupon magazine.

Hot Straw
> http://www.hotstraw.com
> Sells straws safe for use with hot beverages.

How to Cook Everything
> http://www.howtocookeverything.com
> The official website of the best-selling cookbook by Mark
> Bittman.

Hyperpedia
> http://www.hyperdia.com
> A Japanese transportation time-table planning website, available
> in English.

I Love Mama
> http://www.lovemama.net
> A Japanese women's magazine featuring gyaru who are mothers.

IES Abroad
> https://www.iesabroad.org
> A non-profit offering summer, internship, and semester study
> abroad programs across the world for college students.

Immigration Bureau of Japan
> http://www.immi-moj.go.jp/english/index.html
> The official English-language website for the Immigration Bureau
> of Japan.

Imperial Hotel Tokyo
>http://www.imperialhotel.co.jp/e/tokyo
>The official website of the Imperial Hotel based in Tokyo.

Interac
>https://www.interacnetwork.com/recruit
>A dispatch English-teaching company in Japan.

Itoya   http://www.ito-ya.co.jp
>A Japanese stationery store.

Ippodo Tea Company
>http://www.ippodo-tea.co.jp/en
>A Japanese tea company.

iTunes   http://itunes.com
>A downloadable media player and media library.

Japan Pension Service
>http://www.nenkin.go.jp/n/www/english/index.jsp
>The English-language section of Japan Pension Service's official
>website. Provides information in English on health insurance and
>national pension.

Japan Post
>http://www.post.japanpost.jp
>The Japanese postal service.

Japan Rail Pass
>http://www.jrpass.com
>An unlimited travel pass for Japan Rail trains.

Japan Travel Bureau (JTB)
>http://online.jtbusa.com
>A Japanese travel company; the only way to buy Ghibli Museum
>tickets from outside of Japan.

Japanese
>http://www.japaneseapp.com
>An extensive Japanese-English dictionary app.

Japanese Emoticons
> http://www.japaneseemoticons.net
> An English-language directory of Japanese emoticons, ordered by emotion.

Japanese Online Institute (JOI)
> http://japonin.com
> An online Japanese language school.

JAPANiCAN
> http://japanican.com
> A hotel, *ryokan*, and tour booking website sponsored by the Japan Travel Bureau.

The JET Alumni Association International
> http://www.jetalumni.org
> An association for alumni of the JET Program.

JGram http://www.jgram.org
> A database of Japanese grammar with example sentences.

Jobs in Japan
> http://jobsinjapan.com
> A job board featuring employment opportunities for foreigners in

Just Bentō
> http://justbento.com
> A website with creative *bentō* recipes.

Kani Dōraku
> http://douraku.co.jp
> The "Dancing Crab" restaurant.

Kansai Gaidai University
> http://www.kansaigaidai.ac.jp/asp
> A university in Osaka, Japan offering study abroad programs at the undergraduate and graduate level.

Kansai Flea Market
> http://kfm.to
> A classifieds board featuring *Sayōnara* Sales and job opportunities in the Kansai area.

Kansai Scene
>   http://www.kansaiscene.com
>   An English online and print magazine about life in the Kansai region.

Kentucky Fried Chicken
>   http://www.kfc.co.jp/xmas
>   The Japanese branch of the international fried chicken fast food chain.

Konami Sports Club
>   http://www.konamisportsclub.jp
>   A Japanese gym chain.

Kiyomizu Temple
>   http://www.kiyomizudera.or.jp
>   One of Japan's most famous temples.

Koyasan   http://eng.shukubo.net/index.html
>   A guide to *shūkubō* temple lodging, sponsored by the Koyasan Tourist Association and the Shukubo Temple Lodging Association.

Krispy Kreme
>   http://krispykreme.jp
>   The Japanese branch of Krispy Kreme.

Kuro Neko
>   http://www.kuronekoyamato.co.jp/english/services/airport.html
>   An airport *takkyūbin* and package delivery service.

The Japan Exchange and Teaching Program
>   http://www.us.emb-japan.go.jp/JET
>   The only English teaching program sponsored by the Japanese government.

Japan Post
>   http://www.post.japanpost.jp/english
>   The Japanese postal service's English website.

Japan Rail Pass
>   http://jrpass.com
>   Information on the Japan Rail Pass.

Japanese Guest Houses
> http://www.japaneseguesthouses.com
> An easy-to-navigate website offering information on various hotels and *ryokan* throughout Japan.

JET Alumni Association
> http://www.jetalumni.org
> The international association for former participants of the JET Program.

Jet Pens　http://jetpens.com
> An online store of Asian office supplies, including Japanese pens, pencils, and paper goods.

Jim Breen's WWWJDIC
> http://www.edrdg.org/cgi-bin/wwwjdic/wwwjdic?1C
> A free, online English-Japanese dictionary.

Jishu Shrine
> http://www.jishujinja.or.jp
> A shrine in Kyoto dedicated to love and matchmaking.

Kanji Writer
> http://japanese.nciku.com
> A *kanji* recognition website.

Keyhole TV
> http://www.v2p.jp/video/english
> A free, legal way to watch live Japanese television.

Lang-8　http://lang-8.com
> A free, language-learning journal website.

Lawson　http://www.lawson.co.jp
> A Japanese convenience store.

Loft　http://www.loft.co.jp
> A retailer of stationery and assorted goods.

Let's Japan
> http://www.letsjapan.org
> An English-language resource for information on specific Japanese legal procedures.

LINE   http://line.naver.jp/en
         A popular communication app.

Maisen   http://mai-sen.com
         A famous *ton-katsu* restaurant.

MasterCard
         http://www.mastercard.us
         A major credit card company.

The Meat Guy
         http://www.themeatguy.jp/app/en
         An online retailer of meat products.

Meetup   http://meetup.com
         A local interest group-finding website.

Men's Egg
         http://eggmgg.jp
         A Japanese men's magazine.

Metropolis
         http://metropolis.co.jp
         An English-language online and print magazine about happenings
         in Japan, specifically in the Tokyo area.

Miss   http://www.miss.jp
         A Japanese women's magazine.

Mori Art Museum
         http://www.mori.art.museum/eng
         An art museum in Roppongi, Tokyo.

My Language Exchange
         http://www.mylanguageexchange.com
         A penpal exchange website.

My Japan Phone
         http://myjapanphone.com
         A cell phone rental service.

My Shigoto
> http://www.myshigoto.com
> A Japanese job board for foreigners.

Nanka Ii Koto Ga Aru Kamo
> http://blogs.yahoo.co.jp/yasukazutai777
> A Japanese blog featuring different kinds of character-themed *bentō*.

Nanzan Unversity
> http://www.nanzan-u.ac.jp/English
> A Japanese university in Nagoya, Japan well-known for its foreign language program.

Narita Airport
> http://www.narita-airport.jp/en
> A major international airport in Japan.

Narita Express
> https://www.jreast.co.jp/e/nex/index.html
> The express train that leaves from Narita Airport.

Navitime
> http://www.navitime.co.jp
> A Japanese GPS service.

Nihon Nenkin Kikō
> http://www.nenkin.go.jp/n/www/index.html
> The homepage for the Japan Pension Service. The link in the upper-right corner directs you to the English-language pages on the site.

NHK   http://www3.nhk.or.jp
> Japan's national public broadcasting organization.

Nonno   http://www.s-woman.net/non-no
> A Japanese women's magazine.

Oedo Onsen Monogatari
> http://www.oom.en
> A theme park-like *onsen* in Odaiba.

Oggi   http://oggi.tv/index.html
        A Japanese women's magazine.

Oriental Trading
        http://www.orientaltrading.com
        A store that sells party goods, craft supplies, teaching supplies,
        and novelty items.

Osaka Aquarium
        http://www.kaiyukan.com/language/eng/index.htm
        One of the largest aquariums in the world. Located in Osaka,
        Japan.

Osaka Castle
        http://www.osakacastle.net
        The official website of Osaka Castle.

Outback Steakhouse
        http://www.outbacksteakhouse.co.jp/en/index.html
        An Australian-themed steakhouse with branches in Japan.

Pokémon Center
        http://www.pokemon.co.jp/gp/pokecen/about
        The retail location for the Pokémon merchandise line.

Project Gutenberg
        http://www.gutenberg.org
        An online catalog of free, downloadable books.

Quicken
        http://quicken.intuit.com
        Accounting software.

Rakuten
        http://rakuten.jp
        A Japanese shopping site, similar to Amazon.

Read the Kanji
        http://readthekanji.com
        An online tool for studying *kanji*.

Resume Maker
> http://resume.meieki.com
> A Japanese-language site with many free Japanese resume PDF and Word templates available for free download.

Rikai-chan
> http://www.polarcloud.com/rikaichan
> A Japanese-English browser toolbar dictionary.

Ritsumeikan University
> http://www.ritsumei.ac.jp/eng/html/admissions/program_jp/skp
> A university in Kyoto that offers study abroad programs at the undergraduate, graduate, and doctoral level.

Roppongi Hills
> http://www.roppongihills.com
> A major shopping center in Roppongi, Tokyo.

Rurubu   http://www.rurubu.com
> A Japanese travel/lodging planning website.

Sega Joypolis
> http://tokyo-joypolis.com
> An indoor Sega-themed video game amusement center in Odaiba.

Shibuya 109
> www.shibuya109.jp
> A famous department store in Shibuya, Tokyo.

ShopSafe
> http://www.shopsafe.com
> Credit card security software.

Shuminavi
> http://shuminavi.net
> A listing of interest groups and clubs in Japan.

Softbank
> http://mb.softbank.jp/en
> A Japanese cell phone company.

Space ALC
>   http://alc.co.jp
>   An online Japanese-English dictionary intended for native
>   Japanese speakers.

Starbucks
>   http://www.starbucks.co.jp/en
>   An international coffee chain with branches throughout Japan.

Steady   http://tkj.jp/steady
>   A Japanese women's magazine.

Study Abroad 101
>   http://ww.studyabroad101.com
>   A website featuring various study, volunteer, and teaching
>   opportunities in Japan.

Sumida River Cruise
>   http://www.suijobus.co.jp
>   A company that runs waterbuses down the Sumida River in
>   Tokyo.

Supercook
>   http://www.supercook.com
>   A website that finds recipes based on the ingredients you have in
>   your kitchen.

Surviving in Japan
>   http://www.survivingnjapan.com
>   An online guide to living in Japan.

Tabio   http://www.tabio.com
>   A Japanese company specializing in socks and leggings.

Tada Copy
>   http://tadacopy.com
>   A free photocopying service supported by paid advertising.

Tagaini Jisho
>   http://www.tagaini.net
>   A downloadable Japanese-English dictionary.

Tanaka Clinic
> http://www.tanaka-clinic.net/eng
> A medical clinic in Kanagawa with an excellent directory of
> Japanese/English medical translations.

Takarazuka
> http://kageki.hankyu.co.jp
> Women's musical theatre.

Tawaraya
> http://www.kyoto-club.com/tomaru/rkn/tawaraya.html
> One of Japan's best *ryokan*.

Temple University – Japan Campus
> http://www.temple.edu
> A Japanese university open to foreigners.

Tengu Natural Foods
> http://store.alishan.jp
> An online merchant of organic and vegetarian foods.

Tenichi   http://www.tenichi.co.jp
> A Japanese *tenpura* restaurant.

Time Out Tokyo
> http://www.timeout.jp/en/tokyo
> An online magazine for ex-pats living in Tokyo.

Tip-X Gym
> http://tip.x-tokyo.jp
> A fantastic gym with branches throughout Tokyo.

Tofugu   http://www.tofugu.com
> An English-language blog about Japanese culture.

Tokyo Dome
> http://www.tokyo-dome.co.jp/e
> The stadium of the Tokyo Yomiuri Giants baseball team.

Tokyo Imperial Palace
> http://sankan.kunaicho.go.jp/english/guide/koukyo.html
> The official website of the Tokyo Imperial Palace.

Tokyo Metropolitan Health & Medical Information Center
http://www.himawari.metro.tokyo.jp/qq/qq13enmnlt.asp
A resource for foreign residents of Tokyo. Provides English-
language hospital look-up and emergency interpretation by
phone.

Tokyo Yakult Swallows
http://www.yakult-swallows.co.jp/english
A Nippon Professional Baseball team based in Tokyo.

Tsutaya　www.tsutaya.co.jp
An entertainment retailer and bookstore.

Unique Japan
http://new.uniquejapan.com/home
A website that sells authentic samurai swords and Japanese knives.

Uniqlo　http://www.uniqlo.com/jp
A simple, brand name-less clothing store that carries the basics.

VISA　http://usa.visa.com
A major credit card company.

Vista Print
http://vistaprint.com
A custom printing company that produces business cards.

Vivi　http://vivi.tv
A Japanese women's magazine.

Waseda University
http://www.waseda.jp/top/index-j.html
A prestigious Japanese university.

Western Union
http://http://www.westernunion.com
A money transfer company with branches worldwide.

Yodobayashi Camera
http://www.yodobashi.com
An electronics retailer.

Yomiuri Giants
> http://www.giants.jp
> The official website of the Yomiuri Giants, a Nippon Professional Baseball team based in Tokyo.

Yoshinoya
> http://www.yoshinoya.com
> A Japanese fast food chain.

Yukata Kimono Market Sakura
> http://www.kimono-yukata-market.com
> An online store that sells *yukata* and *kimono*.

Zauo   http://r.gnavi.co.jp/g775103/menu1.html
> A popular restaurant franchise where you can fish in the restaurant's moat for your dinner.

Zokugo
> http://zokugo-dict.com
> A free, monolingual dictionary of Japanese slang.

25 ans   http://www.25ans.jp
> A Japanese women's magazine.

ENDNOTES
(in order of reference)

Health and Medical

Koh, Yoree. "Tokyo Snubs Paris (Hilton)." *Wall Street Journal: Japan Real Time.* 22 Sep 2010. 16 Dec 2011 <http://blogs.wsj.com/japanrealtime/2010/09/22/tokyo-snubs-paris>.

"FAQ on Japanese Visa." Embassy of Japan in the United States of America. 5 Dec 2011 <http://www.us.emb-japan.go.jp/english/html/travel_and_visa/visa/faq_new.htm>.

How to Call Home

"How to Call Internationally." Country Code. 7 Oct 2013 <http://countrycode.org/how-to-call>.

At Home

Bird, Isabella Lucy. Unbeaten Tracks in Japan. Project Gutenberg Ebook. 1880. 19 Dec 2011 <http://www.gutenberg.org/ebooks/2184>.

Japan Post, and How to Schedule a Package Delivery

Japan Post Delivery Slip, Yoyogi Branch. 15 Apr 2011.

Garbage Sorting

Shibuya Ward Office. Handout. 2011.

Cooking at Home

Yusa, Kazumi (Monchi). "Mario & Teresa No Obentō" [Mario & Boo Bentō]. Nanka Ii Koto Aru Kamo [Maybe It's a Good Thing]. 27 Sep 2011. 15 Oct 2013 <http://blogs.yahoo.co.jp/yasukazutai777/34920256.html>.

Yusa, Kazumi (Monchi). "Pikachu & Mijumaru Bentō" [Pikachu and
        Oshawott Bentō]. Nanka Ii Koto Aru Kamo [Maybe It's a
        Good Thing]. 24 June 2011. 15 Oct 2013
        <http://blogs.yahoo.co.jp/yasukazutai777/archive/2011/06/24>.

Yusa, Kazumi (Monchi). "Totoro No Obentō & Kēki [Totoro Bentō and
        Cake]." Nanka Ii Koto Aru Kamo [Maybe It's a Good Thing].
        10 May 2011. 22 Oct 2012
        <http://blogs.yahoo.co.jp/yasukazutai777/36541434.html>.

Kazumi Yusa (Monchi). "Rirakkuma No Kawaii Pikku De Rirakkuma
        Obentō" [Rirakkuma Bentō wit h Cute Rirakkuma Picks]. Nanka
        Ii Koto Aru Kamo [Maybe It's a Good Thing].11 Aug 2011. 15
        Oct 2013
        <http://blogs.yahoo.co.jp/yasukazutai777/37081240.html>.

"How Gyokuro is Processed." Ippodo. 2011. 14 Apr 2012
        <http://www.ippodo-tea.co.jp/en/tea/gyokuro_03.html>.

"Genmaicha Green Tea." In Pursuit of Tea. 2012. 14 Apr 2012
        <http://www.inpursuitoftea.com/Genmaicha_Green_Tea_In_
        Pursuit_of_Tea_p/gj800.htm>.

"What is sencha, gyokuro, shincha, matcha etc.?" Japanese Green Tea
        Online. 2012. 14 Apr 2012
        <http://japanesegreenteaonline.com/faq8.htm>.

Becoming a *Sensei*

Namisato, David. "The End." Comic strip. *Life After the B.O.E.* 25 July
        2011. 2 Dec 2011
        <http://www.lifeaftertheboe.com/2011/07/25/theend>.

"Miyako No Kyōin, Tanki-Ryūgaku…Gorin-muke, Eigo Appu [Tokyo's
        English Teachers, Short Term Study Abroad…Aiming for the
        Olympics and Upping English Ability." The Yomiuri
        Shinbun. 8 Nov 2013. 21 Nov 2013
        <http://www.yomiuri.co.jp/kyoiku/news/20131108-
        OYT8T00530.htm>.

Brophy, Barry. "English schools face huge insurance probe." *The Japan
        Times Online.* 12 Apr 2005. 15 Dec 2011
        <http://www.japantimes.co.jp/text/fl20050412zg.html>.

Writing a Resume in Japanese

Kojima, Mitsuko. Saiyō-Sareru Rirekisho Shokumu-keirekisho Wa Kō Kaku
[How to Write a Resume That Will Get You Hired].
Nippon Jitsugyō Shuppansha [Nippon Jitsugyō Publishing].
Tokyo: 30th Reprinting, 2012.

Harlan, Chico. "In Japan, fax machines remain important because of
language and culture." *The Washington Post*. 7 June 2012.
Accessed 15 Feb 2013 < http://articles.washingtonpost.com/2012-
06-07/world/35462783_1_fax-machine-sharp-and-ricoh-
fukushima-daiichi>.

Teaching English

Namisato. "Chopsticks." Comic strip. *Life After the B.O.E.* 16 Sep 2010. 2
Dec 2011
<http://www.lifeaftertheboe.com/2010/09/16/chopsticks>.

"The Japan Exchange and Teaching Program 2012 Application Guidelines."
The Embassy of Japan: The Japan Exchange and Teaching
Program. 30 Oct 2012 <http://www.us.emb-japan.go.jp/
JET/pdfs/2013_Application_Guidelines.pdf>.

Dom. "Kitto Katsu Tō!" Stamanga. 9 Jan 2009. 2 Dec 2011
<http://www.stamaga.net/stamaga/stamp_1054.html>.

Namisato. "Lesson Plan." Comic strip. *Life After the B.O.E.* 16 July 2010.
16 May 2012
<http://www.lifeaftertheboe.com/2010/07/16/lesson-plan>.

At the Office

Namisato. "Talked About Forever." Comic strip. *Life After the B.O.E.*
17 Aug 2009. 2 Dec 2011 <http://www.lifeaftertheboe.
com/2009/08/17/talked-about-forever>.

E. Desapriya, I. Pike, S. Subzwari, G. Scime, and S. Shimizu. "Impact of
lowering the legal blood alcohol concentration limit to 0.03
on male, female, and teenage drivers involved alcohol-related
crashes in Japan." *International Journal of Injury Control and
Safety Promotion*, 14 (2007): 181-187. <http://www.tandfonline.
com/doi/abs/10.1080/17457300701440634?url_ver=Z39.88-

2003&rfr_id=ori:rid:crossref.org&rfr_dat=cr_pub%3dpubmed>.

Money

"Cost of Living—The Most Expensive Cities 2012." City Mayors. 15 Sep
        2012. 16 Nov 2012
        <http://www.citymayors.com/features/cost_survey.html>.

Understanding Your Paycheck

Lloyd, Terrie. "Terrie's Job Tips: Resigning Versus Getting Fired." Daijob. 5
        Dec 2011
        <http://www.daijob.com/en/columns/terrie/article/331>.

The JLPT

"New Japanese-Language Proficiency Test Guidebook: Executive Summary."
        Japan Educational Exchanges and Services. 2009. 17 Dec
        2011 <http://www.jlpt.jp/e/reference/pdf/
        guidebook_s_e.pdf>.

Citing Your Sources in Japanese

Gibaldi, Joseph. MLA Handbook for Writers of Research Papers. New York:
        2003, 6th ed. 147.

Gibaldi 177.

Gibaldi 215.

Tomura, Kayo. "Sankō Bunken No Kakikata [How to Cite Sources]." Meiji
        University. 31 Jan 2005. 8 Oct 2013
        <http://www.isc.meiji.ac.jp/~tomura/references_guide.html>.

Out and About

"Japan Divisions." The University of Texas at Austin: Perry-Castañeda
        Library Map Collection. Public Domain Map Edited by Author.
        22 Oct 2012
        <http://www.lib.utexas.edu/maps/middle_east_and_asia/japan_
        divisions.jpg>.

The Metro

Onishi, Norimitsu. "Never Lost, but Found Daily: Japanese Honesty." *New*

York Times, 8 Jan 2004. 5 Dec 2011
<http://www.nytimes.com/2004/01/08/world/never-lost-but-found-daily-japanese-honesty.html?pagewanted=all&src=pm>.

The Shinkansen

Pavone, Sean. "Fuji and Train." Dreamstime. 10 Feb 2014 <http://www.
dreamstime.com/sepavo_info>.

Visiting a Japanese Temple or Shrine

"Shūkyō Dankai-Zū, Kyōshi-Zū Futatabi Shinja-Zū." Tokyo Ministry of
Internal Affairs: Nihon Tōkei Nenkan [Statistical Yearbook of
Japan]. 2008. 11 Oct 2013
<http://www.stat.go.jp/data/nenkan/23.htm>.

Picture of Shrine Etiquette. Hōgyoku-Inari Temple. Kumagaya, Japan. 8
Aug 2013.

Tokyo Short Guide

"Daruma No Iro Ni Tsuite [About the Colors of Daruma]." Tōichō
Daruma-dera [Toichō Daruma Temple]. 2008. 27 Dec
2012 <http://toi-daruma.jp/?mode=f2>.

"Iro Daruma, Karā Daruma No Shōhin [Colored Daruma]." Kunimine
Bekkō-ya Shōten [Kunimine Bekkō Store]. Takasaki Daruma.
2011. 27 Dec 2012 <http://www.takasaki-daruma.jp/color.html>.

"Japan: Country Specific Information." Travel.State.Gov: U.S. Department
of State. 17 Dec 2011 <http://travel.state.gov/travel/
cis_pa_tw/cis/cis_1148.html>.

"Takasaki No Daruma-ya-san Karā Daruma No Hanbai [Takasaki Daruma
Maker – Colored Daruma]." Takasaki Daruma-ya San
[Takasaki Daruma Maker]. 2012. 27 Dec 2012
<http://www.nextweb.jp/daruma/color_daruma.php>.

"Takasaki Daruma No Gunma-ken Daruma Seizō Kyōdō Kumiai [Takasaki
Daruma's Gunma Prefecture Daruma Doll Manufacturers'
Cooperative Union]." The Gunma Prefecture Daruma
Doll Manufacturers' Cooperative Union. 2012. 27 Dec
2012 <http://takasakidaruma.net/index.html>.

Osaka Short Guide

Cullen, Lisa Takeuchi. "Rent Boys." *Time Magazine*. 21 Jan 2001.
17 Dec 2011 <http://www.time.com/time/magazine/
article/0,9171,193635,00.html>.

"Air Group BEST 10 Ranking." Air Group. 9 Nov 2011
<http://www.air-group.jp/number.html>.

"Seito Bōshū Ni Tsuite [About Admissions]." Takarazuka Ongaku Gakkō.
17 May 2012
<http://www.tms.ac.jp/guidance/admissions.html>.

"Nara No Shika No Rekishi [The History of Nara's Deer]." Zaidan Hōjin
Nara No Shika Aigōkai [Foundation for the Protection of Deer
in Nara Park-Deer Protection Team]. 6 Apr 2012. 11 Apr
2012 <http://naradeer.com/prof-histry.htm>.

"Nara-koen Park (Tōdai-ji Temple)." Japan National Tourism Organization.
18 May 2012
<http://www.jnto.go.jp/eng/location/regional/nara/narakoen_
toudaiji.html>.

Kyoto Short Guide

"Omamori." 19 Feb 2011. 7 Dec 2011
<http://japancategory.com/houkyu/article/view/1.html>.

"Kankō Annai – Fushimi Inari Sandō Shōtengai [Fushimi Inari Tourist
Information]." Fushimi Inari Shrine. 11 Oct
2013 <http://www.fusimi-inari.com/?
page_id=19>.
"Kinkaku-ji No Ayumi"[History of the Golden Pavilion]. Shokoku-ji
Religious Corporation. 24 Jan 2014
<http://www.shokoku-ji.jp/h_k.html>.

"Beautiful kimono woman." Kennosuke. Dreamstime. 10 Feb 2014
<http://www.dreamstime.com/kennosuke_info>.

Onsen— Japanese Hot Springs

Yokota, Tomohisa. "Japanese open air hot spa onsen." 10 Feb 2014
<http://www.dreamstime.com/tomophotography_info>.

Making Friends and Meeting People

Nishi, Fumiko. "Oya to Dōkyō no Mikon-sha no Saikin no Jōkyō Sono 10 [Recent Information Regarding Unmarried Singles Living with their Parents – Part 10]." Japanese Ministry of Internal Affairs: Research Department. 9 Apr 2013. 22 Nov 2013 <http:// www. stat.go.jp/training/2kenkyu/saika.htm>.

Lin, Ho Swee. "Private Love in Public Space: Love Hotels and the Transformation of Intimacy in Contemporary Japan." *Asian Studies Review*, 32:1, 31-56. 2008. 4 Dec 2011. <http://catholic. academia.edu/SweeLinHo/Papers/1100820/Private_Love_ in_Public_Space_Love_Hotels_and_the_Transformation_of_ Intimacy_in_Contemporary_Japan>.

Culture Notes

Shintani, Takanori. Jū-ni-ka-gatsu No Shikitari [12 Months of Cultural Customs]. Tokyo, Japan: PHP Interface, 2007. 1st ed.

Unver, Cenk. "Tea Ceremony, Japan." Dreamstime. 10 Feb 2014 <http:// www.dreamstime.com/zensu_info>.

"The Statistical Handbook of Japan 2012: Chapter Two (Population)." Ministry of Internal Affairs and Communications. 2011. 18 Nov 2012 <http://www.stat.go.jp/english/data/handbook/c02cont. htm#cha2_4>.

Blood Types in Japan

"Karl Landsteiner – Biography." Nobel Prize: The Official Web Site of the Nobel Prize. The Nobel Foundation. Nobel Media. 23 Nov 2008. <http://nobelprize.org/nobel_prizes/medicine/ laureates/1930/landsteiner-bio.html>.

Le Vay, Lulu. "Spirit: Blood Money." *The Independent*. 25 Aug 2005.

"NPO Human science ABO center." NPO Human Science ABO Center. Sep 1999. 23 Nov 2008 <http://www.human-abo.org>.

"What's My Blood Type." What's My Blood Type. The Chambers Group. 2007. 10 Oct 2013 <http://whatsmybloodtype.org/type_a.html>.

Japanese Holidays

"Daijisen Jishō [Daijisen Dictionary]." Yahoo Japan. 5 Dec 2011 <http://dic.yahoo.co.jp>.

Satō, Kōji. Bunka Toshite No Koyomi [Culture as a Calendar]. Sōgensha Publishing: Apr 1999.

Pratt, Yukari. "Osechi – Japanese New Year's Cuisine." 16 Apr 2012 <http://www.bento.com/fexp-osechi.html>.

Wdeon. "Young Women in kimono on Coming of Age Day." Dreamstime. 10 Feb 2014 <http://www.dreamstime.com/wdeon_info>.

Kaneko, Akihide. "Kyō No O-hanashi (Natsu) [Today's Story (Summer)]." Buppo Bunko 5. Suzuki Shuppan: 1984.

Cowardlion. "Shichi-go-shine celebration at Meiji Jingu Shrine." Dreamstime. 10 Feb 2014 <http://www.dreamstime.com/cowardlion_info>.

Sayōnara—Leaving Japan

Bone. "Getting a National Pension Payment Rebate When Leaving Japan as a 'Lump-sum Withdrawal Payment.'" Stippy. 25 Oct 2006. 21 Dec 2011 <http://www.stippy.com/japan-life/refund-get-back-your-national-pension-payments-when-you-leave-japan-lump-sum-withdrawal>.

In Case of Emergency

"Japan: Country Specific Information." Travel.State.Gov: U.S. Department of State. 5 Dec 2011 <http://travel.state.gov/travel/cis_pa_tw/cis/cis_1148.html>.

"Judicial Assistance: Arrests in Japan." Embassy of the United States: Tokyo, Japan. 5 Dec 2011 <http://japan.usembassy.gov/e/acs/tacs-7110b.html>.

"PENAL CODE (Act No. 45 of 1907)." Cabinet Secretariat. 28 May 2006. 10 Oct 2013 <http://www.cas.go.jp/jp/seisaku/hourei/data/PC.pdf>.

Snapshot Guide to Japanese

"Shōgakkō Shidōyōryō Dai Issetsu Kokugo [Elementary School Government
    Regulations for the Study of Japanese]." <u>Ministry of
    Education, Culture, Sports, Science, and Technology</u>. 26 Oct
    2011
    <http://www.mext.go.jp/b_menu/shuppan/
    sonota/990301b/990301d.htm>.
Hadamitzky, Wolfgang and Mark Spahn. *Kanji and Kana*. Tuttle Publishing:
    Singapore, 1997. 1st rev. ed. 7.

"Jōyō Kanji Hyō [General Knowledge Kanji Chart]." <u>Agency for Cultural
    Affairs</u>. 25 Oct 2011
    <http://www.bunka.go.jp/kokugo_nihongo/pdf/
    jouyoukanjihyou_h22.pdf>.

ACKNOWLEDGMENTS

This book would not have been possible without the support of numerous individuals who shared with me their kindness, knowledge, and stories. Thank you for your contributions to this project.

Thank you to the Vassar College Japanese Department, especially Peipei Qiu, Hiromi Tsuchiya Dollase, and Yuko Matsubara. Thank you for first kindling my love of the Japanese language. Your knowledge and encouragement have changed my life.

Thank you to Sarvenaz Allahverdi for her editing expertise and knowledge of Japanese pop culture. You have taught me so much, and this book would not have been possible without you.

Thank you to David Namisato and Kazumi Yusa for letting me share your artistic creations in this book. I know others will enjoy your work as much as I have.

Thank you to Scarlett Rugers at Scarlett Rugers Design for the cover design and interior formatting of this book.

Thank you to my editor, Michael Garrett, for his editorial advice and assistance.

Thank you to Mizuno-sensei, for tirelessly answering my various questions about Japanese culture.

A special thank you goes out to all my Japanese students—you have taught me so much. I enjoyed every moment!

Thank you to Mrs. Tamamura, Mr. Horikawa, Mr. Ishida, Mr. Michihisa, and all the teachers and students in Yao, Osaka for a wonderful year. You taught me so much about what it means to be a teacher.

Thank you to Ochanomizu University and Nanzan University for hosting me as a study abroad student and for all the wonderful experiences that followed.

Thank you to Mr. and Mrs. Mitsutsune Yamaguchi and Sonoko Yamaguchi, who welcomed me into their home and encouraged my studies of Japanese from the very beginning. Your support and kindness helped me throughout all my experiences in Japan.

Last, but not least, thank you to my wonderful family for their support, faith, and for enduring countless discussions on all things Japanese. First, to my sister, Alexandra, for her advice and unique perspective. Thank you to my father, for encouraging me to take risks, and thank you to my mother, for her patience with this project and for being the first believer.

And, of course, thank you Japan for a lifetime of memories and adventures.

謝辞

チュー先生、土屋先生、松原先生、本当にありがとうございました。日本語と日本の文化を私に紹介してくださって、自分の世界が変わりました。先生方のおかげで、いろいろな経験ができ、大変お世話になりました。

堀川先生、石田先生、道久先生、玉村先生、校長先生、教頭先生、八尾市の皆様、一年間、本当にありがとうございました。八尾市の先生も子供もいろいろなことを私に教えてくれましたから、私は毎日仕事を楽しみました。日本でいろいろな町へ行きましたが、八尾市の皆さんの親切さと元気さを忘れません。

水野先生、約3年間、ありがとうございました。先生と一緒にいろいろな話ができたおかげで、私はこの本が作られました。どんな質問をしても、先生はいつもやさしく答えてくれました。本当にお世話になりました。

遊佐和美さん、素敵なお弁当の写真を使わせていただいて、本当にありがとうございました。これから、ブログの活動でがんばってくださいね。

私の元生徒の皆さん、たくさん楽しい思い出を本当にありがとうございました。一緒に過ごした時間は私にとってとても大切な宝です。皆さんの笑顔とやる気は感動しました。これから、勉強でも人生でもがんばってください。応援しています!

山口光恒さん、山口幸子さん、山口園子さん、最初から私の日本語の勉強を応援して、サポートしてくださり、本当に感謝しています。留学のとき、山口さんは私をやさしく迎えてくださいました。いろいろなことを教えてくださって、お世話になりました。

Thank you!

ABOUT THE AUTHOR

Natalia Doan first began studying Japanese at Vassar College, where she graduated with a double major in English and Japanese. She also studied at Ochanomizu University in Tokyo and Nanzan University in Nagoya. She taught English to elementary and middle school students in Osaka, where she lived during the 2011 Tōhoku earthquake. During her time in Japan, she also wrote for an ex-pat magazine in Tokyo, modeled multiple collections for a Kyoto fashion house and for one of Japan's premier women's magazines, and worked for a Japanese company. Natalia currently divides her time between Japan and Virginia.

Made in the USA
Middletown, DE
03 January 2016